Cricket at Scarborough

A Social History of the Club and its Festival

Cricket at Scarborough

A Social History of the Club and its Festival

Ian Hall
with John Found

BREEDON
BOOKS
SPORT

First published in Great Britain by
The Breedon Books Publishing Company Limited
44 Friar Gate, Derby DE1 1DA
1992.

ISBN 1 873626 09 6

Printed and bound by The Bath Press Limited, Bath and London.
Jacket printed by BDC Printing Services Ltd of Derby.

Contents

Acknowledgements

Many people have contributed to this book. Particular thanks are due to the officials and staff of Scarborough Cricket Club, past and present, Mr B.Berryman and North Yorkshire County Library, Mr F.Bowker, Mr D.Briggs, Mr M.Corley, English Heritage (regarding Scarborough Castle), Mr C.W.Foord, The Grand Hotel (Scarborough), Mr L.Halstead, Mrs S.Jackson, Mrs G.Leadbeater, Mr E.Legge, Mr J.Parkinson, and all those people without whose encouragement, help and interest 'Cricket at Scarborough' would not have survived.

Foreword

IT WAS on a rainy day in 1990 that a postcard dropped through the letterbox, informing me that the writer had been to Scarborough and was enquiring when I was going to get 'that piece' published? The postcard was written by Dr Ian Keil, my erstwhile tutor at Loughborough University when, in 1986, I laboriously completed a Masters Degree by submitting a thesis on the History of Scarborough Cricket Club. Shortly afterwards an academic journal arrived on the doormat, a broad hint as to which way the wind was blowing.

I hope that I have not disappointed Ian Keil, but photographs do not figure prominently in academic journals and, for most people, cricket at Scarborough brings to the mind's eye images recalled in a light-hearted rather than in an academic manner. So a book it had to be. The format, which includes many photographs perhaps not published before, means that the book should appeal to the 'dipper-in' as well as the more interested reader.

Without John Found, the book would not have been possible at this time. His sponsored walk from Lord's to Scarborough in 1980, pales in comparison with the amount of leg work which he has done in collating and checking information, 'chivvying' reluctant individuals and preparing the way. He also wrote Chapters Nine and Ten and is also responsible for all the averages in the Appendices. Any mistakes are my own.

Ian Hall
1992

Introduction

FROM its position high on St Nicholas Cliff, Scarborough's Grand Hotel looks down on South Bay and the harbour. Its imposing size, grandeur and dominating presence are reminders of the style and values of a bygone age. For the Victorians were great builders of monuments. Monuments to demonstrate importance, authority and power. Monuments to show that Britain led the world in initiative and enterprise. Like many town halls still in use throughout the country, The Grand Hotel at Scarborough is a monument to Victorian belief in such virtues.

When The Grand Hotel was opened in 1867, Scarborough, the 'Queen of the Watering Places', was at the height of its popularity. From being in the mid-eighteenth century a town with about 6,000 inhabitants, mainly engaged in shipping and fishing, but with an important, exclusive and specialised attraction of spa waters, by the second half of the nineteenth century, Scarborough had grown to three times that population. It had become a thriving holiday and health resort. Furthermore, its inhabitants, in the true entrepreneurial spirit of the time, were determined that the attractions at Scarborough should not be bettered anywhere in England.

It was in such a climate of opinion, just four years after the opening of The Grand Hotel, that the seeds of a idea for a cricket festival at Scarborough first began to germinate. The direct result of the idea was that a small cricket club of minor importance, founded initially in 1849 and reconstituted in 1863, quickly grew to become a household name within cricket circles. In addition, because the Scarborough Cricket Festival blossomed to eventually establish a world-wide reputation, the name of the town has been brought very subtly to the attention of a great number of people for nearly 130 years.

How has this remarkable situation evolved? How has a seaside town with a current

Early lodging houses built around 1840 on the Cliff (now St Nicholas Cliff). The Grand Hotel was later built on the left and opened in 1867.

at Bramall Lane the football pitch encroached a considerable distance on to the cricket outfield. Fielding in the slips at Bramall Lane, with the elevated, reseeded touchline running some three or four yards in front of the crouching fielder, was certainly a hazardous business whenever the ball was edged along the floor.

Parodoxically, it was the failure of football at Park Avenue, rather than its success as at Bramall Lane, which hastened the departure of cricket from Bradford. In 1970, Bradford AFC were not re-elected to the Football League and from that point the ground began to decline until Bradford Cricket Club itself, champions of the Yorkshire Cricket League in 1982 with Martin Crowe as professional, were forced to disband in 1985.

Headingley too, the headquarters of Yorkshire County Cricket Club, is a shared sports arena where football dominates. Here the football code is Rugby League and the Leeds club is one of the top names in the game. The land itself is owned by the Leeds Cricket, Football & Athletic Co Ltd, and so Yorkshire are leaseholders only.

For many years there have been differences of opinion about the provision of cricket facilities on Yorkshire's major ground and, because of the leasehold situation, Yorkshire has limited rights and reduced financial advantages compared to other counties having Test Match arenas. Many members feel that the Leeds club benefits at the expense of Yorkshire cricket and the fact that Yorkshire County Cricket Club does not have a ground of its own is a sore point.

As was the case at Bradford, cricket and football pitches are separated by a dual purpose stand which gives an excellent view behind the wicket on one side and across the rugby pitch on the other, but also as at Bradford, the Leeds Cricket Club, once a powerful member of the Yorkshire Cricket League, has now gone out of existance. At least the cricket club of Sheffield (founded in 1854) has survived to continue to play in the Yorkshire League. It now plays on another ground at Bawtry Road and, by retaining the name of Sheffield United, ensures that cricket memories of Bramall Lane are not forgotten.

Scarborough Cricket Club has not had the association with football which brought problems to the other principal cricket grounds in Yorkshire. It is even probable that the disappearance of Bramall Lane and Park Avenue from the cricket scene, strengthened the position of North Marine Road as a ground for first-class cricket. Despite a body of opinion which favours concentrating Yorkshire matches solely at Leeds, consistently higher

attendances at Scarborough, especially for one-day Sunday League fixtures, has meant that the ground at North Marine Road remains second only to Headingley for the allocation of matches in a Yorkshire season.

The second way in which Scarborough Cricket Club has had a considerable impact on first-class cricket in England is through the staging of the Scarborough Cricket Festival. This event, held towards the end of each season, has secured a unique position in the history of the game. Since 1876, with the exception of only the war years, all the greatest players from every part of the cricketing world have played in the Festival. Other festivals, notably Hastings and Eastbourne, have been launched and have had periods of prosperity, but have since declined to extinction. Only the Scarborough Cricket Festival remains.

It is not only in the Festival that international teams have been seen at Scarborough. The club staged one-day Prudential Trophy matches in 1976 and 1978, featuring England

The Cricketers' Room at the Grand Hotel, pictured at the height of its grandeur.

Since 1980, the Cricketers' Room has been a cafeteria for Butlin's holiday guests.

v West Indies and England v New Zealand. In 1979, a pre-World Cup game saw India v Pakistan playing at North Marine Road, whilst international matches at Under-19 level have regularly been played on the ground since they were first introduced in the 1970s.

In 1951, a women's Test match was played between England and Australia and other women's representative matches have taken place since that date. The initiative of obtaining sponsorship by Rothmans of Pall Mall for The Rest of the World XI at festivals in the early 1960s, when sponsorship of sport was in its infancy, is an indication of the progressive outlook which has been a characteristic of the club throughout its history. The news early in 1992 that the Festival in that year would feature the first major team of South African cricketers to play in England since the country was readmitted to international cricket, further emphasises the club's ability to keep abreast and often ahead of the times.

Thirdly, Scarborough Cricket Club has had a resounding impact on club cricket at national level. In 1965, the National Cricket Association was founded with the aim of promoting club cricket throughout the country. One idea was to organise a national cricket competition for cricket clubs, known initially as the National Cricket Club Trophy. Later, as different sponsors were attracted, the competition featured other names and the Haig, Whitbread and Younger Trophies were followed by the Cockspur Cup and all received extensive national media attention. The Final, played at Lord's, allows club cricketers the opportunity of playing at the mecca of the game and those who have done so are unlikely to forget a memorable experience. Scarborough Cricket Club has been at the forefront of this competition, winning the trophy on no fewer than five occasions and thus emphasising the powerful position the club occupies not only in Yorkshire cricket, but also nationally.

'Early Days' is the title for Chapter One. A brief account of the development of the game of cricket is given, in order to place in context the formation of Scarborough Cricket Club in the nineteenth century. Linked inexorably to the development of the club were the massive social and economic changes taking place in Victorian England, which had enormous consequences for the game of cricket and the town of Scarborough. Scarborough Cricket Club responded to the changing circumstances, took advantage of important economic and social factors and laid down several principles and policies for the administration of the club. Those principles and policies have, by accident or design, been largely adhered to ever since.

Like The Grand Hotel, the foundations of Scarborough Cricket Club were solidly built.

Even so, everything has not always run smoothly. Far from it. Two identities within one organisation is a recipe for conflict. Throughout its history the club has had to balance the interests of club cricket in the highly competitive systems which have long existed in Yorkshire, alongside the demands of the more glamorous first-class game. Sometimes this relationship has been severely tested. Early disputes are referred to in Chapter Two where the contributions of three outstanding secretaries are highlighted and the administration of the club is reviewed.

One of the most obvious questions to ask about Scarborough Cricket Club is how has it managed to maintain its organisational vigour, retain its status and yet remain independent of the main first-class cricket structure. That being the case, the club does not qualify for the direct financial support of a centralised agency like the Test and County Cricket Board (TCCB) which financially underpins all county cricket clubs.

For example, in 1991, some 53 per cent of Derbyshire County Cricket Club's total income came from the distribution of Test match profits by the TCCB. Although over the years, Yorkshire County Cricket Club has contributed generously to the club's finances, especially by means of grant aid for ground improvements, the fact that Scarborough Cricket Club has been able to remain financially stable and secure for nearly 150 years is quite remarkable. At the centre of the conundrum is the beautiful ground at North Marine Road, the development of which has been the focus of much of the organisational energy expended during the club's history. Chapter Three is about the development of the ground and the finances involved.

In the period that Scarborough Cricket Club has existed, cricket itself has undergone considerable changes in technical, organisational and social areas. The holiday resort of Scarborough, like all towns in England, has had to respond to rapid social change. The motor car has replaced the railway as the principal mode of transport and this has had enormous effects on the tourist industry in a seaside town like Scarborough. Self-catering holiday flats have replaced many small hotels and seaside landladies have become a protected species, as many people require more flexibility in their holiday planning, although a considerable exodus of people still takes place from the beaches as five o'clock approaches. Being flexible is fine, but being late for tea is a different matter.

Arrangements for holidays are made much later now than in the days when trains from

King's Cross were specially timed to depart and arrive for the Festival. More holidays are of the short break variety and holiday habits are more variable.

The effects of these changing holiday habits have been felt at North Marine Road. Advance bookings, a feature of the festivals immediately preceding and following World War Two, have declined enormously. In that period, a considerable number of people booked tickets from one season to the next, in order to retain their favourite seat at the Festival and the familiar faces which appeared each year was one of the charms and self perpetuating attractions of the Festival, which became very much a meeting place for old acquaintances. Day trippers are much more influenced by weather forecasts and the committee has become increasingly aware of the need for good weather for satisfactory Festival receipts. In taking account of these social changes, Chapter Four splits the club's history into three chronological periods: pre-1914; between the two world wars; post-1945.

'Cricket on Holiday' is the title for Chapter Five, which explores the origins and charts the progress of the Scarborough Cricket Festival. The amateur involvement, which lay at the heart of much Festival organisation is discussed within the social structure of different periods. Many stories of happenings at different Festivals owe their interest to the rigid social conventions of former times when amateurs and professionals not only used separate dressing-rooms, but entered the field of play through separate gates.

Much of cricket lore is nostalgic. Chapter Six is unashamedly so, as personalities of the cricketing world reminisce about cricket at Scarborough. 'Scarborough Views' is a look through the eyes of people for whom cricket at Scarborough has fond memories.

Chapters Seven and Eight concentrate on the playing side of the Scarborough Cricket Club. The club's heady progress to five Lord's Finals in the national cricket club trophy is described. The important contributions made by cricketers of lesser ability than members of those winning teams is recognised. Their efforts maintained Scarborough Cricket Club's eminent position in leagues as diverse as the Yorkshire Cricket Council, the Yorkshire League, the East Yorkshire Cup, the Ridings League, the Becket League, the Derwent Valley League and various junior competitions. The development of young players has always been a feature of the Scarborough cricketing philosophy.

Several of those young players progressed further. Chapter Nine is a record of those players

North Marine Road, Scarborough. Peter Tinniswood, author of the television series 'Tales from the Long Room' relaxes with the star of the programme, Robin Bailey.

who went on to bridge the gap between club cricket and the first-class game; some who did not; and a few famous names who were happy to play for Scarborough Cricket Club in the twilight of their careers.

Memorable matches are selected for Chapter Ten. Some are club matches, some are just matches. All are a matter of opinion as to the merit of their inclusion. Selection is one of those areas in cricket where everyone is an expert and it is recognised that there will be disagreement. At least the selections represent the wide spectrum of the club's cricketing activities throughout the years.

People who have been in the business of running Scarborough Cricket Club are featured in Chapter Eleven. By means of tape recordings, first undertaken in 1984, fascinating insights have been obtained from people who were not only interested in the club, but had the supreme advantage of being there at the time. Of course,

others from the sharp end could equally well have been included. Like heavyweight boxers, big-hitting batsmen attract most attention and North Marine Road has seen them all. Chapter Twelve looks at the biggest. The final chapter attempts some conclusions to the story of 'Cricket at Scarborough'.

This book is not a blow-by-blow account of matches played at Scarborough. It is not a statistical record and analysis of the Scarborough club. It is more a reminder of the cultural and social influences of changing times, their effect on the game of cricket and how they have influenced the affairs of a unique cricket club in a seaside resort. Scarborough Cricket Club has come a long way since its inception in 1849. In 1999 it will be 150 years old and the twenty-first century beckons. A formidable challenge awaits. Can Scarborough Cricket Club in the future match its own splendid achievements of the past?

Aerial view of North Marine Road, showing just how near the ground is to the sea.

Early Days

THE origins of the game of cricket are obscure, the evidence varied. In 'A History of Cricket' (1926), H.S.Altham states: *The earliest surviving description of a game of cricket is to be found in a Latin poem, written by a certain William Goldwin, a scholar of Eton and King's College, Cambridge, and published with other verses in 1706 under the title 'Musae Juveniles.'*

Benny Green writes in 'A History of Cricket' (1988) that: *In 1654 seven parishioners of Eltham in Kent were fined for playing cricket on the Sabbath. Perhaps their impious athleticism had been inspired by the events in Sussex thirty-two years earlier, when six men were prosecuted for playing the game in a churchyard. About the same time in the same county one Jasper Vinall was accidentally killed through the batsman's attempt to hit the ball twice in order to avoid being caught out.*

In Goldwin's poem there is evidence that, in order to settle a dispute, a *Nestor* (umpire) was asked to impose a *Justas le gas* (rule). This suggests that recognised codes for playing the game were observed long before the first laws of cricket were formally written. It is also certain that such codes were varied and local in their application. Nevertheless, the tactic of a batsman charging a fielder when he was in the process of taking a catch, had become widespread during the seventeenth century and

The Queen Hotel, North Marine Road, where it all started for Scarborough CC in 1849. The name can be made out above the first-floor windows. The ground is opposite and The Cricketers pub now stands on the site of the Queen Hotel.

had undoubtedly led to the death of the unfortunate Jasper.

By the middle of the eighteenth century, charging had been limited to making bodily contact only, thus the chances of further fatalities, due to over-enthusiastic use of the bat, were somewhat reduced! Yet cricket was far from being a gentle activity and the game needed refinement if the upper classes were to take an active part. Gradually the refinements did take place and the first written laws were codified in 1744.

The laws of 1744 were eventually published in 1752 in 'The New Universal Magazine'. The heading was 'The Game of Cricket, as settled by the Cricket Club in 1744 and played on the Artillery Ground, London'. This was because the 1744 code was designed to cater specifically for the challenge matches arranged on the Artillery Ground, but the text indicates it to be a modified version of an oral tradition dating back much earlier.

In that respect, a team game with some claim to be the precursor of cricket, was played as long ago as the thirteenth century, but the evidence is flimsy and so it was not until the late eighteenth century, when written documentation of cricket was thought to be worthwhile, that any degree of certainty can be established about the early days of cricket history.

There were many local variations of the 1744 code. One such variation is featured in a striking picture in the MCC archives at Lord's. An early eighteenth-century wicket, one foot high and two feet wide, has a hole in front into which the ball had to be 'popped' to secure a run out. In the picture a determined fielder and an equally determined batsman are engaged in a desperate scramble to reach this popping hole and it is worthwhile noting that even in modern times the batting crease is sometimes referred to as the 'popping crease'.

In 1744 the length of the pitch was confirmed at twenty-two yards. In some parts of the country the pitch length had been twenty-three yards, but the pitch length is generally recognised as being either Tudor in origin, four gads, or the Saxon equivalent of one chain, and it soon became normal to see groundsmen marking out pitches using a chain measure. Had twenty-three yards been adopted for the length of the pitch, it is possible that the game might have progressed differently. For example, the problems associated with the use of short-pitched bowling which has afflicted cricket at various times, would be rather less acute on a pitch measuring twenty-three yards in length.

The Hambledon Club of Hampshire is usually credited with the development of 'modern' cricket. According to Altham: 'If they did not find out cricket, they raised the game into an art.' From around 1768 and for about twenty years, the men of Hambledon, John Nyren, William Fennex, John Small, David Harris and others, immortalised in John Nyren's 'Young Cricketer's Tutor' and 'The Cricketers of My Time', became dominant figures in the early history of the game.

Harris, in particular, was important as *he was the first of all bowlers to combine length and direction with real pace and above all, to make the ball 'lift' quickly from the pitch.*

For this quality his peculiar action was responsible and Nyren's description is famous: *He would bring it from under the arm by a twist, and nearly as high as his armpit, and*

Cricket in 1750, a match in a holiday setting at Brading on the Isle of Wight.

with this action push it, as it were, from him. How it was the balls acquired the velocity they did by this mode of delivery I could never comprehend.

From this example, although it is clear that over-arm, or even round-arm bowling, was not permitted, the Harris style of bowling did force changes in the way the game was played. Defence, forward play and cutting were introduced and technical aspects of the game began to be taken more seriously. The shape of the bat was modified, as the curved club for dealing with under-arm bowling along the floor, was rather too cumbersome to combat the likes of David Harris. Ironically it was John Small, a teammate of Harris, who first used a straighter blade and so a 'straight bat' as a term to describe defence, became part of cricket language.

These developments highlight a deceptively simple, but fundamental relationship in the contest between bat and ball. Quite simply, the ball has to be bowled before it can be batted and the way the ball is bowled necessarily conditions the batting response. Sometimes referred to as the 'spirit of the game' attitude is all important in preserving what can be a delicate balance. When the 'spirit of the game' is ignored the game suffers and the law makers intervene. Since 1744, cricket laws have changed considerably, but perhaps not always with the successful outcome anticipated.

At times in the history of cricket, public reaction against certain methods of bowling has forced a change in the attitude with which the ball is bowled. In the famous 'Bodyline' series between Australia and England in 1932-33, passions were aroused to such an extent that an international 'incident' was only narrowly averted. It meant that not for another forty years was consistently short-pitched bowling revived as a method of attack.

Ironically, it was Australia who then led the way through the superbly fluent Dennis Lillee, aided and abetted by the raw power of Jeff Thomson. They were followed by the relentless four-man pace attacks of the West Indies which, under the captaincy of Clive Lloyd and Viv Richards in the 1970s and 1980s, slowed down over rates to the general detriment of the game and hastened the move towards batsmen's helmets, plus all the other protective equipment which is now part of modern cricket.

Inevitably, in 1991, the International Cricket Conference (ICC) acted to restrict the use of intimidatory bowling by limiting the number of 'bouncers' able to be bowled in an over.

Despite the significance of such happenings, it is unlikely that the world of cricket reverberated more than it did around 1790,

when round-arm bowling was first introduced. This new style was usually frowned upon as being ungentlemanly, although by the early 1800s there was several notable exponents of it. One of the reasons for the 'ungentlemanly' label, was because the move towards round-arm bowling had been influenced by ladies. Ladies cricket was very popular in villages in many parts of the country, but due to the voluminous nature of dresses of the period, under-arm bowling was difficult and many ladies had resorted to a round-arm bowling method. The advantages became quickly obvious and more and more male bowlers began to use it until, in 1827, the new style of round-arm bowling was legalised. The round-arm method lasted until 1864, when the laws were changed again, this time to allow over-arm bowling.

Another example in modern times of an adjustment being made to defeat the cunning intentions of bowlers, has been the change in the no-ball law. This made the placing of the front foot in relation to the batting crease the determining factor in deciding fairness when bowling the ball. Previously the law had required the back foot to be behind the bowling crease at the point of delivery.

The change was brought about by a number of fast bowlers 'dragging' the back foot and so effectively releasing the ball from less than the required distance. Photographs show great fast bowlers like Ray Lindwall and Fred Trueman gaining advantages of pace by 'dragging', a style which enabled the front foot to be well over the batting crease at the moment of delivery.

In the 1960s, the Australian bowlers Ian Meckiff and Gordon Rorke were bowling from more than a yard over the batting crease. To compound the difficulty for batsmen, both these bowlers also contravened the law on throwing. Others like Cuan McCarthy and Geoff Griffin from South Africa, Charlie Griffith from West Indies and Harold Rhodes in England, were amongst several international bowlers who were also found guilty of 'throwing' or 'jerking' the ball, with disastrous consequences for their careers. Did David Harris 'jerk' the ball? How would he have fared today? Providing that the umpire is informed, there is still no restriction on under-arm bowling.

The fascination of cricket depends on preserving the balance between ball and bat. Bats have been regulated, stumps too. An early attempt to have a bat the same width as the stumps was quickly defeated, with the restriction on the bat's width being set at four and a half inches. In recent years in Australia, the aforementioned Dennis Lillee tried to introduce an aluminium bat, presumably with commercial possibilities in mind. He failed.

Much earlier, in 1775, a third stump was introduced to combat the fact that a number of matches were being won or lost, because of the ball passing between the two stumps without removing the bail. Today, no small boy would ever think of not checking the distance between the stumps when he sets them up on the beach at Scarborough.

Inevitably, throughout cricket history, technical and technological development have affected the balance of the game. Laws have been adapted and modified. The makers of the laws have been criticised as the laws are always open to debate and discussion. Undoubtedly the debate will continue. W.G.Grace was said not to like defensive shots, because according to the great man 'he only got three off them'. Wielding modern, superbly balanced heavy-weight bats, with increasingly large 'middles' or 'sweet spots', many players now score three runs from little more than defensive pushes. Increasing power could become the latest threat to the balance of the game and a challenge to the lawmakers. No doubt the good 'Doctor' would have made suitable comment.

Changes in the laws have long been the responsibility of committees based at Lord's, which since about 1800 has been the centre of cricket influence previously concentrated

Thomas Lord, the York-shireman who gave his name to the most famous cricket ground in the world.

around Hambledon. Two significant elements combined to transfer power from Hambledon to London. Firstly, in 1774, the Revision of the Laws of the Game was undertaken by a committee of noblemen and gentlemen, which met at The Star and Garter club in Pall Mall. This was also the meeting place of a select London social group called the 'Je ne sais quoi' club and the cricket enthusiasts of this group formed the White Conduit Club, which played matches at White Conduit Fields, Islington.

Secondly and crucially, the White Conduit Club members began to resent the fact that their matches at Islington were played wide open to public scrutiny and curiosity. Neither were they too happy with the rather primitive facilities which existed. Accordingly, two members, The Earl of Winchilsea, himself a patron of Hambledon and Charles Lennox, later Duke of Richmond, took steps to acquire a ground more in keeping with the club's perceived exclusive status. They approached a man called Thomas Lord.

Thomas Lord, born in Thirsk in Yorkshire and the son of a farmer, was a worker on the ground at White Conduit Fields. It was as much by chance as anything that Winchilsea and Lennox happened to commission him to find a more private ground to play on which needed to be suitably nearer to town. The opportunity proved to be the making of Thomas Lord, as later he went on to build a successful business career dealing in property all over London. None of his future deals, however, was to leave such an indelible mark as his intitial venture on behalf of the White Conduit Club members. Interestingly, Lord also became a wine merchant, successful enough to provide wines for the table of King George IV. He was clearly a man of energy and ambition.

Lord approached the agent of the Portman family and arranged to rent some land from them in what is now Dorset Square. Throughout the winter and spring, Thomas Lord worked hard to get his ground ready for the coming season and on 31 May 1787 the first ever match was played at Lord's. This match was between two so called county teams, Middlesex and Essex, but by June 1787 it was the White Conduit Club itself which was playing against Middlesex at Lord's.

A year later the White Conduit Club became the Marylebone Cricket Club (MCC) the ground being situated in the parish of Marylebone and by 1800, Lord's was established as the centre of cricket influence. The MCC quickly became recognised as the supreme authority on the game, including the laws and the power base for control of the game had clearly changed.

Sadly for romantics, Hambledon played its last recorded match against an All England XI in 1793, significantly and somewhat ironically, at Lord's. Despite two changes of venue — the present Lord's ground was opened in 1814 — the centralisation of cricket authority at Lord's was to have enormous consequences for future developments in cricket. Lord's influence spread to all parts of the country. Nowhere did it become more significant than at Scarborough.

Important as the technical and organisational changes were in the development of the game, the social and cultural effects were equally influencial. The initial effect of the move of cricket's power base from Hambledon to London and the formation of the MCC was to add emphasis to the 'upper social class' control of the organisation of cricket in England. This was vitally important for the establishment of cricket on a national basis. As in horse racing, it was only members of the upper social class who, in the early part of the nineteenth century, were sufficiently mobile, interested and interactive to make national organisation possible. In contrast, many other games and sports, such as skittles, marbles and wrestling, which had been equally as popular as cricket with village people, remained strictly local.

It is also significant that the national organisation of cricket in the later nineteenth century developed through the agencies of county shires, rather than urban towns as in football. This county and village club emphasis tended to reinforce upper-class control and highlighted the rural origins of the game in local parishes, as illustrated in the Hambledon story.

Within the framework of a country village community it had been possible to play the game with class lines adhered to, but with different social classes taking part. This was possible because cricket is a non-contact game, at least in a personal physical sense. Different social classes were able to participate on the field without coming into direct physical contact with each other and so dignity, an essential ingredient for class distinction, was maintained.

At the same time, suitable arrangements were made to retain off the field class differences. These were reinforced in segregated changing and dining arrangements, which were preserved even until the late 1950s in the first-class game. Examples of the paternalistic and more tolerant attitude of the upper classes towards the workers when on the cricket field and the intermingling of the classes in village communities are recorded in H.S.Altham, on Hambledon:

That plain-spoken little bumkin has not yet learned his lesson; an hour or two hence he will miss by a hair's breadth the leg stump of the Duke of Dorset and 'forgetting' in his eagerness and delight the style in which we were always accustomed to impress our aristocratical playmates with our acknowledgement of their rank and station, he would ball out "Ah, it was tedious near you, sir," and so set the whole field laughing.

Or, John Nyren writing of his father.

He could differ with a superior, without trenching upon his dignity or losing his own, I have known him maintain an opinion with great firmness against the Duke of Dorset and Sir Horace Mann; when, in consequence of his being proved to be in the right, the latter has afterwards crossed the ground and shaken him heartily by the hand.

This sense of community is strongly emphasised in all early accounts of cricket, although

John Nyren, a man of Hambledon, traditionally the cradle of English cricket.

this did not prevent landowners attempting to 'poach' outstanding players from other landowners.

(Richard Nyren) . . .has had words, firm but respectful, with the great Sir Horace Mann, of Kent, about that rising young batsman, James Aylward, whom Sir Horace is trying to filch away from Hambledon with the lure of a bailiff's post on his own estate at Bishopsbourne (and lure him away he did; but the best batsman made but a poor bailiff, we are told).

At the same time as cricket authority was being transferred from Hambledon to London, general attitudes towards leisure were also changing. At the end of the eighteenth century, concern for social control of the poorer classes, who were perceived to be a potential threat to authority following the French Revolution, is well documented in religious and educational literature. Added to this establishment concern for social control is the view expressed by Hugh Cunningham in 'Leisure in the Industrial Revolution' that because the new factory system occupied working people's time much more than before, the upper classes were the only people with time available and so they retreated to their own leisure activities. The end result was that leisure participation became far more segregated and increasingly dominated by considerations of class.

Furthermore, the greater privatisation of property taking place during this period, witness the ambitions of the White Conduit Club, meant that *the privatisation of property . . .entailed for all classes a privatisation of leisure, privatisation in the sense that leisure became class-bound and impenetrable for those outside the class in question.*

The consequence of these social changes was that class consciousness increased throughout the nineteenth century. Nowhere was this more apparent in society than in the cricket world and in particular in the contrast between Gentlemen (amateurs) and Players (professionals). Scarborough Cricket Festival became an outstanding example of this social structure in operation and so deeply embedded was the division between the two groups, that it was not until 1963 that the distinction between amateurs and professionals was finally abolished.

The first match between Gentlemen and Players was played in 1806 at Lord's (Dorset Square). Despite the presence of the Gentlemen amateurs in that match, surprisingly most cricket at the time was played by professionals. In fact, when Surrey played England at Lord's in 1807, not a single amateur was included in the Surrey team and England included only four amateurs, two of whom batted at ten and eleven.

Before the coming of W.G.Grace in the 1860s, The Gentlemen versus Players matches were able to take place only by virtue of the Gentlemen being allowed odds, or given men, or both. The reason for this state of affair was that gambling was intrinsically linked to the game of cricket. Most of the gambling was done by the gentry and the association with horse racing was close, even to the extent of bookmakers being a prominent part of the cricket scene in the nineteenth century.

According to Cunningham: *Just in front of the pavilion at Lord's at every great match sat men ready, with money down, to give and take the current odds on the play. Many well-known bookmakers were to be found regularly amongst them and even the famous Crockford and Gully occasionally appeared there.*

Single-wicket and double-wicket matches were also popular as betting mediums, with one of the most celebrated taking place in 1810 between George 'Squire' Osbaldeston and the professional William Lambert versus Reverend Lord Frederick Beauclerk and T.C.Howard. When Osbaldeston fell ill, Lambert took on the opposition single-handed and won the match. Despite this loss, Beauclerk went on to dominate affairs at Lord's, which he treated much as his own personal club, behaving with a combination of autocracy and arrogance.

With gambling rife, corruption and dishonesty often threatened single-wicket matches and a number of incidents were reported of individuals being 'warned off' grounds. Gambling at cricket matches became a feature of the Victorian period and some of the sums involved were very large. George Atkinson, a Yorkshire player of the mid-nineteenth century, recalled in the 'Yorkshire Evening Post' (1897): *One of my earlier exploits in cricket was fielding in a single wicket match on the Leeds Clarence old ground in 1857, when Jim Sadler beat John Grange in a contest for £200 a-side.*

Likewise: *No doubt many cricketers of the past generation will remember the great single-wicket match at Stockton played in 1861. It was for £400 between the Cambridge Three, R.Carpenter, G.Tarrant and T.Haywood and the Stockton Five, W.Halton, T.Robinson, T.Hornby, T.Darnton and myself. The match caused a lot of excitement and betting. Mr Jackson the backer of the Cambridge Three made some extraordinary bets and won a lot of money. One of the bets was £1000 to £1 that neither of the Five got 100 runs and at one stage of the match could be heard shouting, in stentorian tones, "£1000 to £500 on the Three".*

Atkinson went on to say that, in his opinion *there is no doubt that these money matches did harm to the games in that they created a lot of heavy gambling and unhealthy excitement.*

It is only since 1973 that gambling has reappeared on the cricket scene with the admittance of Ladbrokes the bookmakers, firstly to Test matches and then to county games. At Leeds in 1976, it was discovered that Australian players Rodney Marsh and Dennis Lillee had attempted to place a bet on the Test match in which they were taking part, a move which adds piquancy to the views of Atkinson on cricket and gambling a hundred years before.

The early part of the nineteenth century saw cricket developing rapidly on three fronts. In the south of England, strongly influenced by MCC from Lord's, the gentry administered cricket at county level. Kent became a stronghold of the game, thanks to notable performers like Alfred Mynn, 'Champion of English Cricketers', a reference on his tombstone to his victories in single-wicket matches, and Fuller Pilch, one of the great batsmen of the century. The third member of the Kent triumvirate was Nicholas Wanostrocht, who played under the alias of 'Felix' but whose manual on the art of batsmanship, 'Felix on the Bat' was the first textbook on the subject, whilst his artistic illustrations in other books were to become collectors' items.

'Felix' was the 'nom-de-plume' adopted by Wanostrocht because, being a schoolteacher, he was anxious to avoid difficulties with parents about his activities, due to cricket's

distasteful association with gambling. Despite this moral handicap, official county cricket clubs began to be formed, as distinct from the previous loose groupings of players playing under county headings. Sussex were the first county club in 1839, although not recognised as such until 1864. The first University match between Oxford and Cambridge took place in 1827. Life in nineteenth-century England became nothing if not organised. Cricket, as always, reflected the changing social structure.

Beside the 'organised' cricket influenced from Lord's, Mary Russell Mitford writes in 'Our Village' of a different kind of cricket played in the 1820s:

I doubt if there can be any scene in the world more animating or delightful than a cricket-match. I do not mean a set match at Lord's

Left: Nicholas Wanostrocht — 'Felix' — author of the first textbook on batting. Right: Alfred Mynn, the 'Champion of English Cricketers'.

Lunchtime promenaders at North Marine Road in the 1930s, carrying on a tradition begun many years before.

Ground for money, hard money, between a certain number of gentlemen and players, as they are called, people who make a trade of the noble art of sport, and degrade it into an affair of bettings, and hedgings, and cheatings, it may be, like boxing or horse-racing; nor do I mean a pretty fete in a gentleman's park, where one club of cricketing dandies encounter another such club, and where they show off in graceful costume to a gay marquee of admiring belles . . .No! The cricket that I mean is a real solid old-fashioned match between neighbouring parishes, where each attacks the other for honour and a supper, glory and half-a-crown a man. If there be any gentlemen amongst them, it is well, if not, it is so much the better.

Mitford is scornful of the way in which much cricket had been appropriated by the gentry for the purposes of gambling, with the support of the MCC at Lord's. In her view, the game had been degraded from what previously was a noble sport. References to honour and disparages against 'so called gentlemen' were to anticipate the ethos of the public schools' approach to sport, which developed later in the century and was much more in sympathy with Mitford's ideals.

As might be expected, the approach was rather different in the north of England. Here, cricket was emerging as a spectator sport, but from a different base. Publicans were central figures. They often took it upon themselves to organise matches in the locality as a means

of contributing to trade and it was largely from these origins that the appeal of the game began to take hold in the north.

Cricket rapidly grew in popularity. As early as 1825 there was a reported attendance of between 14,000 and 20,000 at Darnall in Sheffield for a match between the Rest of Yorkshire and All England. In 1835, some 20,000 people watched the Nottingham versus Sussex match in which Nottingham beat Sussex, the first time a northern team had beaten either Kent or Sussex, the two great southern counties.

More parochially, Nottingham versus Sheffield matches had been played since 1771. Nottingham had become the northern centre of cricket, so much so that when the second North versus South match was scheduled to be played in 1836 at Leicester, rather than Nottingham, a public outcry forced a meeting presided over by the Mayor of Nottingham. This meeting passed three resolutions deploring the choice of venue and the burghers of Nottingham may have had a good case, for the South won the match at Leicester, so reversing the result of the match played at Lord's earlier in the season which the North won. The North versus South matches became very important in the cricket calendar and such a match became a feature of the Scarborough Cricket Festival.

Nottingham reinforced its position as the leading centre of cricket in the north of England when, in 1837, a bricklayer named

North Marine Road in 1992. The Cricketers pub stands on the site of the Queen Hotel, where Scarborough CC was founded in 1849. The ground is immediately opposite and the cliff top at the rear of the pub over-looks North Bay.

Castle Hill looking towards the castle itself. High winds and rifle practice were hazards when Scarborough CC staged early matches here.

William Clarke married the widow who kept the Trent Bridge Inn. Clarke became respon-sible for establishing county cricket at Trent Bridge, but it was not until he was engaged by MCC as a practice bowler at Lord's, that he had a wider impact on the game.

Although he was 48 years old at the time, he soon established himself as the leading slow bowler in England, largely because he cleverly reverted to under-arm bowling when round-arm bowling was the normal style. Confused batsmen were unable to counter his method,

but Clarke was not just a cunning cricketer, he was a shrewd entrepreneur. He saw the opportunity of using cricket for his own profit and in 1846 he organised a number of professionals into a travelling group which he called the All England XI.

This group toured the country playing challenge matches against all and sundry, often against opposing teams of up to twenty or more players and in H.S.Altham's words became 'truly missionaries of cricket'. There had, of course, been England sides before, often produced by private individuals, or MCC for individual events, but a permanent touring team composed of the country's best players was a completely new venture.

A fee of £4 to £6 per match was paid to the players, depending on the length of journey involved, but eventually, tired of Clarke's arrogance and meanness, several of the players broke away in 1852 to form a rival group, the United England XI. The leader of this equally successful group was John Wisden, who in 1864 published 'The Cricketer's Almanack', which has become the 'bible' of cricket.

Interestingly, between 1856 and 1859, these two sides participated in a series of matches at Lord's against each other, in which amateurs were not allowed to play. Amateurs were included when the Elevens were touring. Other touring professional groups were formed. In 1858 a 'New All England XI' was formed by Messrs Sherman and Chadband, and in 1862 Fred Caesar organised 'Another All England XI' followed in 1865 by the very popular 'United South of England XI'. Roger Iddison, a famous name in the history of Yorkshire cricket, was principal organiser of the United North of England XI, formed in 1869, and was co-secretary of the Yorkshire United XI.

The most important point about these XIs was that they established the principle of teams playing outside their locality and for significant periods of time. In 1859 this idea was extended when the first England team to play abroad set sail for Canada, captained by George Parr, one of William Clarke's original All England XI.

The Rifle Volunteers whose practice on Castle Hill often interfered with the cricket there.

The first tour of Australia took place two years later in 1861. The precedent set by the professional touring teams of playing away from their own neighbourhood was also to be a necessary requirement for teams playing at the Scarborough Cricket Festival later in the century.

It was against this early background of the development of modern cricket that Scarborough Cricket Club was formed in 1849. The club was originally called Queen's Club and played on land opposite the Queen Hotel on North Marine Road. As was often the case in the North of England, the landlord, John Bell, could well have been involved in the organisation, as he opened the innings in the first recorded match played between Scarborough and Visitors and Filey and Visitors, at Filey, in late August 1849. A return match took place on Monday 3 September, at Scarborough, and from the very first, the influence of visitors was apparent.

The land on which early matches were played was little more than a rough field. Eventually it was to become the site of the present ground on North Marine Road, but many of the important matches were played at Castle Hill. This tended to produce a conflict of interest, because the Army owned the land and the Army needed rifle practice.

The reason for having a cricket field there at all was that Lord Hill, Commander-in-Chief of the Army, had ordered the preparation of a cricket ground as near as possible to every Army barracks in the country. It was this directive, issued in 1841, which really estab-

lished cricket as an important leisure activity and went a long way towards making the game an accepted part of the social fabric of the nation. As far as Scarborough Cricket Club was concerned, the presence of riflemen at practice had a rather more inhibiting effect and partly contributed to the club eventually abandoning matches at Castle Hill in favour of developing its own ground on North Marine Road.

Besides Filey, other local sides against which Scarborough played in those early days were Setterington, Castle Howard, Wykeham, Sherburn, Pickering and Hutton Buscel, whilst another stalwart of the period was John Mackereth. He was a brewer and it is quite likely that he supplied John Bell with beer at the Queen Hotel. His name became associated with the club for more than 40 years

as player, committeeman and vice-president and this trend towards longevity of service has become a recurring feature throughout the history of the club.

Without doubt, the first major turning point for Scarborough Cricket Club came in 1863. Then the club was reconstituted and Lord Derwent (then Sir Harcourt Johnstone, Bart) became president. The reason behind the move was that in 1862 the All-England XI had been attracted to Scarborough to play against Twenty (Players) of Scarborough. The match was a great success, so much so, that it became an annual event and as was normal in the later nineteenth century, proper formal organisation was required, especially when finance was involved.

A report in the 'Scarborough Post' of 1867

Left: Paxton's Saloon c.1858, now The Spa. Right: More origins of The Spa, the Gothic Saloon, c.1841.

The golden era of The Spa, an illustration showing the complex c.1900.

Scarborough Railway Station, opened in 1856. Behind the station is the Pavlion Hotel, built in 1870.

stated: *Never since it has been the annual custom of an All-England Eleven to visit Scarborough have they been so signally favoured with weather . . . large companies have assembled in the Castle Yard than have ever been witnessed on similar occasions.*

The match took place on 19, 20 and 21 August and the All-England XI won by eight wickets.

The benefit to the club of the game was highlighted in the report of the 'annual soiree and dinner' held at the Queen Hotel when ' . . . *a highly respectable, though not very numerous party of gentlemen assembled and rejoiced over the sumptuous banquet before them.*

The treasurer, Mr Hick, presented the financial state of the club from the year 1864, when there was an adverse balance of £1 13s

0d, to the present situation where the balance in hand was about £20.

'The Scarborough Post' was complimentary about the success of the club's venture: *This success was due to the proceeds of the All-England match and a concert that was given in aid of their funds. Besides this balance they now have a handsome pavilion in the field and they had also the service of professional cricketer, Mr King.*

In the chairman's toast the moral benefits of cricket were stressed: *It stood alone among all sports in its power of giving spirit and emulation to youth. Even its danger (for there was certainly at least some danger in the game) commended it to Englishmen.*

Some fundamental issues are raised in these reports, which were to have considerable significance for Scarborough Cricket Club.

The North Bay in 1870 showing steps leading from North Marine Road down to the beach. Bathing huts on wheels were a feature of this period. The North Pier, opened in 1869, was destroyed by a storm in 1905.

The height of the season. Promenading on South Bay c.1900.

The emphasis on moral values, inherently attributed to cricket, became a considerable factor in promoting the game in the second half of the nineteenth century, particularly through the influence of the public schools, and Scarborough people were well aware of such trends and attitudes and strongly supported them.

In more practical terms, the finances of the club were already being centred around matches involving representative teams from outside the town and this source of income became increasingly a vital part of the club's development. This state of affairs was reinforced by a match which had become traditional by 1867, between Scarborough Cricket Club and Scarborough Visitors, and it was from this match that the seeds of the festival idea germinated, culminating with the famous challenge match in 1871 between Lord Londesborough's XI and C.I. Thornton's XI.

By playing the Visitors match towards the end of August, when it was hoped that weather conditions would be most favourable, the club attempted to take maximum advantage of being a seaside resort. In any analysis of Scarborough Cricket Club's longevity, the

Looking over Scarborough from the Spa Gardens in the late 19th century.

attractions of sunshine, sea and sand should not be underestimated.

By far the most unusual and spectacular match in the early years of Scarborough Cricket Club, took place on 27, 28 and 29 August 1869, at the Castle Hill Yard. This match was played between Scarborough Cricket Club and a team of Australian Aborigines. According to the 'Scarborough Post'.

This interesting match, between eleven members of the Scarborough Club and the same number of black cricketers from Australia, was begun on Thursday in the Castle Yard. Notwithstanding the boisterous state of the weather, a large concourse of spectators assembled to witness the novel sight; and they were well rewarded, for some very good cricket and shown by the dark-skinned players.

The Aborigines team, according to the scorecard was:
Shepherd
Twopenny, plain
Tiger, pink
Cuzens, white
Mullagh, blue
Red Cap, black
Lawrence, captain
Peter, green
Dick-a-Dick, yellow
Charley, brown
Mosquito, magenta

Presumably the colours were items of clothing, perhaps a cap, or more likely a belt or tie around the waist, to make identification easier for the scorers. The Aborigines won the match by 10 wickets: Scarborough CC 90 and 109. Aborigines 148 and 53 for 0 wicket.

The 'Scarborough Post' reported: *On Saturday afternoon the most interesting portion of the proceedings, namely, the English and Australian sports, came off in the Castle Yard, in the presence of about 4,000 spectators. The English sports came first on the programme and consisted of 100 yards flat race for £1; standing high jump for 10s; vaulting with pole; running high jump, 10s; 150 yards steeplechase over four hurdles, £1; 100 yards backwards race, £1; running long jump and throwing the cricket ball.*

From the results listed it would appear the Aborigines were equally as successful in these events as they were at cricket and afterwards.

. . .a splendid display of Australian sports were shown by the Aborigines, who dressed in their native costume, performed feats with spears and boomerangs with a precision and grace which was both pleasing and surprising to behold . . .Altogether, the Blacks have given us a good three days' amusement and it is satisfactory to know that they and our enterprising local cricket club have been amply repaid for their labour.

It is clear from these reports that Scarborough itself reflected the colonial outlook of the period. The reports also indicate that, from the very beginning, the club had acquired another main characteristic of Victorian England, the keen and hard-nosed entrepreneurial outlook.

It is generally agreed that the mid-nineteenth century marked a turning point in the history of leisure. In 'Mid-Victorian Britain 1851-1875', Geoffrey Best writes: *The leisure patterns of modern industrial urban society now begin to take shape.*

There were many contributory factors, but the opening of the York-Scarborough railway line in 1845 would be high on the list of important happenings and it certainly heralded a new era in the development of the town. Visitors were brought to Scarborough from far afield and from a broader social background. Industrial workers from Bradford, Leeds, Sheffield and the West Riding gained welcome relief from the factory and the pit in a trip on the train to the seaside. The rapid expansion of the tourist trade stimulated the growth of facilities, both in number and range. Spectator sports were quickly recognised as being a useful attraction to bring additional trade to the resort.

At the same time as working class people began to take advantage of changing working and leisure patterns, the gentry was still drawn to the town by Scarborough's past reputation for upper-class sophistication. Such a reputation was established through the highest credentials, for since the early sixteenth century, Scarborough had always been associated with the Crown. Scarborough Castle, now a ruin, dominated the headland dividing the North and South Bays and was an important royal and baronial government centre for the north of the country.

The connection with royalty was to remain until late into the nineteenth century, but by 1850, the reason for the visits to the town by 'the quality' had radically changed, socialising was the purpose and the Spa was the focus.

The development of the Spa had assumed three stages. The first stage was in 1626, when a Mistress Barrow discovered some wells with

The Aborigines team which met Scarborough CC in 1869 at the Castle Hill Yard.

*The Church Parade,
Scarborough, c. 1900.*

supposedly medicinal properties and a public well was established in 1698. An establishment was erected to serve the patrons, but the tortuous path down St Nicholas Cliff proved to be a great deterrent to many, consequently, it was not until the new Spa Bridge was opened in 1827 that the Spa became truly popular.

The second stage in the growth of Scarborough as a spa town had taken place at the end of the eighteenth century when coastal resorts began to overtake inland spas in popularity, because sea water was considered to be even more benefical to health than inland waters. As Scarborough was already recognised as a major spa, the town quickly seized the opportunity to consolidate its reputation with the 'new' seabathing and set out to expand its facilities for, although the mystical powers of spa and sea waters had many advocates, it was shrewdly recognised by the town worthies that the primary and overiding importance in the life of any resort was social.

At Scarborough both the pump room at the Spa and the beach soon became the focus of

activity for a variety of visitors, often equipped with strange contraptions, such as bathing machines and bathing chariots complete with awnings. It became quite clear that in the matter of social advantage, the transfer of affection from inland spa to coastal resort, gave Scarborough a head start over most competitors.

The long tradition of the gentry visiting Scarborough was a crucially important element in the development of Scarborough Cricket Club. This was particularly true in the formative years when patronage of the club was provided largely by visitors from outside the town, who recognised certain social advantages in being involved in the affairs of a cricket club at Scarborough. The fact that some of the visitors also had influence and power at cricket's administrative centre, Lord's, gave Scarborough Cricket Club a tremendous advantage as the destiny of the club became shaped in the wider cricket world.

On the other hand, local concern was focused more on the day-to-day practicalities of what

was to become undoubtedly a very successful business venture. By combining two virtues of nineteenth-century England, upper-class influence and business acumen, Scarborough Cricket Club was able to fulfil two requirements.

These were to provide entertainment of the highest quality for visitors to the town and by so doing, Scarborough Cricket Club added considerably to the attraction of Scarborough as a major holiday resort. At the same time, the club was able to satisfy local demand for cricket, a sport that was rapidly becoming a popular leisure activity in Victorian England.

South Bay c.1900. Cockles and whelk stalls in the foreground with the Grand Hotel (background left) overlooking the Baths and the bay.

Three Wise Men

I T IS with feelings of satisfaction to myself that I rise tonight to take leave of you as your secretary, but before so doing perhaps you will pardon me if I claim your indulgence for a few moments whilst I look back over the long period during which it has been my privilege as well as pleasure to serve you. I think it is now close upon twenty years since I entered on the important office which I am about to relinquish, having been appointed in the year 1869 as honorary secretary, a period when the club, through various causes, had fallen to a rather low ebb, the income of the club not exceeding £30 annually and when the members had many and great difficulties to contend with in the shape of the ground and other embarrassments.

Some of you here tonight will remember the old ridge and fur to say nothing (of) other nuisances from cows, pigs and other livestock which used to form such a barrier to good batting and fielding in the old days and, to use the words of your respected patron Charles Legard Bart, 'where the cow and all the accompaniments of a cow were to be seen on the Scarborough Cricket Ground'. But I am happy to say, gentlemen, this has passed away for ever as far as the Scarborough Cricket Club is concerned.

The above is part of the prepared retirement speech of Robert Baker, who became the first paid secretary of Scarborough Cricket Club in 1872 at a salary of £10 per annum. Baker died from Bright's disease, or kidney failure, in 1896, after a painful two-year illness. Tragically, it was at the early age of 46. He was succeeded by William Leadbeater.

A little luck is a vital ingredient in the cricket mixture and Scarborough Cricket Club had a large helping when Richard Bent, the original appointee to the secretaryship when Baker died, had to leave Scarborough for business reasons. Thus Leadbeater, almost by default, took the job. He had already been assistant to Baker for nearly nine years between 1884 and 1893 and was well-versed in the requirements of the position. He was also a member of the committee for about a year before he became secretary. He was to remain secretary until he retired in 1930.

Robert Baker and William Leadbeater rightly take much of the credit for providing the direction, guidance and firm leadership that any successful organisation requires and which was so important in the formative years of Scarborough Cricket Club. These two forceful, but very individual characters were able to establish sound principles and influence club policy, particularly in respect of ground development and club membership. These foundations of policy were consolidated in later years by a third man, who was equally influential. His name was Alfred Rutherford.

When 'Alfie' Rutherford became secretary in 1949 he was, naturally, a product of a more modern age. He contributed greatly to revitalising the club in the early post-war period by continuing the policies carried out by Baker and Leadbeater regarding the ground, but he made increased membership a particular target. When Rutherford left in 1961, to become general manager to Leeds Cricket, Football & Athletic Co Ltd, the landlords of Yorkshire County Cricket Club's headquarters at Headingley, membership of Scarborough Cricket Club had rocketed to over 4,500 and the health and welfare of the club had never been better.

It is one of the intriguing aspects of the history of Scarborough Cricket Club that, despite the inevitable change of personnel over such a long period, the two basic planks of club policy — ground improvement and high membership — have remained constant. Two examples suffice. In 1870, a report in the 'Scarborough Gazette' identified two elements in what later became future policy of the club: *What the club requires is a good ground and a good professional bowler. Were we in possession of these necessities we would feel quite confident of rendering a satisfactory account of ourselves against some of the best clubs in the district.*

In 1948, J.M.Kilburn wrote: *The committee's policy has always been to invest in improvements rather than preserve a heavy cash balance.*

Undoubtedly, the ground at North Marine Road has been the cornerstone from which the club has progressed. Ideally situated, just across the road which runs along the cliffs overlooking North Bay and close to the town centre, the policy of investing in improvements to the ground has been vindicated many times over. The link with good players, identified in 1870 as a good professional bowler, is also significant. A good ground attracts good players, a first-class ground even better. Baker, Leadbeater, Rutherford and Scarborough Cricket Club committees through the years have understood that simple but vital relationship.

Robert Baker

Whether Robert Baker actually gave his prepared resignation speech is unlikely. He did not relinquish the post of secretary until his death in 1896, a period of twenty-four years, which is rather longer than the 'close upon twenty years' referred to in his speech. Evidence suggests that Robert Baker was not inclined to contemplate resignation lightly. It was more likely he felt strongly about something or other and had the resignation speech drafted to be used if necessary to force the issue.

Born in 1849 at Hunmanby, a village just

outside Scarborough, Baker came to Scarborough from Bridlington, where he had lived since an early age. He was eighteen years old and, remarkably, had already been secretary of Bridlington Cricket Club for four years. Baker's keenness led him into disputes with people on a number of occasions and it would appear that it was a disagreement between himself and J.R.Dippie, a good playing member and, briefly, joint honorary secretary, which led directly to Dippie being replaced by Baker as secretary in 1872.

The position of secretary had been one of a shared nature since 1863, with W.Wharton and Charles Haig being the first occupants of the post. As mentioned in the speech, Baker was first appointed in an honorary capacity in 1869, jointly with H.Blanchard. Minutes of meetings in 1871, however, list H.O.Welburn and J.R.Dippie as joint secretaries, with Baker elected to the committee on 18 October 1871. It would seem, therefore, that Baker's honorary service as secretary was interrupted when he and Dippie came into conflict about the ground. It was concern about the standard of playing conditions which was at the root of the argument.

It was no accident that Robert Baker took

Scarborough Cricket Club in 1873. Robert Baker is standing extreme right. J.R.Dippie is sitting extreme front right. Here is the full line-up. Back row (left to right): J.King, W.Sanderson (captain), M.Wheaton (umpire), T.Yeoman, Dr J.W.Taylor, C. Smailes, R.Baker. Middle: J.Dickinson, J.Mackereth, G.Dippie, R.Iddison. Front: W.Wright, G.Watson, J.R.Dippie. Baker and J.R.Dippie had a dispute about the ground. John Mackereth supplied the landlord of the Queen Hotel, John Bell, with beer. John King was club professional. Roger Iddison was captain of many 'Yorkshire' teams and a leading figure in cricket in the county.

The ground at North Marine Road after it had been levelled. The occasion is the opening of the new Pavilion in 1874.

such a close interest in the playing conditions. He was the outstanding player in the club and played for Yorkshire in three matches in 1874 and 1875. He made the first-ever Scarborough century, 127 not out in 1874, and the following year took nine wickets whilst playing for a Yorkshire XI against Hampshire at Lyndhurst.

In 1922, S.F.Yeomans, who played for Scarborough for 41 years and knew Baker well, wrote: *Robert Baker was a man who liked and generally got a good deal of his own way and would not allow any interference from anyone in matters connected with the Scarborough Club.*

Yeomans went on to describe how on one occasion, Baker had banned R.W.(Roberty) Frank from playing for Scarborough, because Frank had elected to play for North Riding rather than Scarborough at a previous time. Later that season, Middlesbrough invited Frank to play for them at Scarborough, much to Baker's annoyance. That annoyance knew no bounds when, amazingly, Frank made a record score of 309 out of a total of 382!

On another occasion, a fielder named Bird missed a catch off Baker's bowling, whereupon Baker called out, "Go off the field Bird, we can do without you." The next the team saw of Bird was on the station at York that evening,

the wretched fielder having caught the first train out of Darlington after his dismissal.

Baker was extremely energetic and of a practical nature. The ground became his abiding passion. According to Revd R.S.Holmes in his 'History of Yorkshire Cricket (1833-1903)', Baker *practially lived for the game and club, and the present ground will ever remain a memorial of his work and forthought and devotion.*

Even so, the initiative for ground development did not lie only with Robert Baker. A meeting of the committee held on 17 October 1871 — the one at which Baker was elected to the committee after being joint honorary secretary — resolved that secretaries Welbourne and Dippie should *write to Henry Walker Esq, requesting him to inform Lord Londesborough that in the opinion of the committee the most desirable course to adopt with reference to the laying down of a new ground is to enlarge the present ground of the club by levelling a part of the next field.*

Later, at a meeting in November, Baker, now a committee member, moved a resolution that a deputation consisting of the president, Mr Bedford, Dr Taylor, Mr Delamere and Mr J.R.Dippie, should speak to Mr J.Woodall, the owner, and Mr Millhouse, the tenant of the field on which the club played, with a view to improvement work being carried out. The deputation did reach agreement with Mr Millhouse and work began to get the ground at North Marine Road into a fit state for first-class cricket.

Robert Baker clearly influenced the decision to develop the site on North Marine Road, but there were other factors which the club had to take into consideration, and powerful ones at that. Since the reconstitution of the club in 1863, the ground at North Marine Road had been rented at £15 per annum, but it was in a very primitive state, being little more than a meadow with plenty of livestock in attendance.

Moreover it was not enclosed and so the taking of gate money was difficult, a vital consideration when much of the club's income depended on it. Important matches, therefore, were played at Castle Hill, although conditions at Castle Hill Yard were also far from satisfactory. The problems there were concerned first with the high winds which sometimes necessitated iron bails being used on the stumps; and second, a conflict of interest with the military. The Army owned the land and according to J.M.Kilburn: *On more than one occasion, there was a difference of opinion between those who wanted to play cricket and those who wanted to practise rifle shooting. Range as often as rain stopped play.*

With this as the background, a match of crucial significance in the history of Scarborough Cricket Club took place at Castle Hill on 11 and 12 September 1871. The match was played between Lord Londesborough's XI and Scarborough Visitors (C.I.Thornton's XI) and it was the forerunner of the Scarborough Cricket Festival.

Lord Londesborough's role in the development of the Festival is examined in more detail later, but there is no doubt that the match in 1871 was instrumental in shaping the destiny of Scarborough Cricket Club. The important point is that as a direct consequence of the match, the club came under pressure from Lord Londesborough to improve facilities both on and off the field; specifically to find a new ground.

Robert Baker's influence was probably decisive at this point for, despite schemes to the contrary, including one to lay down a new ground at Castle Hill, the club decided to develop their existing headquarters at North Marine Road and ignore other suggestions, even from Lord Londesborough. This decision was perhaps the most important in the entire history of Scarborough Cricket Club and the evidence is that Robert Baker had a major influence in the making of it.

Robert Baker, the first paid secretary of Scarborough CC.

Another offshoot of the 1871 match at Castle Hill was the start of matches between Yorkshire and Middlesex at Scarborough, the first of which took place on the redeveloped ground at North Marine Road in September 1874. In this match, Baker made one of his three appearances for Yorkshire, going in at number eight and making 22. The following year the Scarborough Cricket Festival began and has only been interrupted since by two world wars.

By January 1872 work had begun on the levelling and reconstruction of the ground at North Marine Road, with Baker a member of the sub-committee charged with supervising the work, which included enclosing part of the ground. On 15 April the secretary, J.R.Dippie, reported to the general committee that a complaint had been made to him that Baker was playing on the new ground. After consultation with two or three members of the committee, he had written to Baker to tell him to stop doing so, as he was retarding progress and if Baker persisted, then he (Dippie) would 'have no alternative to bring the matter before the committee forthwith'.

Baker replied to the effect that Dippie could do what he liked, but it would not prevent him (Baker) continuing to play on the ground. The outcome of this confrontation between Baker and Dippie was that several members sided with Baker and threatened to resign from the club unless Mr Dippie withdrew his letter to Baker. Further correspondence ensued until Dippie offered to withdraw, providing that all other correspondence was withdrawn also, including the resignations.

Sometime following a meeting on 17 May, Baker and Dippie exchanged roles with Robert Baker assuming the position of secretary and Dippie taking Baker's place on the committee. A significant difference in the arrangement was that the new occupant of the secretary's chair was paid.

This did not seem to please Dippie. A minute of 3 October 1872 records: *In consideration of Mr Baker assuming the duties of Secretary of the Scarborough Cricket Club (under premise of remuneration) at a critical period when that office became vacant, it is proposed by Mr Yeomans and seconded by Mr Mackereth, that the sum of £10 be given to Mr Baker for his sevices during the present year.*

An amendment was then put to reduce this amount to £7 10s, but this was lost by four votes to three. Naturally, J.R.Dippie voted as one of the three. Tenacious as ever, Dippie refused to let the matter rest and so it was brought again to the vote at the next meeting, whereupon Dippie proposed an amendment that the issue be left over to the annual general meeting on 23 October, presumably so that more members could vote.

This too was defeated and at that 1872 annual general meeting, Robert Baker was re-elected as secretary of Scarborough Cricket club, at an annual salary of £10 per year. This

salary remained in force until the annual meeting of 1874, when Baker asked for £20 per year, refused the £15 per year offered and settled for £10 per year plus 10 per cent of subscription income. Increasing membership in order to provide a core income was already an important aim of the club and was to remain fundemental policy in the future.

Throughout the formative years of the 1870s, Baker's business acumen was to stand the club in good stead, although because the postion of secretary was an elected one, he was challenged at various times. The most notable of these challenges was in 1878, when he received 41 votes against 36 cast for a Mr Dickinson, but despite these conflicts of opinion and personality, Baker continued his forthright administration of the club's affairs and improved financial figures supported his methods. These figures show that in 1872 the income to Scarborough Cricket Club from membership subscription was £51.

By the time Baker presented his last annual statement of accounts in 1895, membership income had risen to £267. Along with profits from the festivals, membership continued to be one of the two main sources of income to the club until the advent of commercial sponsorship in the 1970s. Baker's eye for business had much to do with establishing and developing these sources and the shrewd negotiation of a percentage of subscription income as part of his salary, was an indication of the confidence he had in his own judgement and ability.

When Robert Baker died in June 1896, Richard Bent was appointed secretary. As luck would have it, he soon had to leave the town because of business commitments and that cleared the way for W.W.Leadbeater to become secretary in 1897.

William Leadbeater
William Leadbeater remained secretary until his retirement in 1930. Then he was awarded a testimonial in recognition of his services to Scarborough Cricket Club and received £275 together with a souvenir of the presentation in the form of a leather-bound volume containing a list of subscribers to the testimonial fund. He and Mrs Leadbeater were also made honorary life members of the club.

Unlike Baker, Leadbeater did not claim to be a cricketer, although he came from a cricketing family and did play a little. His brothers, R.W. and H.Leadbeater, were both members of the committee at various times and Harry Leadbeater was one of the finest left-handed batsmen that the club produced. William Leadbeater, however, walked with a pronounced limp, due to having a club foot, and he was seldom seen without his trusty stick. His stick earned almost as much respect as he did, for he was reputed to have made full use of it on any unfortunate small boy who misbehaved on the cricket ground.

In his younger days he did play for the club on occasions, modestly describing himself as 'just an emergency man', but perhaps it was misplaced modesty, for he took 8-26 for Scarborough 'A' team against York Revellers with his slow bowling. He is credited with forming the Reserve team, to give the club three senior sides, and his encouragement to young players was often kindly. Less kindly was his approach to more senior players if he felt that they were not performing satisfactorily, or with the degree of loyalty to the club which he demanded.

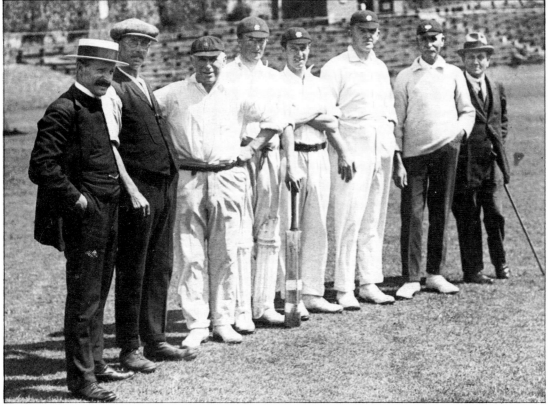

William Leadbeater with some Scarborough greats. From left to right: W.S.Robinson, Alf Fattorini (groundsman), George Hirst, the Allen family, David Hunter, W.W. Leadbeater.

On Festival duty in 1924. William Leadbeater (extreme left) outside the Festival marquee with H.D.G. Leveson-Gower (centre, in blazer), Labour MP Ramsay MacDonald and C.I.Thornton.

*William Leadbeater,
secretary of Scar-
borough CC from 1897
to 1930.*

'W.W.', as he was often referred to in the Press, was a dominant figure with a flair for originality and showmanship. He also had great organising ability and, having been assistant to Robert Baker for nearly nine years, understood the intricacies and workings of the club. There is ample evidence to show that he could be a prickly character. Yet, when given the right opportunity, he could be suitably diplomatic. At a farewell dinner to mark the leaving from the town of a former captain of the 2nd XI with whom he did not always see eye to eye, Leadbeater proposed a toast and gave a clue that he understood his own personality quite well: "My friends tell me that I am a difficult man to get on with. Yet in the five years I have known Mr Briggs there has never been a jarring note."

Leadbeater was well prepared for jarring notes if necessary, even with founding fathers

of the Festival like C.I.Thornton. After his playing days were over, Thornton had been responsible for gathering together Festival teams, in particular those that played under the banner of MCC. He was not always too punctilious in this task, which led to some anxious moments at Scarborough, as Festival publicity and arrangements had to be made and Leadbeater's impatience increased. To overcome this problem, Leadbeater proposed the formation of the 'London Committee' consisting of Thornton as chairman, H.D.G.Leveson-Gower (who eventually took over from Thornton as team organiser), Lord Londesborough and Lord Hawke, the Yorkshire captain. Thornton was not too happy about the idea, but despite his objections, the London Committee came into being and was a clear indication of Leadbeater's forcefulness.

Several other evidences suggest that William Leadbeater did not suffer fools gladly, but, as J.M.Kilburn points out: *William Leadbeater entered no easy inheritance. The increasing importance of club and Festival brought increasing work and responsiblity to the officials and though many think alike on many points sometimes they do not think at all and have differences of prejudice.*

Leadbeater recognised, as had Baker, the necessity of a strong membership to provide a financial base for the operation of the club. By this time, around the turn of the century, Scarborough Cricket Club had taken its place as an integral part of the cricket scene, in a period known as 'The Golden Age of Cricket'. The membership total was rising, from 250 to over 1,600 during Leadbeater's period in office, which meant that by 1930, half the club's income came from membership.

At the same time as membership income was increasing, the policy of ground improvement continued on a substantial scale. In this, Leadbeater was strongly supported by W.S. (Robin) Robinson, who was not only captain of the first team for a period, but was also chairman of the committee for thirty-seven years until 1940. In 1902, new seating for the Enclosure was purchased (cost £142), a new Press box was built in 1903 (cost £250), additional seating in the Enclosure was installed in 1907 (cost £136), complete reseating of the Popular Bank was undertaken in 1922, a new tea-room built in 1924 and the new Concrete (North) Stand was constructed in 1926 (cost £6,700).

These were substantial sums of money at the time and were clear indicators of the ambitions of the club and Leadbeater's resolve.

J.M.Kilburn summarised Leadbeater's style of management: *Much of his work lay in the consolidation of the position of Scarborough Cricket Club in matters financial and the 'filthy technical'; therefore a good deal standing to his honour cannot be recorded because it consists of the persuasive word here, the watchfulness there, that means so much in the smooth running of affairs.*

In 1930, Leadbeater resigned. He characteristically refused persistent attempts to persuade him to continue and was given a testimonial by the club. Eventually he was presented with a cheque for £275 and a leather-bound volume containing the names of subscribers. In making the presentation, Viscount Downe declared that William Leadbeater would go down in history as one of the greatest of cricket secretaries.

The secretary who followed Leadbeater was J.Lucas Goodall, later to be a prominent property owner in the town. He remained secretary until 1949 but, because of business interests, did not have the time or commitment which was available to William Leadbeater. Neither did he have the extrovert personality of the man who was to succeed him. That man was Alfred Rutherford.

Alfred Rutherford

Rutherford was not a Scarborough man. He came from Thirsk, where he had been a clerk in the North Riding County Council at Northallerton. As a physical-training instructor in the RAF, he was posted to Scarborough during the war and afterwards he became

Alfred 'Alfie' Rutherford (second left) in jovial mood at the Grand Hotel. Scarborough CC chairman Frank Winn is at right.

honorary secretary of Thirsk Athletic Club. From a list of seventy-nine applicants he was appointed secretary of Scarborough Cricket Club on 3 January 1949. There was an immediate and considerable impact.

The 'Yorkshire Illustrated' was enthusiastic: *The Festival seemed to wake up with a bang! Amenities improved for players and spectators alike. The Festival instead of swimming along on an even keel suddenly got a jerk from outside, from Alfred! There was a clamour for reserved seats and last season's takings for these (£1,544) were more than double what they were in 1949 (£749).*

Alfred Rutherford's great assets, apart from considerable organising ability, were energy, drive and enthusiasm. He created a mood of optimism and he had a flair for publicity and, like William Leadbeater, he paid great attention to detail. There was never any danger that small, but vitally important items would be neglected when Alfred Rutherford was in charge. It was even said that if toilet paper was required in the ladies' loo, 'Alfie' would be aware of it!

Rutherford was helped during this period in office by two major factors. First, he became secretary at a time when attendances at sporting

events had never been higher. Early post-war Britain saw people flocking as spectators to all kinds of entertainment. Many of the record attendances at sporting events were set in the 1940s and 1950s, when people packed together in antiquated stadiums, with two or three policemen as interested bystanders. For people who watched football and cricket matches in that era, it is ironic that as facilities have improved, attendances have declined and the number of policemen has increased.

Second, Alfred Rutherford was supported by a committee eager to rebuild the image and status of the club following the war years. Yet Rutherford and the committee were sensible enough to realise the wisdom of the policies adopted by the club in the years of Baker and Leadbeater, particularly regarding membership income and ground improvement. The net result was that membership increased in almost every year during Rutherford's period in office, from a figure of 1,852 in 1948, to a total of 4,564 in 1961.

The 'Yorkshire Illustrated' commented: *In case you should think these are mere figures, other things have been moving too in a practical way on the Scarborough Cricket Ground. The players' changing-rooms have*

Alfred Rutherford in conversation with Viscount Downe in 1955.

been enlarged, new shower baths built, a new dining-room built on top of the Pavilion and behind the dining-room a luxury bar and club room. The Pavilion frontage has been increased, too, to make room for spectators.

Based on the prosperity enjoyed at the time, the West Stand was built, seating 1,700 spectators, and the ground assumed the outline which it presents today.

Alfred Rutherford eventually left Scarborough to take up the position of general manager of Leeds Cricket, Football & Athletic Co, Ltd, owners of Headingley. In that year of 1961, HRH the Duke of Edinburgh was president of Scarborough Cricket Club and travelled from Balmoral to be present at the Festival. The following year, The Duke of Edinburgh accepted an invitation to become the fourth honorary life member of Scarborough Cricket Club. 'Alfie' Rutherford became the fifth.

The Ground — and Finance

ONCE the committee took the decision not to seek another ground elsewhere and eventually purchased the freehold of the land on North Marine Road in 1877, the following words could have been written at any period in Scarborough Cricket Club's history:

The Committee continues to give much thought and consideration to ground development and maintenance. The building programme envisaged many years ago is almost complete and it will be the future task of the Ground Committee to develop the remaining space available, to the best purpose. Progress, will of course, depend entirely on the financial position of the club.

In fact, the words are taken from the 1957 Annual Report, shortly after the completion of the West Stand. They once again emphasise the importance of investment in the ground,

which has formed the basis of the Scarborough club's policy since the early days of its existence and highlight the necessity for financial stability to bring that about.

The original purpose of playing at the partially-enclosed Castle Hill Yard, rather than at the open field opposite the Queen Hotel on North Marine Road, was to take advantage of the increasing number of visitors to the town and charge gate money. It was also very apparent that the ground on North Marine Road was not a very good advertisement for an aspiring club and Scarborough Cricket Club was certainly that.

In a newspaper article in the 'Scarborough Post' in 1905, George Watson, a playing member of the club who joined the committee in 1864 and remained on it for sixty years, recalled a match he played on the ground opposite the Queen Hotel in 1866:

Castle Hill. The ground where Scarborough played important matches — and where gate money could be collected — before the development of the ground at North Marine Road.

At that time, we had not even a hut upon the ground and Mr Bainbridge kept our cricket material for us in Mrs Greenbury's out-house in Trafalgar Square. In those days the playing field was so small that the long-stop used to stand in the ditch. By the way, the present cricket field consists of two fields and fifteen yards of a third. There were not above twenty-four members belonging to the club and only about eleven players all told, so we often had to call upon the stonemasons, who had a team at that time, to make up our team.

It was after the season of 1872 and the altercation between Robert Baker and J.R.Dippie which led to Baker becoming secretary, that the club seriously tackled the problem of improving the ground and the facilities, Lord Londesborough had made it plain after the challenge match in 1871, that without such improvements, or preferably another ground, he would not be interested in continuing his association with the club.

So once the decision was taken to remain at North Marine Road, immediate further attempts were made to improve the ground by levelling part of the area and adding a substantial perimeter fence at a total cost of £195 15s 2d. Of this sum, £170 was raised by public subscription, the list being headed by Lord Londesborough and Mr John Haig. In addition, in the winter of 1873, a new pavilion was erected at a cost of £234.

Already the club was engaged in what today would be classed as 'marketing' with two 'spelling bee' contests organised, one of which was held at the Town Hall, and determined attempts to increase membership. Increased gate receipts at local matches also contributed to club funds, so that by the end of 1877 the debt at the bank was down to £38.

Despite all the encouraging progress, problems at the ground remained. Being a tenant, rather than the owner of the ground, the club was restricted in its ambitions. More particularly the ambitions of the gentry, headed by Lord Londesborough and C.I.Thornton, had been stimulated by the success of the fixtures in 1876, when it is widely accepted that the true Scarborough Cricket Festival began. Matches took place between Scarborough and New Forest Rangers and, even more important, between MCC and Yorkshire. This match, first proposed for 1875, had been a victim of bad weather in that year, but soon became a traditional Festival fixture.

Meanwhile, the sticky problem of ownership of the ground was finally solved in 1877, when at the annual meeting the chairman, Mr W.E.Woodall, made an announcement:

. . .suggestions had been offered by The Right Honourable Lord Londesborough, Sir Charles Legard, Sir Harcourt Johnstone (later Lord Derwent) and others for the purchase of the cricket field in order to make it available

for first-class matches between Marylebone and other Southern County Clubs and those of the Northern Counties, which suggestions had resulted in Mr Woodall, the owner of the field having most liberally offered to sell in perpetuity to the above name Noblemen and Trustees for the use of the club as a Cricket Ground on such Terms as appeared to the meeting highly advantageous and worthy of prompt acceptance . . .if suggestions of the promoters were fairly and honourably carried out, the Club would soon be in possession of one of the most beautiful and complete grounds in Yorkshire.

The chairman then went on to read a draft of the proposed contract in which it became known that £350 had been temporarily advanced as a deposit by the above 'Noblemen and Gentlemen Members of the Club'. A discussion was held to decide how the total purchase money of £3,500 might be raised and the outcome was that a Scarborough Cricket Club Improvement Fund was set up and a letter to potential subscribers was issued in November 1877.

In the letter it was explained that the club had purchased the ground from John Woodall Esq, for £3,500, and in due course of time it would be conveyed to Lord Londesborough, Sir Charles Legard Bart MP and Sir Harcourt Johnstone Bart MP in perpetuity as Trustees. It was further hoped that £2,500 would be raised

by the sale of building land fronting North Marine Road, but that upwards of a further £1,000 would be required *to make the ground suitable for the best matches.* The following donations had already been promised.

Rt Hon Lord Londesborough	£100
Sir Harcourt Johnstone, Bart, MP	£50
Sir Charles Legard, Bart, MP	£50
E.H.Hebden Esq	£50
George Salt Esq.	£50
W.E.Woodall Esq (the president)	£20
Henry-Walker Esq	£20

The letter went on to state that the estimated value of the land for building purposes was £5,000, thus Mr J.Woodall was sacrificing £1,500 for *the benefit of the Club and Town generally.* The specific reference to the possibilty that the town might benefit from having a successful cricket club was to become a continuous theme and the rest of the letter amplified the basis on which the club saw itself in relationship to the town:

As it is a matter of great importance not only to the club, but also to the Town of Scarborough and the county generally that this undertaking should be successful and speedily carried out in order that the Ground may be ready for the great Matches proposed by Lord Londesborough to be played at Scarborough next season, we trust that a strong effort be made to effect the above arrangement. We have not the least hesitation in saying it will greatly

A 19th-century photograph which shows the wooden Pavilion in the background and the slope of the ground. J.King is the umpire and Roger Iddison is sixth from left. In front George Atkinson holds the ball.

On the steps of the old Pavilion. Scarborough CC v Masonic XI in 1890.

Scarborough Railway Station in the late 1890s.

benefit the Town at large as well as providing for the amusement and comfort of the visitors to our popular watering place.

The statement highlighted the thinking of all future committees. First, that if the club aimed to attract good teams to play at North Marine Road, the ground had to be of a high standard. If those teams were sufficiently attractive, they would encourage visitors to Scarborough, who would benefit the club and increase business in the town. The argument was circular, the ground a vital component.

Second, there was recognition of the necessity for a close liaison with Lord's, the administrative centre of the game. This was achieved over the years through individuals like Lord Londesborough, C.I.Thornton, H.G.D.Leveson-Gower, Lord Hawke, T.N.Pearce and others, who were able to exert sufficient influence to make sure that teams and individuals took part in the Festival. Not by accident were Viscount Downe (1872), Sir Charles Legard (1875) and Lord Londesborough (1876) all MCC presidents who also had close ties with Scarborough Cricket Club.

The initiatives taken in 1877 proved to be inspired. Of course, the climate of opinion was eminently favourable. The later Victorians were always anxious to promote town identity, none more so than the aldermen of Scarborough, and in what better way to do so than by taking advantage of the popular upsurge of interest in spectator sports. A sport like cricket, with its favourable moral connotations, fitted extremely well with Scarborough's perceived image of gentility. At the same time, cricket would contribute to taking commercial advantage of the new wave of tourism which was becoming apparent in the second half of the nineteenth century.

Likewise the continued attention given to the town by the Londesborough family, along with other nobility, was distinctly advantageous and flattering. The result was that the cementing of the early relationship between

cricket club and the town authorities was not difficult; it would have been surprising indeed had it been so, for quite often they were the same people.

The total cost of the purchase and renovation of the ground came to just over £7,000. Of this sum £750 was raised by subscription and about £2,500 was obtained from the sale of twenty-six plots of building land on the north-east side of the ground. Eventually, a number of small hotels were built on those plots and they conveniently overlooked the ground. Needless to say the owners of those hotels in future years had cause to be grateful to the decisions made at Scarborough Cricket Club in 1877; a free seat at a bedroom window to watch Hobbs, Bradman, Hutton, Sobers or Richards bat, and Rhodes, Lindwall, Trueman, Verity or Hadlee bowl, were at a premium long before the days of private boxes and corporate hospitality.

The debt to the club of the purchase of the ground was £3,000 and the success of the venture was assured when W.G.Grace played in the Festival in 1885 and receipts soared. The presence of 'W.G.' the greatest name in cricket, was final confirmation that Scarborough Cricket Club was recognised at national level. The 'Doctor' did not let anyone down either — he made 174.

In 1878, the principle of letting catering rights on the ground was adopted and other lettings were taken at various times, even to the extent of football being allowed on the ground at a rent of £10 per year. The FA Cup had begun in 1872, initially for the benefit of

amateur and public school teams, but football was developing rapidly in the industrial towns of northern England, especially Lancashire, and the Football League was formed in 1888.

Ever the imaginative entrepreneur, Lord Londesborough suggested to the committee that electric lights should be installed on the ground for a football match. Experiments had been held at Bramall Lane, but had been a financial failure and so the matter was not proceeded with, but it is interesting to speculate whether floodlight cricket at North Marine Road might be a viable proposition for the club in modern times. Certainly the ground would be an ideal setting and the proprieters of those small hotels would undoubtedly be in favour.

In later years, hockey and tennis were also played at North Marine Road and in 1901 a bowling green was constructed for the use of members. A charity baseball match, staged in 1918, brought into the club's coffers the not inconsiderable sum of £6 3s 0d, whilst in more recent times, fund-raising events like donkey derbies have been equally successful, Lord Londesborough might well have approved.

The year 1896 saw further development with the construction of the present Pavilion at a cost of £2,150. This imposing red-brick building was a substantial structure at the time and has been expanded and developed since, without losing its original outline. The Pavilion proved to be Robert Baker's final contribution to the club he had worked so hard to establish, for he died in that year. Yet there

Scarborough's North Marine Road ground in the early 1950s. The Festival marquees are in the foreground, including the band-stand. The band played during the intervals, sometimes during play and always the national anthem at the close of play.

A view of the ground before the concrete North Stand was built in 1926. Note the old 'Cowsheds' and the sightscreen. Woodall Avenue is in the background. The red brick Pavilion was built in 1896 to replace the wooden structure which had stood since 1874.

was no disputing that Scarborough Cricket Club, from being a small club for a handful of enthusiastic members had by the time of his death, become an important institution requiring a progressive commercial outlook. It could truly be said to be in the leisure business.

Leisure and Finance

By the second half of the nineteenth century, the twin forces of competition and self-help, forerunners of the free-market economy, were well established in Victorian consciousness. It happened also that there was an increase in leisure time for a greater proportion of the population, largely due to new laws being passed which brought a reduction in working hours for many people.

This developing situation in the new urban, industrial towns of the North, led to a sharp distinction being drawn between working time and leisure time, which was in complete contrast to that which had existed in pre-industrial England in the days of Hambeldon. There, in a more rural England, the time division between work and leisure was much less defined. People could pass the time of day, take a break, have a chat and be more in control of their time. It was the raucous sound of the

factory hooter, clocking-in and clocking-out, along with hourly rates of pay, which put an abrupt end to that style of working life for a great number of people.

Much of the reduction in working hours came less within the working week itself and more through increases in blocks of free time, such as Saturday afternoons. Of even greater significance in giving people more leisure time was the coming of regular annual holidays. Lowerson and Myerscough make the point:

Leisure time became the subject of crucial debate about how people should make use of their leisure time, both for the good of their souls and the good of their country . . . improving leisure could be used to transform the 'swinish multitude' into the 'respectable working classes'.

The authorities in Victorian England perceived possible dangers in the new 'leisure age'. Idle hands were thought to be the recipe for trouble. On the other hand, rising demands for increased respite from the coal face, or the factory floor, could no longer be safely ignored. Increases in leisure time, therefore, were justified as being necessary for social control and, furthermore, should be used to raise the moral outlook of the nation. Emphasis on morality in leisure activities was a path already being followed by the public schools and the

A view taken from over the North Bay in 1953, before the West Stand was constructed in 1956. Also not yet built is The Cricketers pub opposite the main entrance on the site of the former Queen Hotel where the club was founded in 1849.

A view towards North Bay. The North Marine Road ground in 1953. The occasion is the visit of the Australians. Note the spectators sitting on the grass.

publication of the best selling 'Tom Brown's Schooldays' in 1857 further popularised the philosophy.

It was natural that this belief should be used to try to 'transform' the masses and sport was seen as an ideal instrument through which to transmit such a moral concept. 'Playing the game' in both meanings of the phrase, became obligatory; it was considered to be good for the soul and to be good for the country.

A further effect of the increase in leisure time was the development of competition between those agencies involved in formal leisure provision, both at individual and community level. Theatres, music-hall, circuses, working men's clubs and many other commercial enterprises flourished as increased leisure provision was seen to be profitable. The area which profited most, however, was that of holiday provision and nowhere were the results felt more profitably than at Scarborough.

There is no doubt that one of the great inventions which transformed society in the nineteenth century was the steam engine and the railway. In the half-century following the opening of the York-Scarborough railway line in 1845, Scarborough's population grew rapidly from under 13,000 in 1851 to more than 33,000 in 1891.

The prosperity brought to the town by the influx of holiday makers in that half-century, also brought a huge demand for more accommodation and leisure provision. The Spa entered a new era of popularity as a place of entertainment and became noted for its high standard of music and the quality of recitals and concerts. The music-hall was at its zenith and the popular theatrical presentations, a feature of the late nineteenth century, found expression at the Prince of Wales Theatre, erected in 1877, the Theatre Royal, reconstructed in 1886 and the Londesborough Theatre, established in 1891.

The Londesborough influence, having being crucial to the cricket festival, was felt also in the world of theatre. This was mainly through the efforts of Lady Londesborough, who had long been a patron of amateur theatricals. The mutual benefits of such were touched upon in the 'Yorkshire Post's' observations on the Festival in 1905:

Amongst those who lunched with Lord and Lady Londesborough, besides the amateurs at the Festival, were Lady Chelsea and Lady Angela Forbes, who are included in Lady Londesborough's house party for the Festival and Lady Londesborough's amateur theatricals next week.

Naturally, the inter-relationships between pleasure and business had become an increasing fact of life. What could be more congenial than to indulge in a spot of both at the cricket festival? Was this the beginning of corporate hospitality? Certainly the increased business activity in the town was not unwelcome at Scarbrough Cricket Club.

Given the social and economic changes, it was apparent that the financial structure of the club was becoming crucial. The ground development served two functions. It attracted good players and teams to play on it, who attracted spectators to generate sufficient income to enable such matches to be staged.

It was quickly apparent, however, that gate receipts alone did not provide sufficient income to cover the costs of administering such ventures and, whilst the early Festivals benefited considerably from the generosity of Lord Londesborough, Robert Baker saw clearly the dangers of relying solely on gate receipts and Festival profits and he identified the need for a more stable and reliable form of income.

The answer came in the form of increased club membership. Along with Festival profits,

The 'Cowsheds' before the West Stand was built.

The West Stand, constructed in 1956.

All hands to the roller. Bernard Pearson, the groundsman from 1960 to 1980, is at the right rear as Jack Meads keeps an eye on the gang from the rear. Pearson succeeded Meads as head groundsman.

they were to be the backbone of the club's finances until the advent of sponsorship in the 1970s. Club membership was to eventually stretch far beyond the confines of Scarborough and district, becoming countrywide and even international, to a peak figure of 4,527 in 1961. That figure being above the membership of many county clubs.

In 1863 the income of the club was approximately £30. When Robert Baker presented his first statement of accounts in 1873 it showed gate receipts of £20; membership income of £51. In 1876 the first nine-day Festival took place, gross takings £158, but the club was still indebted to Lord Londesborough for defraying all costs incurred by players, a situation that was to occur at many subsequent Festivals.

By 1877, the total gross income of the club had risen to £287. In the last statement of accounts presented by Robert Baker in 1895, total income had climbed to £770; £292 was net profit from the Festival and £267 was from members' subscriptions, these two sources accounted for 73 per cent of income. Festival profits and members' subscriptions continued to provide the foundations of the finances of the club, until commercial sponsorship in the 1970s defrayed Festival costs, much as Lord Londesborough had done a hundred years before.

Top left: *The Commit-
tee Room downstairs
with sponsors' lounge
leading off. This facil-
ity was built in 1981
and greatly extended
the club's commercial
activities.* Top right:
*The old bar in the Pavil-
ion dining-room up-
stairs. It was situated at
the rear of the building
and has now been
replaced and refur-
bished.* Bottom left: *The
Pavilion at North
Marine Road, pictured
in 1992. Developed
and modernised over
the years, the roof was
completely replaced in
1991-2.* Bottom right:
*The popular Tea Room
in the Trafalgar
Square Enclosure. Built
in 1924 to replace a
previous building, it
was refurbished in
1991. Many people
claim that the best view
of the ground is from
the Tea Room
verandah.*

Year	Members' subscriptions (£)	Festival profit (loss) £
1900	401	566
1910	988	901
1930	1,358	764
1939	1,458	†(150)
1947	1,674	1,093
1950	3,099	2,804
1960	6,314	1,087
1970	5,789	(1,148)
1980	20,798	(4,731)
1990	41,993	63,238
1991	52,815	52,695

†Festival cancelled.

Discussions about finance are always likely
to bring about disagreements and Scarborough
Cricket Club has seen plenty of those. The twin
forms of income, Festival receipts and membership income, reflect and highlight a double-
edged sword dilemma, which has posed a
problem for club administrators throughout
the club's history. The problem has been that
increased involvement in the first-class game
has, at certain times, brought allegations of
a lack of attention to local needs. A recurring
theme has been criticism, often by outsiders,
of local people's lack of interest in the club,
represented by poor attendances at local
matches and reduced numbers of local
members.

Two discussions from the minutes of the
annual meeting in 1888 illustrate the conflict.
The first account centres on a match in which
Scarborough Cricket Club was invited to play
against MCC at Lord's in 1888. Expense was
the major issue, but also the matter of
strengthening the side with outsiders was
raised. Members Hudson and Sanderson led
the attack:

*Mr Hudson brought forward the question
of the Marylebone match. It was to him a
matter of finance as to whether the club should
be at the expense of £20 to £30 for — to the*

Scarborough people — an inviable match at Lord's cricket ground . . .The last season one man was pitched out of the team who had been chosen to play.

The response to this objection put the opposing view:

The Chairman thought the match was the greatest advantage in the world to the club. The Revd F.G.Stapleton said the real question was whether the members of the club got satisfaction for the amount of money they expended . . .It was, however, desirable that it (the club) should take its place amongst other large clubs in the country.

In a second discussion, finance was again mentioned, but antagonism towards the Festival and its influence on a local club like Scarborough was strongly voiced:

Mr W.Sanderson said that he had been noticing the balance sheet of the Scarborough Cricket Club. They would see that if they compared the receipts of this year with some years back that they had been greatly falling off. It was very well to say many gentlemen who visit the cricket matches were annual members, but that did not account altogether for the falling off in the attendance . . .There was a want of enthusiasm in the town on belief of cricket, though how it arose he did not know. He suggested they might do a little in playing clubs nearer home . . .The Festival did a great deal for cricket, but it did not do everything (hear, hear), and if they could arouse some sort of enthusiasm in the town and district it was worth the while of the club to try.

Mr Sanderson then went on to propose that a cricket association should be formed with other neighbouring clubs, with a challenge cup to be played for and rules to debar professionals. Scarborough Cricket Club itself had employed a professional, John King, since 1867; in 1873 he was paid 30s per week and he was to remain with the club as professional and groundsman until 1912.

As tempers began to fray following the somewhat controversial proposal by Mr Sanderson, an important statement was made about what some people perceived to be the real purpose of Scarborough Cricket Club. A fundamental difference in attitude and tone was revealed in the response by a Mr Allinson:

Mr Allinson said it would be very derogatory for the club to take up anything of the kind proposed. Surely the Scarborough Cricket Club had not come down so low as that? He could not see what object he gained by it.

Who was Mr Allinson? Since the purchase of the ground in 1877, the trustees of the club had been allowed a representative on the committee and Mr Allinson was that required representative of the trustees. More signifi-

cantly, he was Lord Londesborough's representative and his remarks graphically illustrate his lordship's view of the club as being exclusively a 'gentlemen's club'.

The 'Leeds Mercury' was clearly in no doubt as to what the real purpose of the Festival was, as it made constant reference to *Lord Londesborough's Cricket Week* at Festival time. The erstwhile Mr Hudson had a reply for Mr Allinson:

. . .in 1887, 838 persons paid for admission. Last year there were 309, showing a falling off of 479 people. Mr Sanderson was, in his opinion, quite right (hear, hear). Now it seemed to be all lawn tennis, which was not a manly game (oh!).

Whether the club was to be a 'gentleman's club', or a cricket club, was certainly a matter of some dispute. What was not in dispute was that cricket should be considered a 'manly' occupation, this being one of the values justifying taking part in sport in Victorian England and was strong reason for playing cricket at all. Not so tennis. The tennis club referred to had been formed in 1878, when the principle of letting the ground was established, initially for catering rights, but it seemed that the playing of tennis was frowned upon by some local members and the views of Mr Allinson were not too popular either.

Social and Cultural Factors

Despite the problems which have arisen from time to time about finance and the dual purpose of Scarborough Cricket Club, it remains an organisation which has survived for nearly 150 years from its origins in 1849. Robert Baker was quick to realise that the club could only survive on its chosen path by adopting business strategies and a commercial outlook. A testimony to that approach is that during the period of the club's existence, a vast number of other business ventures have failed.

It is equally true that many sporting organisations, founded in the second half of the nineteenth century, have survived; first-class football clubs, first-class county cricket clubs, several race courses, have all managed to survive less prosperous times, in a way that other business organisations have failed to do. Why should that be? The simple answer is that the demand and market for this type of business has remained more constant than for most other business ventures and there may be two reasons.

First, although sporting organisations can justify claim to be businesses, their *raison d'etre* is not solely profit. The disastrous experiences of a football club like Tottenham Hotspur, which attempted to use football as a tool for commercial profit, ought to serve as a warning

to sporting authorities of the dangers of such an approach which can soon become unbalanced.

Second, there may be a factor of longevity within the inherent nature of sport and games, which cannot be explained in organisational language. Other claims made for games at various times in the past are unlikely to have any special long-term significance. Claims in support of character building, health, social control and even incitement to revolution, have largely been the consequence of social circumstances at the time.

Why people play games, or why people go to watch others playing games, is a complex, psychological phenomenon which has not been adequately explained. Perhaps it is just that the primitive concept of striking an object with an instrument, the hunting instinct, in an open space outdoors, is sufficient to ensure a constant supply of people to become involved in the manifestation of that idea in such games as cricket, football and golf.

The general terms used in the analysis so far do not in themselves account for the longevity of Scarborough Cricket Club. There are more specific reasons.

First, the club has demonstrated an ability to adapt and even anticipate social change. This has meant that over the years members and the public have been provided, at any particular time, with what they have required.

In financial terms, for example, the club took advantage of the patronage available in the late nineteenth century, moved through a period of self-sufficiency before and after World War Two and then tapped the reservoir of commercial sponsorship in recent years.

In cricketing terms, the provision of traditional, leisurely, three-day cricket for the weekly visiting cricket connoisseur who travelled by train, has been supplemented with the more immediate, instant, one-day match, which attracts day-trippers in motor cars.

Second, high quality at the right price is usually successful. Scarborough Cricket Club has invariably succeeded in attracting the highest quality players to the Festival. From Grace to Bradman and Sobers to Botham, all the greatest players of the time have played at Scarborough; so have the best teams from home and overseas. Furthermore, the consistent support of Yorkshire CCC in playing first-class county matches on the ground, together with its financial support grants for ground improvements, has been of inestimable value.

Third, the siting of the ground at North Marine Road, within a few dozen yards of the beach and a few hundred yards from the town centre, has been enormously advantageous in attracting the casual spectator.

Fourth, Yorkshire cricket is taken seriously; so is a Yorkshire holiday. Being able to combine the two at Scarborough Cricket

Festival, or when a first-class cricket match is taking place on the ground, has been a continued source of reconciliation between family commitments. The beach and first-class cricket seem to complement each other ideally.

Finally, any organisation is only the sum of the people in it. Scarborough Cricket Club has been fortunate in attracting hard working people who have contributed qualities of leadership over long periods of time. The result has been continuity and the cultivation of a collective will to maintain and also build upon the achievements of previous generations.

Like all organisations in modern times, Scarborough Cricket Club has had to cope with inflation and rising costs, not only in ground maintenance and administration costs, but also an enormously increased outlay in attracting players and teams to play in the Festival. In former times the honour of being invited to play in the Festival, for a small fee and expenses, was usually sufficient; the Invitation XI versus the Tourists match was often referred to as 'the Sixth Test Match'.

Now the requirements of modern professional players and teams to play at Scarborough go far beyond honour alone and without the aid of sponsorship on an increasing scale, the continuation of the Festival would not be possible. It must also be said that, contrary to some misguided opinions, most players do recognise the unique contribution made to cricket by the Festival and Scarborough Cricket Club and the efforts made by individual players and county and international teams to take part in the Scarborough Cricket Festival are often very considerable.

Despite modern publicity, the financial problems of today are neither more, nor less, than those experienced when the club was reconstituted in 1863; or when the Festival first began in the 1870s. The problems are just different for a different era. The balance between membership subscriptions and Festival profits as the main sources of income, has been one of ups and downs. In 1877, members' subscriptions contributed 63 per cent of the total income of the club; the Festival 21 per cent. In 1900, members' subscriptions were down to 39 per cent of total income; the 'patronaged' Festival up to 44 per cent.

By 1960, due to the efforts of Alfred Rutherford, members' subscriptions accounted for 68 per cent of total income, the Festival just 12 per cent. The year 1970 saw members' subscriptions being even more crucial to survival — 66 per cent of total income, the declining Festival, hit by bad weather, lost £1,148. Even so, the Festival of the previous year, played in better weather, had only made a profit of £43! Something had to be done and

done quickly to revive the financial fortunes of the club. At that point, Scarborough Cricket Club moved swiftly into the field of commercial sponsorship.

The club was not new to sponsorship. In the 1960s, the Festival had welcomed the assistance of sponsors, with the Carling Black Label single-wicket competition an innovative venture in 1963. Likewise, the result of sponsorship by Rothmans of Pall Mall of a World XI to play an England XI, between 1965 and 1968, and an International XI v Barbados in 1969, was to bring to North Marine Road some of the most memorable cricket seen for many years. In addition, live television was attracted for the first time.

During this time, Scarborough Cricket Club could justifiably claim to be providing a lead to the rest of the cricket world in respect of these sponsored ventures, which were made possible by the independence of the club from the slower moving established cricket administration who tended to view commercial involvement in sport with suspicion.

It was the 1970s, however, which consolidated the role of the commercial sponsor at North Marine Road. The Fenner Trophy Knock-Out Tournament in 1971 featured four county teams, including Yorkshire. Members' subscriptions were now 50 per cent of total income, a revived Festival 26 per cent.

The Fenner sponsorship lasted ten years and established the pattern of a knock-out tournament for part of the Festival and that has continued. Since then other sponsors have been involved, so that by 1990, members' subscriptions had again fallen to 26 per cent of total income, the sponsored Festival receipts having increased to 40 per cent.

Finally, it is interesting to compare financial statistics for 1900 and 1990. Membership accounted for 39 per cent of total income in 1900, 26 per cent in 1990. The Festival was 44 per cent of total income in 1900, 40 per cent in 1990.

Membership, although reduced, still contributes a healthy proportion of the club's total income. The Festival profit has remained steady and the reason is clear. Lord Londesborough's patronage in the late nineteenth century has been replaced by commercial sponsorship in the late twentieth century. The wheel has turned full circle.

Yet the basic principles still remain. If first-class cricketers are to play at Scarborough, first-class facilities are required and they cost money. Robert Baker, William Leadbeater and Alfred Rutherford identified the need for members' subscriptions to provide a core income, patronage, self-help; or sponsorship was to be the icing on the cake. At times the

The Cricketers pub opposite the main entrance to Scarborough CC on North Marine Road. It stands on the site of the Queen Hotel, where the club was founded in 1849. Note the proposed development of self-contained flats on behalf of the club.

proportions may have changed, but if either of those two sources of revenue is lost, Scarborough Cricket Club will be left with a beautiful ground on which to play club cricket, but a ground that will inevitably fall into disrepair.

The problem for Robert Baker in 1872 was that the club had access to first-class players, but without a first-class ground. The potential problem for Scarborough Cricket Club in the future is that the situation could be reversed.

Periods in History

THERE can be little doubt that modern cricket evolved during the later Victorian and Edwardian periods. Eric Midwinter in 'W.G.Grace: His Life and Times' claims: *The emergence of the game of cricket in a shape recognisable to modern ages occurred around 1830 to 1835 and cricket was being played in thirty-seven English counties.*

Midwinter reasons that 1835 saw the overhaul of the laws of cricket in the same way that the Municipal Incorporations Act saw the more rational management of English Boroughs. In the expanding commercial climate of the nineteenth century, ledgers of credit and debit were required to be kept strictly in order in all trading activities.

It was the beginning of a period when the principle of formal law and order was established in English society. This was due to the work of Sir Robert Peel at the Home Office in the 1820s and highlighted by the passing of the Metropolitan Police Act in 1829, which replaced the romantically named, but largely ineffective, Bow Street Runners. Initially it was not a popular measure.

A Parliamentary committee set up to consider the problem of crime in London reported: *It is difficult to reconcile the effective system of police with that perfect freedom of action and exemption from interference which are the great privileges and blessings of society in this country.*

Despite the past traditions of freedom and exemption from interference, centralisation and collectivism increased in all social organisation in England throughout the nineteenth century. Sport was no exception. Midwinter expands his thesis:

Put briefly, demographic, industrial, political and administrative revolutions meshed to create the Victorian state which had its cultural dimensions too. Its dour religiosity, its harsh manners, its stern adherence to the work ethic and, above all, its bounding self-assurance and complacency had already settled into discernable shape by the accession of Queen Victoria in 1827 and it was not to be fundamentally disturbed until the Edwardian decade and the trauma of World War One.

It is arguable whether the process started in the cricket world quite as early as Midwinter suggests. Nevertheless, it was in harmony with such cultural influences that the game of cricket developed. Allied, too, were vital characteristics which Midwinter claims to be outstanding qualities of leading Victorians such as Florence Nightingale, Thomas Arnold, General Gordon, George Hudson and others. The two characteristics attributed to these people were first, single-mindedness and zealousness to their chosen duty; second, total commitment, which in some cases made them over-specialised as human beings.

It was the degree of competitiveness which was most significant. According to Midwinter, this competitiveness at national level had not really been seen before and the total commitment of the participants helped to create a special significance. This competitive zeal was further emphasised in cricket, when political, diplomatic and even military overtones were introduced to justify the game later in the century and it was expressed particularly in the cult of 'Muscular Christianity', courage and morality, in the public schools.

The public schools had great influence in Victorian England, although it is doubtful whether as many battles were won on the playing fields of Eton as were claimed.

All forms of human activity depend for their importance and popularity on the achievements of their leading exponents and the larger-than-life figure who came to dominate cricket in the Victorian age was Dr.W.G.Grace.

Prince Ranjitsinhji, who is recognised as one of the most stylish of all batsmen and whose career was beginning as Grace's was ending, paid 'the Doctor' a supreme compliment: *Before W.G., batsmen did not know what to make of batting . . .He revolutionised batting. He turned it from an accomplishment to a science, he turned its many straight channels into one great winding river.*

Midwinter says: *Grace, in large part, created modern cricket and established it as a social and cultural reflection of his age . . .Grace was the complete Victorian. Accomplished, egocentric, bumptiously confident, madden-*

ingly fit and untiring, boyishly high-spirited and, by that token, deceitful, extremely money-minded and, for good and ill, paternalistic. Maybe it is the other way round; maybe it is because of W.G.Grace and a few others of the same ilk we conceive thus of the Victorian male.

Whatever the merits, or otherwise of that particular view, there is no doubt at all of

W.G.Grace, the legendary figure in the game of cricket.

W.G.Grace's standing in cricket history, or of his influence on the development of cricket in the pre-1914 period.

Grace, however, required no competitor nor complement to perform at the most titanic levels and be judged accordingly; batsman and bowler; captain, selector and manager; bearing forward the past and looking to the future. Indeed it is not often, in any walk of life and over such a sustained period that one man has so dominated it. He was both Gladstone and Disraeli to cricket and he played Sullivan to his own Gilbert.

It is not known whether Disraeli had any views about cricket. In his novel 'Sybil', written in the 1840s, he did have a view about society. That view, encompassed in the sub-title 'The Two Nations', reflected a view of Conservatism based on paternalistic control of society by those born to rule.

Taken from this starting point there can be little wonder that the aristocracy and upper classes regarded the distinction between amateurs and professionals, Gentlemen and Players, as a reflection of the natural order of things and a mark of cricket's superiority over other games. With the public schools believing that qualities of manliness and leadership were being promoted, cricket rapidly assumed institution status, rather than being simply a leisure pursuit.

Furthermore, by the turn of the century, cricket had even assumed political significance, being described as 'the flower of the Empire', whilst numerous references were made to the military analogies of cricket and war. In this climate the 'golden age' of amateurism flourished.

As described earlier, William Clarke formed his All-England XI in the mid-nineteenth century. The immediate result was that a period of professional domination of cricket followed. Clarke's travelling players promoted professionalism around the country in what was still essentially a village and community pastime.

The change to a wider stage for the game of cricket came largely through the influence of the network of public schools and their connection with the organisational centre at Lord's, and the presence of W.G.Grace. These two forces moved the destiny of the game away from the travelling professionals and back into the control of the Establishment.

This shift in power was reflected in two ways. On the playing side, the balance of results in the Gentlemen v Players matches swung back towards the amateurs after the disastrous start of only seven wins in the first twenty-eight games to the professionals' three between 1865 and 1885. On the administrative side,

The Australian team, pictured in 'mufti', which played at the Festival in 1888. Back row (left to right): J. McBlackham, J. Worrall, A.H. Jarvis, H. Trott, C.T.B. Turner, H.F. Boyle. Front: C.W. Beal (manager), A.C. Bannerman, P.S. McDonnell (captain), G.J. Bonnor, F.J. Ferris, J. Edwards.

county cricket expanded from a total of twenty-five matches recorded for the season in 1872, to a Championship consisting of fourteen first-class counties in 1900.

The MCC further reasserted its position at the centre of cricket influence with a revision of the laws of the game in 1844, when, for example, boundaries were mentioned in the laws for the first time.

The re-emergence of the MCC as the controlling body in the game of cricket was of paramount importance. Membership of the MCC rose from around 650 in the 1860s to over 2,000 in the 1880s, more than 700 of which were owners of titles. The county game became organised and gradually the professionals accepted that the county clubs were their natural employers.

In his book 'English Cricket', Christopher Brookes expresses the view: *The subtle 'divide and rule' strategy enabled a deeply conservative institution to withstand the challenge.*

Thus the later Victorian and early Edwardian period became known as the 'Golden Age of Cricket', when amateurs were dominant and aristocrats prevailed. Around 1880, Lord Enfield was president of Middlesex; Lord Monson of Surrey, with the Prince of Wales as patron; Nottinghamshire had the Duke of St Albans; Gloucestershire, the Duke of Beaufort, and Kent had the Marquis of Abergavenny with the Duke of Edinburgh as patron. The Earl of Sheffield was president of Sussex and the Earl of Cork and Orrey was president of Somerset.

In 1881, apart from HRH the Prince of Wales being its patron, the MCC had Lord George Hamilton as president, with five other lords and three honourables on the committee. In this period the ranks of county sides were swelled by public school masters and products of Oxford and Cambridge, who became free to play during their vacations. The consequence was that the number of professionals was drastically reduced.

Midwinter states: *In effect, the systematic establishment of the county circuit was tantamount to the formation of a cartel, which rigidly controlled the provision of labour ...The cricket establishment gradually assumed a monopoly; it presumed to adopt the style and the statutory commitment of the royal chartered company of a century or so earlier.*

Derek Birley in 'The Willow Wand' (1979) supports the Midwinter thesis and claims that in association with the counties, MCC produced leaders who were able to translate the early Victorian Tory vision of a natural order of things into institutional terms. Lord Harris was its chief advocate.

Harris took hair on the Anglo-Saxon chest for granted, in particular, the gentlemanly Anglo-Saxon chest. If cricket had not existed one feels that Lord Harris would have found it necessary to invent it as an outlet for his moral, social and political values. Conversely, so much does he epitomise the game at its high point, if Harris had not existed, cricket would have needed to invent him. The amalgamation of Englishness, nobility and virility was never more complete.

The result of such a set of social class values was that professionals were expected to uphold the honour of the side at all costs. In 1909, Harris wrote to 'The Times' and in a letter illustrating how arrangements for dividing amateurs and professionals were so much better in cricket than in football, he outlined the contemporary upper-class definition of the two:

The real distinction is not whether 'A' receives £5 or £2 for playing in a match, nor whether 'B' received £200 and his expenses . . .for representing England in a tour; but does he make his livelihood out of playing the game, is it his daily occupation in its season? If he does, then he is a professional and he knows he is a professional.

Further to this, Lord Harris remarked that the professional . . .*recognises as convenient and bows to these social regulations which distinguish the amateur from the professional at cricket.*

The rigidity and forceful expression of such an outlook was not unusual at the time. In Yorkshire cricket, during the last decade of the nineteenth century, the equivalent of Lord Harris was Lord Hawke.

The well-known, but unwritten rule that only individuals born within the Ridings are eligible to play for Yorkshire was held to be a cornerstone of Yorkshire cricket culture until it was modified amongst great controversy in 1991 to allow the county to recruit their first overseas player, the Australian Craig McDermott. In the event McDermott suffered an injury before he was due to fly to England and the Yorkshire committee opted instead for the brilliant young Indian Test batsman, Sachin Tendulkar.

Yet despite the restriction being ostensibly adhered to up to that time, the person who represented more than anyone the aristocratic and autocratic approach to obeying the rules was born in Lincolnshire. The Hon Martin Bladen was born in 1860 and succeeded as Baron Hawke in 1887. He attended Eton and Cambridge and between 1881 and 1911 played 513 matches for Yorkshire. Lord Hawke captained Yorkshire from 1883 to 1910 and captained England on four of the five occasions

he played. In 1898, whilst still an active player and captain of Yorkshire, he also became president and remained so until his death in 1938. Throughout those years he virtually controlled the county's affairs.

Lord Hawke was in many respects a benevolent dictator. He is credited with introducing winter payment for professionals in Yorkshire and he instituted strict codes of conduct for the players under his command. He sat on various MCC committees and it was at his suggestion that Test selectors were appointed for a full series, rather than allowing the county on whose ground the match was to be played to pick the team to represent England.

Yorkshire's pre-eminence in the period was a direct result of Lord Hawke's authority and his great interest in the Scarborough Cricket Festival was of great value in linking the Yorkshire and Scarborough clubs for mutual benefit.

People like Lord Harris and Lord Hawke not only consolidated the position of the amateur in the cricket world, but reinforced the role of the captain in cricket and his complete authority in the administration of county cricket clubs. Although the totally powerful position of a captain in the Lord Hawke style declined after World War Two, the all-round importance of the captain still remains in cricket, as distinct from many sports, despite the recent trend in some counties to appoint cricket managers.

Two further points are worth making about the captain's changing role and the Lord Hawke influence. In 1953, Sir Leonard Hutton became the first professional captain of England; he never became captain of Yorkshire. It was not until 1960 that Yorkshire appointed a professional captain and then there was much opposition. Second, it is arguable that when the distinction between amateur and professional was abolished in 1962, to become effective in 1963, with several professional captains taking over the leadership of many county clubs, a certain style of captaincy was lost forever.

It is easy to overstate the case, but professionalism is essentially about the elimination of risk and that approach can breed a cautious outlook. Many people, on reflection, are inclined to believe that the amateur captain did bring to the game a degree of independence and objectivity which is not given to many professional captains.

Between the Wars 1919-1939
If the Edwardian period was the age of the gentleman amateur, the period between the wars saw the rise of the modern professional.

There were sound social reasons for the changing pattern.

World War One had huge detrimental economic effects for the country and the number of men who could spend the whole summer playing cricket was greatly reduced. Complementing the reduction of amateur cricketers was the increase in professional players, who saw in the game of cricket a chance to escape from the pit, or the factory and were proud to be paid for doing so. Many of those professionals were conscious of wage levels and the need for financial security during the massive unemployment periods of the 1930s. They were not as ready to accept the previously accepted practice of being automatically replaced in the summer holidays by undergraduates and schoolmasters, many of whom were not good players. Members of county clubs, too, wanted a winning team, so with Press and members being more sensitive to the issue, amateurs increasingly had to win their places in straight competition with professionals. The move towards a more pragmatic outlook, plus the influence of committed professionals from the urban industrial areas, meant that between 1922 and 1939 the County Championship was never taken south of the Trent. Along with the increase of professional players in the leagues which sprang up rapidly in the north of England, a seemingly endless supply of good quality players was guaranteed to keep the men in possession of first-team places in a county side well on their toes. Cricket in the North began to be taken very seriously indeed.

Another significant factor during the inter-war period was the growth of international cricket. The former Dominions of the Empire began to challenge the supremacy of the Mother Country. West Indies, New Zealand and India began to compete with England, Australia and South Africa and were awarded Test Match status and this heightened public awareness and interest in the game.

At the Scarborough Cricket Festival, the two main changes in the cricket world were clearly reflected. Some of the most competitive matches in Festival history were played during this period. Gentlemen v Players and Leveson-Gower's XI v Tourists, especially when the visitors were Australia, were fiercely fought. Notable sides such as Warwick Armstrong's 1922 team and Donald Bradman's 1938 team, previously unbeaten outside the Test matches, tasted defeat for the first time at Scarborough.

Also in the period between the wars, the club's own domestic cricket activities began to

Lord Hawke, Lady Londesborough and Lord Harris pictured at the 1929 Festival.

Left: *Lord Hawke (left, minus spats) socialising at the Festival.* Right: *One of Yorkshire's all-time greats, Maurice Leyland (1920-1947), in conversation before a match at North Marine Road in 1923.*

move out of the shadows of the Festival in a more public way. The Annual Report of 1922 recorded, for the first time, the records of the 1st XI, 'A' team and Reserves, along with averages of individual players of each team and a report of progress. The total number of matches played by each of the teams in the season was twenty-two, twenty-five and twenty-one respectively, all on a friendly basis, although league cricket was soon to be tasted. A further development was the playing of four

Watching a match from the Popular Bank in the 1930s.

matches by The Possibles, a junior team, captained by a senior player, which began a tradition of promoting junior cricket.

Eventually, the club re-entered the Yorkshire Cricket Council, which operated a differential league system based on percentage results, with home and away fixtures against Sheffield United, Leeds, Hull, York, Barnsley, Wakefield, Castleford, Harrogate, Pontefract and Lofthouse. Of these clubs, only Pontefract and Lofthouse no longer play in the Yorkshire Cricket League, which is one of the two major leagues in the county, the other being the Bradford League.

By 1925 The Possibles' fixture list had increased to eighteen matches and two professionals were engaged to play in the First XI, one of which was the redoubtable and legendary George Hirst, who had retired from county cricket at the end of the 1921 Festival but who was to give inspirational guidance to the young cricketers of Scarborough Cricket Club.

The Yorkshire Cricket Council at this time contained a total of eighty-three teams in only one division. Most teams played between twenty and twenty-five matches, with a percentage points scoring system to decide placings. At the end of the season the top four clubs played two semi-finals, followed by a Final to decide the champion club.

The big weakness in this system was that by careful selecting of opponents, clubs could gain a high percentage of wins not commensurate with their true standard, thus it is likely that the strongest clubs did not often become champions. In 1926 even a Scarborough fifth

Major A.W.Lupton, Yorkshire's captain from 1925 to 1927, leads out his team at North Marine Road, followed by Wilfred Rhodes.

team, The Occasionals, played two matches, but this experiment was not continued after 1928.

More important was the appearance in 1928 of J.A.Richardson, who was to become one of the outstanding club cricketers in Yorkshire in the 1930s and, but for his business commitments as a farmer and auctioneer, would probably have made more than ten appearances for Yorkshire.

How far the great economic and social changes of the inter-war periods had any effect on the Scarborough Cricket Club is difficult to estimate. The club had never relied for its finance on gate receipts at local matches and throughout the history of the club there were occasions when the alleged lack of local support for the club was the subject for criticism. At the Festival, financial returns show that the years of the Depression were no

Jack Hobbs and Percy Holmes batting for the Players v the Gentlemen in 1927.

George Hirst (umpire) passes a word with H.D.G.Leveson-Gower (facing) at Scarborough in 1928.

Listening to a radio commentary on the St Leger at North Marine Road in September 1927.

bar to attendances, which indicates that followers of Festival cricket were less affected than others by the consequences of unemployment and hardship in the inter-war years.

Festival Finances

	Profit/Loss		Profit/Loss
	£		£
1919	632	1928	502
1920	901	1929	299
1921	1,325	1930	764
1922	840	1933	607
1924	433	1934	892
1925	1,044	1935	432
1926	919	1938	990

Note: Members were not charged for admittance to the Festival

As if to emphasise the point of relative prosperity, the club felt sufficiently confident in 1925-6 to erect the North Stand at a cost of approximately £6,750, whilst a number of other improvements and developments to the ground took place throughout the period.

The other form of income to the club during the inter-war years was, as always, members' subscriptions.

Members' Subscriptions £

1920	988
1925	1,380
1930	1,358
1935	1,345
1939	1,458

Many of the members came from places other than Scarborough and it is this 'outside' membership following which has been a feature of the club through its history.

Comparative figures for 1920 and 1939 – Total Receipts

1920 Receipts £2,601 including credit balance of £355

1939 Receipts £3,948 including credit balance of £1,762 (These receipts include net profit/Loss on Festival. Festival did not take place in 1939 and expenses incurred were £159).

The conclusion to be drawn from the figures is that the Scarborough Cricket Club continued to consolidate its position as a viable and soundly structured institution during a period when many businesses found great difficulty in surviving. Not only did it survive. According to Kilburn: *Between the wars Scarborough had perhaps the best of the cricket of a plebeian period.*

During this period it would seem that the Festival began to have a stronger influence on people's holiday patterns, with many followers booking seats for the Festival a year in advance.

Year by year the Festival crowds grow larger and more and more people began to build their annual engagements round a holiday in early September...The town of Scarborough means much to the Festival; the Festival in turn is

The Popular Bank, as crowded as ever between the wars.

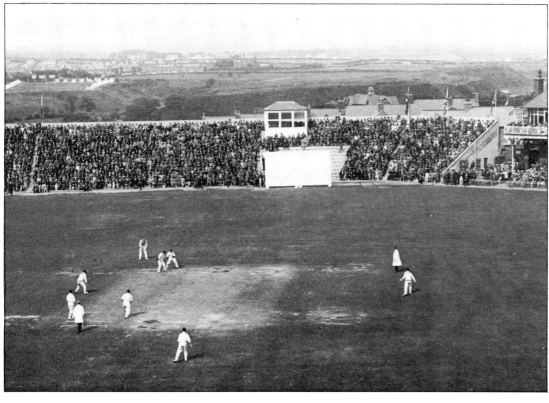

The North Stand is also full for this match in 1926. The Press box overlooks the sight-screen. It is one of the best press box views in cricket.

one of the assets of the town. *In combination the two are irresistible.*

Post-1945

In the immediate post-war years, Scarborough Cricket Club continued to build on the solid foundations laid down since 1863. The Festival was revived immediately in 1945 and, despite a loss of £139 in that year and the resignation of Mr W.S.Robinson, chairman of the committee for 37 years, it soon became apparent that the club was in good health and could look forward confidently to the future.

In 1946 the Festival made a profit of £489 and subscriptions totalled £1,388. In 1947 the figures were £1,093 and £1,674 respectively; and in 1948, on the occasion of the visit of Donald Bradman's all-conquering Australian team, £1,035 and £2,463. In 1949 the Festival profit increased to £1,915. These impressive figures enabled the club to continue its long-established policy of ground improvement.

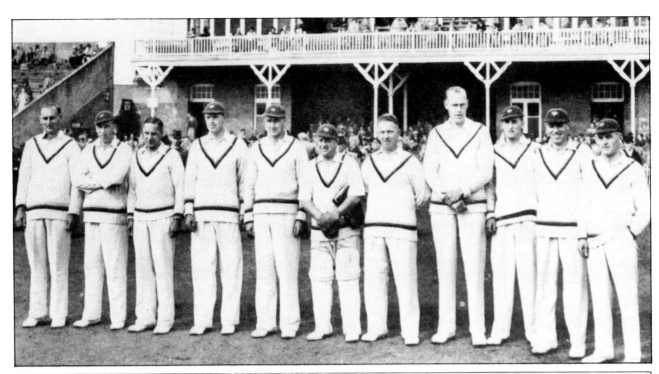

Top: *County Champions Yorkshire line up at Scarborough before their match against MCC at the 1938 Festival.*

Bottom: *Bill Edrich and R.E.S.Wyatt at the wicket for MCC on the first day of the match.*

The repairs to the North (Concrete) Stand alone cost £6,436 in 1948.

The early post-war years were notable for huge attendances at sporting events. Scarborough Cricket Festival was no exception. Photographs taken at the time show several rows of spectators sitting on the grass at many matches, well inside the normal boundary perimeter. Faced by the steep North Stand and surrounded by the Popular Bank and Trafalgar Square Enclosure, the compact playing area must have felt exceedingly small to the players.

In 1953 the club was able to report a working profit on the general account of £1,002 and on the Festival account of £6,413. The membership income was £4,889 from 3,126 members and so the club felt able to reiterate established club policy of ground improvement.

The Annual Report of 1953 stated: *The*

Committee continues its declared policy of ploughing back all available funds into the club's ground and equipment.

The main entrance was entirely rebuilt and in 1956 the West Stand was constructed at a cost of £16,000. These improvements meant that Scarborough Cricket Club owned a ground which could compare favourably with any ground of similar size in the country.

Between 1950 and 1963, the format of the Festival remained unchanged: MCC v Yorkshire, Gentlemen v Players, T.N.Pearce's XI v the Tourists. The Festival continued to flourish.

Sir Leonard Hutton was the first professional captain of England but he never skippered his native county. This photograph was taken at Scarborough in 1947.

The main entrance off North Marine Road pictured before the 1955 development.

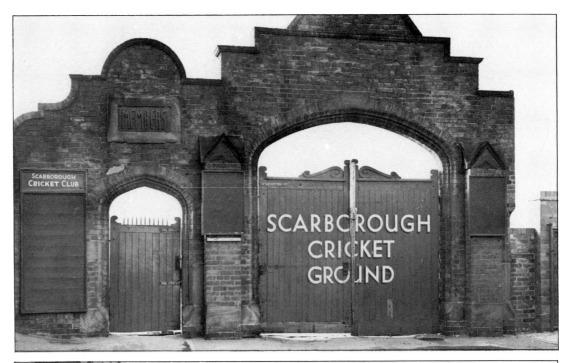

Getting into the match after the opening of the new entrance.

At local level the club advanced rapidly. The First XI won the Yorkshire Cricket Council in 1957 and, when a Yorkshire League was formed within the jurisdiction of the Yorkshire Cricket Council, but consisting of less teams, the club won that in 1957 and 1959. In addition the 'A' team carried off the East Yorkshire Cup title in five years out of seven.

Outstanding club cricketers in this period were Alan Richardson, who continued his pre-war success, Ted Lester, who was to become a valuable member of the Yorkshire County team, and a pair of formidable bowlers in Geoff Dennis and Bill Foord. The latter also played with distinction for Yorkshire.

Young players destined to make their mark in later years included Ken Stockwell and Tony

Moor, who were outstanding products of the club's youth policy. During the 1960s four more Yorkshire League Championships were won, confirming the club's reputation in Yorkshire club cricket.

The 1960s brought a number of structural changes which were to alter the face of first-class cricket and which had a significant effect on the Festival format in the 1970s. At the same time as the first-class game was undergoing change, so too were moves being made to co-ordinate club cricket.

In 1965, the National Cricket Association was formed. Its function was to act as an umbrella under which all non-first-class cricket could operate and so qualify for government aid, which had not been possible

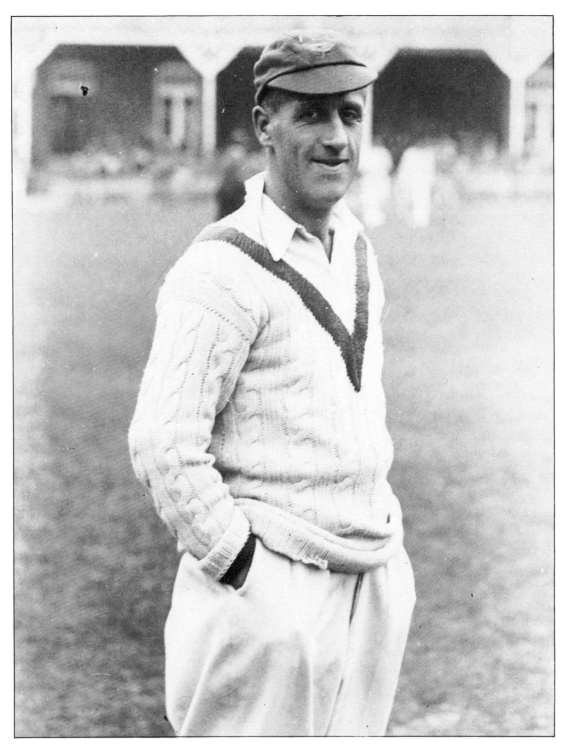

Percy Holmes (York-shire and England) taught cricket at Scarborough College in the 1950s.

through MCC, a private members' club. At first, the fifty-two county cricket associations from all over Britain were serviced by MCC secretariat, but in 1974, the NCA began to operate with its own staff.

In keeping with the trend towards limited-overs knock-out competitions, the NCA instituted the National Club knock-out competition, sponsored by 'The Cricketer' magazine in 1969, with the Final played at Lord's. Scarborough Cricket Club entered the new tournament.

The 1968 Annual Report stated: *This is an exciting concept involving the leading clubs throughout the country, and it will be interesting to test the belief that our First XI is one of the finest club teams in the country.*

The club soon emphasised this belief by winning the competition in 1972. When John Haig & Co took over the sponsorship, the trophy was secured on four occasions in seven years up to 1982, including successive years 1981 and 1982. Such a record far outstripped any other club side in the country.

At the same time, Scarborough Cricket Club enhanced its local reputation by continued

Massive crowds in the 1950s. Spectators sitting on the grass meant that the playing area was relatively small.

Scarborough CC in 1952, members of the Yorkshire Council League. Back row (left to right): A.Marston (wicket-keeper), G.H.Dennis, B.C.Moor, E.McKenna, K.C.Stockwell, R.A.Diggle, scorer. Front: J.Cammish, R.Halton, J.A.Richardson (captain), G.Shepherdson, J.Lister. Joe Lister later became secretary of Yorkshire CC.

success in the Yorkshire League, being champions thirteen times between 1957 and 1984. The club even found time in 1976 to win another NCA innovation, the Wrigley National six-a-side competition.

Throughout the post war period the club continued to stage County Championship matches at North Marine Road, with gate receipts generally being far in excess of those collected on other Yorkshire grounds, especially after Bramall Lane, Sheffield, ceased to be a venue for Yorkshire cricket in the 1960s.

Scarborough, for obvious reasons, also became a favourite venue for John Player Sunday League matches, with queues often forming before 10am for a 2pm start. Needless to say the gates were closed on several occasions, with the ground capacity of about

14,000 being achieved and with the visiting team being left in no doubt that the expected result of the contest was a Yorkshire victory.

Strong backing for Scarborough Cricket Club by Yorkshire County Cricket Club has always been a central feature in the club's history and the benefits have been mutual. Yorkshire has collected substantial gate receipts and Scarborough Cricket Club has profited from ancillary takings when first-class cricket has been played at North Marine Road. Even more important have been the grants which the Yorkshire club has sanctioned to aid the ground improvement programme at various times.

Given the place of cricket in the collective Yorkshire consciousness, two effects were manifest in the post-war period.

First, the policy of the Yorkshire club to

play matches around the county, in order to satisfy its widespread membership, resulted in many members organising their cricket-watching arrangements to coincide with a visit to Scarborough. This following for Yorkshire cricket occured much in the same way as the traditional following for the Festival was built up.

Second, drawing on the experience of the Festival, the ability of the Scarborough club to organise important matches, such as Gillette Cup semi-finals, meant that the county club was able to confidently allocate important matches to North Marine Road.

This was confirmed when the Annual Report of 1975 recorded: . . .*26 August 1976 — England v West Indies. The club is proud to accept this one-day official Test match, which is a wonderful recognition of the*

Top: *Scarborough CC 1st XI in 1964. Left to right: G.A.Harling (scorer), C.W.Foord, J.Oxley, A.Marsden, B.E.Moor, G.H.Dennis (captain), J.Hutton, G.R.Bloom, G.Downes, K.C.Stockwell, C.C. Clifford, K.A.Calvert, H.Halliday (coach).*

Bottom: *Scarborough CC 1st XI in 1969. Back row (left to right): M.Kirkland, C.Moor, K.C.Stockwell, C.A.Hurd, C.C.Clifford, K.A.Calvert. Front: J.Hutton, M.Heath, C.W.Foord, G.H. Dennis (captain), R.Bloom, C.Oxtoby.*

Opposite: The Fenner Trophy, competed for between 1971 and 1981.

Top: Brian Close and Phil Hart before their sponsored parachute jump at Grindale in 1980.

Bottom: A sign of the times. John Foord (left) and André Meunier complete their sponsored walk from Lord's to North Marine Road in 1981, to raise money for club funds. Some spectators even came for the match.

standing of the club, the amenities of the ground and the ability of its committee to organise first-class cricket.

To further enhance the club's reputation, the president-elect for 1976 was HRH The Duchess of Kent, who followed a distinguished list of past presidents of Scarborough Cricket Club, including HRH The Duke of Edinburgh in 1962.

In 1978 the club staged its second one-day Test match, England v New Zealand, sponsored by Prudential Assurance Company, and also a three-day Under-19 Test match, England v West Indies, the first of a series of three for the Agatha Christie Trophy.

Thus, the 1970s was a period when the club established itself as an organisation capable of dealing with international cricket at the highest level outside full Test matches. It was all a far cry from the days when Robert Baker began his plans for the improvement of a rough field on North Marine Road.

At the same time as first-class cricket was thriving on the ground, cricket at the other end of the scale was organised every bit as meticulously as for Festival occasions and international matches. The Primary Schools Knock-Out competition, with twelve or more competing schools, provided entertaining and skilful cricket on two evenings of the week during June and July. In front of the Popular Bank, populated by several hundred holiday-makers and with a rope to reduce the playing area to an appropriate size, great deeds were done.

Tears, too, were sometimes shed, but all was forgiven after the presentation of the trophy, when winners and losers celebrated in the Pavilion, usually with a banquet of Rennard's fish and chips.

Yet, in spite of all the playing successes, warning signs were apparent on the financial horizon. Increasing costs of maintaining a ground suitable for first-class cricket were beginning to be keenly felt. Waterproofing and safety measures for the West and North stands became a continuous problem in the 1970s and around £90,000 was required to complete the work, with little obvious benefit. General running costs were rising and it was clear that the club, in common with many other sporting organisations, had to increase its income. The members' clubroom accounts are an indication that the committee was aware of the problem.

County Championship cricket at Scarborough. David Bairstow grimaces as Warwickshire's Andy Moles flounders at North Marine Road in 1987.

Surplus from members bar £

1951	114
1960	370
1970	297
1974	998

In 1975 alterations were made to the clubroom

1976	2,676

In 1977 it was decided to open the clubroom during the winter months as well as the summer.

1978	3,014
1980	3,234
1982	3,429
1986	3,161
1990	9,423
1991	6,018

In 1978 an analysis by the secretary of the club's financial situation was presented to the committee in an attempt to stimulate action to reverse the trend towards increasing financial problems.

The central theme was that the traditional forms of income to the club needed to be supplemented. The result of the initiative was that a fund-raising sub-committee was established and, for the first time, the club entered into various money raising activities unassociated with cricket.

An agreement was reached with Scarborough Football Club to sell lottery tickets on the ground during the season. Other events began to be staged on the ground, including

Yorkshire v Leicester-
shire at North Marine
Road. Umpire Jack
Van Gelovan and
bowler Ray Illingworth
watch David Bairstow
attempt a catch.

a 'donkey derby', designed to attract holiday-makers. Sponsorship of local matches was introduced and developed, 'other income' began to make an appearance in the accounts. Once again Scarborough Cricket Club was moving with the times.

Other Income £

1979	3,963
1980	3,764
1981	4,169
1982	12,349
1983	12,103
1984	10,969
1991	15,666

Whether by accident or design, Scarborough Cricket Club has always produced the right men at the right time to administer the club's affairs. The post-war period has seen an enormous change in social and recreational patterns. For an organisation like Scarborough Cricket Club these changes have forced responses on the cricket and administration fronts.

One no longer determines the other in that cricket revenue alone cannot sustain the organisation as it did in the past. Patronage of cricket is no longer in the hands of the wealthy aristocrat of the 1890s, but in the hands of the commercial manager of the 1990s. Returns on investment are paramount.

Scarborough Cricket Club's need is to produce people with the ability to deal with the harsher cricket, economic and social requirements of the future and be equally as successful as in gentler times in the past.

That is not to suggest that the task of solving the problems in the future will be more difficult than in Robert Baker's time. The problems will just be different.

It would also be a mistake to suppose that the Victorians had any less appreciation of the value of a sovereign, than the marketing men of the twentieth century have of a pound. When about to win a Test Match against South Africa with a leg-bye off his thigh-pad, Cliff Gladwin memorably quoted, "Cometh the hour, cometh the man," That could well be the motto of Scarborough Cricket Club.

The Festival — Cricket on Holiday

IN ITS simplest form, Scarborough Cricket Festival is a series of matches between invited teams, or teams consisting of individually invited players, which takes place towards the end of each season at the North Marine Road ground, the home of Scarborough Cricket Club. The Cricket Festival has taken place every year since the early 1870s, except for the years of the two world wars.

There are many reasons why the Festival has survived for such a long period of time. Perhaps the most satisfying explanation is contained in J.M.Kilburn's view that *Festival cricket, as Scarborough knows it, is first-class cricket on holiday.*

Certainly, Festival cricket at Scarborough has always been played with a certain emphasis. First-class cricketers have been encouraged to demonstrate their skills freely, without the restrictions often imposed by the tight competitive matches from which they earn their living. At the Festival, cricketers too are on holiday, able, according to Kilburn, to indulge in *casting of work-day shackles.*

Of course, many people subscribe to the notion of working hard and playing hard. At times, Festival cricket has been very competitive, During the inter-war years and for sometime afterwards, the H.D.G.Leveson-Gower's XI v Tourists match was often referred to as the 'Sixth Test Match'. Donald Bradman, remembering how the Australians had been beaten at Scarborough in 1938, insisted that Leveson Gower's XI at Scarborough in 1948, should not include more than six current Test players.

This additional fixture at the end of a long tour contributed to the Australians finally refusing to participate in the Festival after 1965. Despite this and other difficulties arising in the modern game, the spirit in which cricket has been played at the Scarborough Festival has largely survived. Kilburn summarises festival cricket as *Cricket played wholeheartedly but lightheartedly; with ambition, but without recrimination or fear of it, for its intrinsic purpose but with an awareness of obligation towards those who pay to see.*

How far this central unifying force has been under threat, particulary in recent times, is discussed later.

The first 'legitimate' Festival took place in 1876. There were, however, a sequence of events and precedents, which can fairly be regarded as being the true origins of the Scarborough Cricket Festival. Reference has been made to club matches being played at Castle Hill rather than the ground opposite the Queen Hotel on North Marine Road. These important matches usually featured visitors to the town, sometimes as collective teams. From 1862 to 1870, the famous All-England XI visited Scarborough to play against varying numbers of Scarborough residents, sometimes as many as sixteen or twenty-two.

These matches highlighted the problems of playing at Castle Hill, for, apart from rifle practice and the small playing area, it was reported: *In 1869 the match was played in a furious gale of wind from the north-east and steel bails were used, this being an innovation not relished by the players.*

Clearly, although Castle Hill was less than ideal in cricketing terms, there were other more influential factors involved which contributed to cricket not continuing at that venue.

The visiting teams which played at Castle Hill had a certain social standing. This was the inevitable consequence of the structure of society in mid-Victorian England, whereby formal and organised groups were usually the result of upper-class initiatives. Furthermore, the historical development of Scarborough as a spa resort, meant that the established influences of the gentry still predominated over the newer social forces introduced by working-class people, who flooded the town during the summer season, transported by trains from the urban industrial areas of the West Riding.

There was also in that social mix an element of patronage. The second half of the nineteenth century had witnessed a swing back to the pre-industrial era of patronage. If not quite on the Hambledon model, patronage had nevertheless been brought again to prominence by upper-class concern about lower-class working conditions in factory towns, especially if those conditions either threatened a reduction in profits, or encouraged unrest amongst the workforce.

Patronage was not, however, confined to industrial areas. A town like Scarborough was particularly ripe for a substantial patron figure as there were a number of possibilities to which a patron could contribute and justifiably claim to be benefiting the community.

If such patronage could raise the social standing of the patron figure, so much the better. Sport was the ideal vehicle for such an arrangement and the patron figure to emerge was the first Earl of Londesborough.

William Henry Forester Denison (1834-1900) was descended in direct male line from the Burtons of Buncragg, County Clare. They assumed the name of Conyngham in 1781, when succeeding to the Conyngham estates. Lord Albert Conyngham was an entrepreneur who earned great wealth in manufacturing cloth in Leeds and this wealth was invested in land in Yorkshire.

In 1849 the name Denison was assumed by Royal Licence on the succession to property owned by an uncle, William Joseph Denison MP of Denbies, and William Henry Forester

Denison, as he was now called, was created Baron Londesborough. He became related to the Sitwell family on the marriage of his daughter to Sir George Sitwell in 1886; in 1887 he was made Earl of Londesborough. He represented Beverley in the House of Commons as a Liberal MP before becoming a Conservative at the time of the Irish problems.

The Londesborough estates were at Grimston Park, Tadcaster, at Market Weighton in the East Riding and at Seamer, just outside Scarborough. Besides being an agriculturist, Londesborough himself was a successful horse breeder and a strong supporter of the Turf. He was also an all-round patron of sport, especially sailing and cricket.

Lord Hawke recalled: *Lord Londesborough's hospitality was unbounded. He was an enthusiast for Yorkshire cricket and when the county came to Lord's he always drove up in his four-in-hand, drew up at the Players' end of the pavilion, watched the horses taken out and then came into the club wearing his long box-cloth coat which reached almost to his heels.*

The Londesborough name in Scarborough became strongly represented in several areas of public activity like The Londesborough Theatre, opened in 1871, and The Londesborough Rooms. His lordship's Scarborough residence, Londesborough Lodge, overlooked Valley Park Gardens and led directly down to

Lord Londesborough (left), one of the founding fathers of the Scarborough Festival with C.I.Thornton (right), who was regarded as the doyen of the Festival.

the Spa and was another example of the Londesborough influence.

It was here that the Prince of Wales stayed as a guest during visits in 1869 and 1871, although after the latter visit he contracted typhoid, for which the drains at Londesborough Lodge were blamed by critics of the Londesborough family. Nevertheless, it was these visits by the Prince of Wales which established the reputation of the magnificent Grand Hotel as the centre of Scarborough society. The Grand, opened in 1867, was to play a prominent role in the development of the Scarborough Cricket Festival.

The matches played at Castle Hill in the 1860s, along with his lordship's interest in sport and increasing family involvement in the Scarborough social scene, provided the springboard for a cricket match played in 1871 which is often referred to as being the true origin of the Festival.

This notable challenge match was between Lord Londesborough's XI and C.I.Thornton's XI. Thornton had been a member of one of the Scarborough Visitors teams in previous years. Educated at Eton and Cambridge, he had the reputation of being an immense hitter of

the ball and on that score alone he was to inscribe his name indelibly in the folklore of the Scarborough club. He also played for Kent and Middlesex and in a match at Canterbury hit a ball 152 yards.

In practice he hit balls over 160 yards on several occasions and whilst an undergraduate at Cambridge had driven a ball over the pavilion at Lord's. At Scarborough in 1886, whilst playing for the Gentlemen of England v I Zingari, he achieved universal fame by striking a ball delivered by A.G.Steel over the roof-tops of the houses which line the south side of the ground and into Trafalgar Square beyond. Countless discussions have been held as to whether or not this extraordinary feat has since been repeated and evidence for two of the claiments is examined later. It is worth recording that in that innings Thornton made 107 in twenty-nine strokes, including eight sixes and twelve fours.

Before the historic match in 1871, two other important matches had taken place at Castle Hill. The first of these was in 1869 and was between Grimston Park and Scarborough Incogniti. The Grimston Park team contained five Yorkshire county players and the Incogniti

Londesborough Lodge. His lordship accommodated members of his teams here at various times. A footpath from the Lodge led directly down to The Spa.

numbered sixteen players, but the real significance was that all the expenses of the Grimston Park team were met by Lord Londesborough.

The second match took place in 1870 and was between Scarborough and Visitors and a United South XI. It was in this match that W.G.Grace made his first appearance at Scarborough. 'The Doctor', as he was often referred to, was undoubtedly the most influential and popular figure in Victorian and Edwardian society and his presence at Castle Hill did much to consolidate Scarborough's reputation as an important up-and-coming cricket centre.

Grace's influence on cricket was immense. Suffice to say that his appearance in Scarborough stirred in the mind of the erstwhile Robert Baker several ideas of what might be possible in the future, given a little help from wealthy aristocracy.

In order to raise a team for Lord Londesborough's challenge match in 1871, C.I.Thornton approached the MCC at Lord's for assistance. This action was to have enormous consequences for the development of the Festival. Thornton's approach established a link between Scarborough Cricket Club and Lord's and set a precedent which was to be observed thereafter.

Thornton was given three professionals by MCC and told to do his best. On arriving at Castle Hill, Thornton's XI was confronted, not

by a team of nondescript players, but by almost the whole of the Yorkshire county team masquerading as Lord Londesborough's XI. Thornton was not pleased and, in later years, was known to have claimed victory in the contest. Actually, the match ended in a draw.

A condition of this match, laid down by the War Office, who owned the land at Castle Hill, was that there should be no charge for admission. Lord Londesborough, therefore, defrayed all the expenses incurred and also indulged in some especially lavish hospitality, which also did no harm to the occasion.

Lord Hawke recalled: *In the years when I wore short frocks, old Roger Iddison used to be commissioned by Lord Londesborough to get a side together at some place of other; one, for example, in the New Forest, another time at Grimston Park, or again at Scarborough, Lord Londesborough never bargained, but simply gave him a cheque for whatever he asked, which once indicated Roger to say, "His lordship just 'angs' 'is purse on the gate and lets anyone 'elp 'imself as likes"*

Following the match between Lord Londesborough's XI and C.I.Thornton's XI, which was held in early September, a crucial committee meeting of the Scarborough Cricket Club was held on 18 September 1871. At that meeting the existing rules of the club were revised. It was resolved that the Right Honourable Lord Londesborough, E.H.Hebden Esq and certain Borough members become patrons of the club.

Also at the meeting, a letter was read from his lordship about the possibility of finding another ground on which to play matches with which he might be associated. His lordship had clearly become impatient with the problems associated with Castle Hill. The committee decided to instruct the two joint secretaries to reply to Lord Londesborough with suggestions for the development of the existing club ground opposite the Queen Hotel.

It is interesting that, despite pressure from Lord Londesborough, the club members were sufficiently independent to resist the idea of a change of venue from the club's headquarters, despite the obvious difficulties caused by the poor state of the ground. Even so, the new patron's influence was beginning to be felt; the principle of playing matches outside the immediate club fixture list had been established and once Robert Baker got to work as secretary in 1872, the idea of a festival of cricket at Scarborough was soon brought to reality.

Lord Londesborough's contribution in those early days was very great. He brought patronage and a stamp of respectability, prestige and status to the Scarborough Cricket Club. On the other hand, his motives were not entirely, or even necessarily altruistic. The theory that around the latter part of the nineteenth century the aristocracy attempted to appropriate certain leisure pursuits for their exclusive benefit seems particularly plausible in the context of the Scarborough Cricket Festival.

Neither can there be little doubt that the cricket itself was a vehicle for indulging in the more serious business of social inter-action. But patronage had its price. More and more newspapers and minutes of committee meetings began to make reference to 'His Lordship's Festival'.

In 1898, the 'Scarborough Mercury recalled: *It was Lord Londesborough who made the Scarborough Cricket Festival possible. He brought here for many years the Gentlemen Players and at his own expense entertained them. Those he was unable to entertain at Londesborough Lodge he provided for at hotels and even went as far as to keep a house in The Crescent specially for the use of the cricketers. In addition to this great expense his lordship and the countess daily entertained during the Festival the cricketers and distinguished visitors on the ground and there is no doubt they were the means of getting together for many seasons the parties which gave the annual Festival a name throughout the country.*

Londesborough undoubtedly saw the Fes-

tival as an ideal instrument for promoting his own social standing and the club also benefited. Yet it is rather curious that, despite the massive contribution of the First Earl of Londesborough to the establishing of the Scarborough Cricket Festival, he never became president of Scarborough Cricket Club itself. Furthermore, there is no record of his ever being invited, despite the fact that in 1876 he was made president of MCC. Were the Scarborough officials making a point? Interestingly enough, the Second Lord Londesborough, who married the eldest daughter of the Earl of Westmorland in 1887 and succeeded his father in 1900, did become president of Scarborough Cricket Club on two occasions, in 1904 and 1912. Perhaps the club were simply putting the record straight.

The other leading figure in the early history of the Festival was C.I.(Buns) Thornton, who after the initial 'trial' match of 1871, became responsible for organising teams for the Festival. C.I.Thornton's XI, then H.D.G.Leveson-Gower's XI, followed by T.N.Pearce's XI, were indelibly associated with cricket at Scarborough and for the greater period of Festival history they played matches against touring teams from all over the cricketing world.

To be invited to play in such teams was an honour much sought after and valued only slightly less than playing for England itself. In latter years, D.B.Close's XI and Michael Parkinson's XI have also featured in matches against touring teams.

Thornton established the important link between Scarborough Cricket Club and the MCC in the match of 1871, by recruiting players for his team from MCC. Eventually, the MCC v Yorkshire match became one of the cornerstones of the Festival programme and lasted until 1971. MCC always regarded the fixture as its responsibility.

In 1898, the MCC attempted to transfer the whole of the expense of the match to the Scarborough club, but a special committee meeting of the club resolved: *A letter signed by the president and secretary be forwarded to Mr Lacey (secretary of MCC) asking him, in view of the fact that the match had been played under existing circumstances for upwards of twenty years, not to press the suggestion advanced to Mr Thornton.*

And the matter was never raised again. In 1921, C.I.Thornton had conferred upon him the Freedom of the Borough of Scarborough and joined the very short and select list of Freeman of Scarborough.

Thornton was succeeded in the role of teams' organiser by H.D.G.Leveson-Gower. 'Shrimp' Leveson-Gower went to Winchester and

Arm in arm. H.D.G.
Leveson-Gower (left)
and Lord Hawke out-
side the Festival mar-
quee. Without their
support it is unlikely
that the Festival could
have been such a
success.

Oxford and captained his university and Surrey. He also led various MCC teams at home and abroad and was an England selector for many years. His association with Scarborough lasted 51 years, from 1899 to 1950, and he, too, was made a Freeman of Scarborough in 1930.

Leveson-Gower's XI v the Tourists XI was undoubtedly one of the highlights of the inter-war years when Leveson-Gower *pursued my object that the public should have the chance of seeing as many first-class cricketers as possible during those nine days.*

Leveson-Gower's successor was T.N.Pearce. A former captain, chairman and now president of Essex, Tom Pearce was an England selector and held many offices in the administrative structure of MCC. He was also a former international rugby referee. When he finally stepped down as teams' organiser in 1981, the

Left: *Tom Pearce succeeded Leveson-Gower as teams' organiser in 1950. He was only the third occupant of the post. He stepped down in 1981. Right: H.D.G. 'Shrimp' Leveson-Gower, whose association with the Festival lasted 51 years from 1899 to 1950.*

Festival lost only its third occupant of the post in over one hundred years.

The continuity established by such influential figures in the cricket world had many advantages for the Festival. First, the best quality players were always able to be contacted and made available to play at Scarborough. Not that much persuasion was usually required, but if there ever was the need . . .!

Second, in the sometimes delicate matter of negotiations with touring teams, the MCC was always prepared to act as intermediary. Third, three-day matches at the Festival have always had first-class status, whilst the scheduling of the county programme, to take account of Festival dates, has always been given careful consideration by the appropriate authorities at Lord's.

Complimenting the support from Lord's, created and consolidated by the efforts of Thornton, Londesborough, Leveson-Gower, Pearce and others, has been the unwavering backing given to the Festival by Yorkshire County Cricket Club. Yorkshire CCC was formed officially in 1863 and reorganised in 1891, but various Yorkshire teams had played against other counties since 1833 and many Yorkshire players were familiar with playing at Scarborough in a variety of visiting teams. As previously mentioned, Lord Londes-

Lord Hawke's XI of 1889.

Parading at the Festival in 1892. The view is towards the Festival marquee from the Popular Bank.

Eager young autograph hunters at the 1923 Festival visit of the West Indians.

borough's XI of 1871 was almost entirely the Yorkshire team.

At a committee meeting held in January 1873: *A letter was also read from Roger Iddison (Yorkshire captain) stating that the Middlesex County Club were anxious to arrange the return match with Yorkshire to be played at Scarborough the latter part of August next.*

The committee, being concerned about the financing of such a match, requested more information. The information must have proved to be satisfactory, as in 1874 the first official county cricket match at Scarborough took place between Yorkshire and Middlesex.

Also at that January meeting: *Letters were read from Roger Iddison stating that Lord*

Londesborough was anxious to arrange a North and South match to be played at Scarborough on 25, 26, 27 August 1873, his lordship offering to pay the North XI if the club would consent to pay the South.

This offer was accepted and the North v South match became an integral part of many Festivals.

The individual who did most to cement the relationship between Scarborough Cricket Club and Yorkshire was Lord Hawke. Lord Hawke made his first appearance for Yorkshire at the Festival of 1881 and, as captain of Yorkshire, was instrumental in making the county a force in the cricket world. His influence also extended to committees and

councils of MCC. He was elected president of the Scarborough Cricket Club in 1929, and in 1930, when he was made a Freeman of the Borough of Scarborough.

Lord Hawke led Yorkshire to the County Championship in 1898 and William Leadbeater saw the opportunity of indulging in a public relations exercise with the county at the end of the Festival. He took the calculated risk of arranging a special banquet to celebrate the winning of the County Championship, although he could not be certain that the county would actually do so.

The 'Scarborough Post' admired Leadbeater's initiative: *It seldom falls to the lot of a cricket club to be able to gather together at one time such a brilliant company as that which assembled at the Balmoral Hotel on Friday night to pay a tribute to the abilities of Lord Hawke and other members of the Yorkshire County Cricket XI and the president of the Scarborough Cricket Club (Captain Darley J.P), the secretary (Mr W.W.Leadbeater) and the committee may fairly congratulate themselves upon the success of the bold and ambitious step they took some months ago, when a deputation was sent to Sheffield with the object of interviewing Lord Hawke and inducing him to accept, on behalf of the Yorkshire XI and himself, the invitation to attend the banquet.*

This type of initiative was characteristic of Leadbeater's style and did no harm to the relationship between the two clubs. That is not to say that the relationship was not put to the test at various times. A good example of such an occurence came with the 'covered wicket incident' of 1908.

For many years the wicket at the Festival had, when necessary, been covered overnight against the elements, in order that spectators seeking to attend the following day would know that play was certain. Lord Hawke was vehemently opposed to the idea as it was not the normal cricket practice at the time. So when Yorkshire scored 325 on the first day of the match against MCC, heavy overnight rain followed by bright sunshine left his lordship eagerly anticipating a difficult wicket for the MCC to bat on.

No doubt the thought of a few strategic pre-match wagers had also sharpened his appetite. William Leadbeater, however, was more mindful of the gate receipts and, unbeknown to Lord Hawke, had ordered the wicket to be covered overnight. The following day a furious Lord Hawke almost refused to allow Yorkshire to play and some skilful diplomacy was called

C.I.Thornton's England XI v the Australians at Scarborough, 1926. From left to right: H.Strudwick, E. Tyldesley, W.Rhodes, G.T.S. Stevens, A.E.R.Gilligan, C.I.Thornton, V.W.C.Jupp, G.O.Allen, J.B.Hobbs, H.Sutcliffe, P.Holmes, M.Tate.

for. Fortunately, the matter was resolved without getting out of hand and the custom of covering the wicket at the Festival became established. The cricketer's view and the administrator's outlook is a recipe for disagreement and is not entirely a modern phenomenon.

The MCC v Yorkshire match was a cornerstone of the Festival programme until 1971. Gentlemen v Players and North v South were other fixtures which took place over many years, although they have now been consigned to the history books. The other traditional fixture was the match involving the current international touring team and that match still survives.

As Kilburn observed: *Much of the charm of the Festival lies in repetition. Every Festival has within it something from every other Festival, yet far from familiarity breeding contempt the appeal is cumulative.*

That observation would undoubtedly be true until about 1960, after which the Festival underwent a number of fundamental changes. Certainly the regularity with which many cricket followers returned to Scarborough year

after year, confirmed Kilburn's opinion of the Festival format.

The most eagerly awaited tourists at Scarborough Cricket Festival in those years were the Australians. They first played at North Marine Road in 1878, but as tours became more demanding, both in time and intensity of play, attitudes began to change. The prospect of playing virtually a 'Sixth Test Match' at Scarborough at the end of a long, hard tour was not one which the Australians always relished.

On the 1948 tour the Australians were unbeaten, with Lindwall and Miller undermining the English batsmen with fast bowling and Bradman, Morris and the young Neil Harvey leading the batting line-up. Bradman remembered the defeat suffered by the Australians ten years earlier in 1939 at the hands of Leveson-Gower's XI at the Festival. That was the only defeat incurred on that tour, apart from the final Test at The Oval — Hutton's match — and Bradman was determined that the 1948 Australians would remain unbeaten.

So he refused to consider playing at Scarborough, unless Leveson-Gower's XI was

HRH Princess Mary with H.D.G.Leveson-Gower (right), who is wearing his famous spats. The photograph was taken at the Grand Hotel during the 1927 Festival.

restricted to not more than six current England Test players. Leveson-Gower agreed to the condition, although he did cheat a little by including in his team the world-class New Zealand batsman Martin Donnelly!

The Australians were in no mood for frivolity and made a first-inning total of 489-9 declared to ensure that the match was drawn. Barnes made 151 and on his last appearance in England, Bradman made 153. Bradman was satisfied and 15,000 people attending the final day's play were happy with what they saw.

During the match Bradman was made an honorary life member of Yorkshire County

Festival scenes from the 1920s and '30s. Left (top to bottom): Time for tea and a cigarette; George Hirst (left), Wilfred Rhodes (centre) and Lord Hawke; Festival spirit; Waiting to bat. *Right (top to bottom):* K.S.Duleepsinjhi; Alderman Whitfield (1927 president) accompanies Princess Mary. *opposite page left (top to obttom):* Billy Griffith; Princess Mary greeted by Alderman Whitfield and Mrs Whitfield. *Right (top to bottom):* 1929 dignitaries (from left): H.D.G.Leveson-Gower, J.W.H.T.Douglas, Lord Harris, Lord Hawke and Lord Downe; another 1929 group (from left): H.G.D.Leveson-Gower, Lord Hawke, Lady Hawke, C.I.Thornton, Lady Downe, Mrs J.W.H.T.Douglas, Mrs Leveson-Gower, Mrs Nigel Haig; the Australians take the field against Leveson-Gower's XI on a chilly day in 1930. Don Bradman is extreme right.

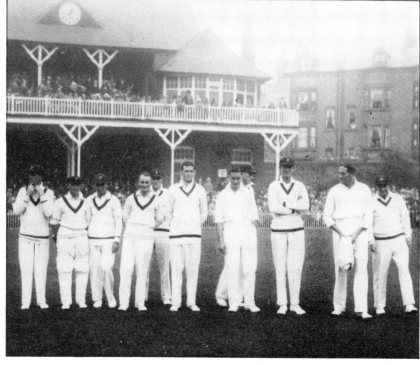

A strong Festival
team from the 1940s.
From left to right:
T.Pritchard, J.Walsh,
T.G.Evans, L.Hutton,
W.J.Edrich, N.Yardley,
F.R.Brown (captain),
R . T . S i m p s o n ,
T.E.Bailey, A.V.Bedser,
T.W.Graveney.

A strong Festival team from the 1940s. From left to right: T.Pritchard, J.Walsh, T.G.Evans, L.Hutton, W.J.Edrich, N.Yardley, F.R.Brown (captain), R.T.Simpson, T.E.Bailey, A.V.Bedser, T.W.Graveney.

The 1948 Australians
v Leveson-Gower's XI.
From left to right:
S.G.Barnes, K.R.Miller,
S.Loxton, D.Tallon,
R.N.Harvey, I.W. John-
son, R.R.Lindwall,
W.A.Johnston, D.G.
Bradman (captain),
A.R.Morris, A.L.Hassett.
This was Don Brad-
man's last appearance
in England.

The 1948 Australians v Leveson-Gower's XI. From left to right: S.G.Barnes, K.R.Miller, S.Loxton, D.Tallon, R.N.Harvey, I.W. Johnson, R.R.Lindwall, W.A.Johnston, D.G. Bradman (captain), A.R.Morris, A.L.Hassett. This was Don Bradman's last appearance in England.

Cricket Club, an honour which he values greatly. Later that evening, at The Grand Hotel, the foyer and hall-way was crowded, the chairs and seating places all occupied. Bradman appeared at the head of the main staircase to make his way to dinner and everyone rose as one to give 'The Don' a marvellous standing ovation. Sadly, largely due to commercial reasons, the Australians have not appeared at the Festival since 1964.

Gentlemen v Players was always a popular match at the Scarborough Cricket Festival. Introduced in 1885, it survived until 1962, after which the distinction between amateur and professional players was abolished. From about 1920, these matches became part of the established pattern of the Festival programme. Thirty-nine matches were played in total with the Players winning fifteen, the Gentlemen four and nineteen were drawn. When special occasional matches were played, for example featuring the outgoing English touring side,

these matches tended to replace the Gentlemen v Players fixture.

During the long settled period up to the 1960s, income from the Festival provided the Scarborough Cricket Club with sufficient funds to implement the established policy of ground improvement. The North (Concrete) Stand was built in 1926 at a cost of £6,700; new seating was installed in the Trafalgar Square enclosure and a Tea Room added; the Popular Bank was re-seated. These improvements made between the wars were the consequence of successful Festivals in a period when the Scarborough Cricket Festival had become a very important event in the cricket calendar. Invitations were sort and valued for two main reasons.

From the professionals' point of view, the first-class status of matches at the Festival provided an extension to the season in which personal milestones of runs and wickets could often be achieved. The invitation teams

sometimes contained the names of players on the fringe of international recognition and so provided an opportunity to catch the eye of the selectors, especially when a winter touring team was due to be announced. This applied equally to amateurs and Ted Dexter felt that his 80-odd made when he volunteered to open the batting in the second innings against Fred Trueman and Frank Tyson in 1957, may well have been to his benefit when the selectors were considering him for the captaincy at a later date.

Crowds were large and the general holiday atmosphere was a welcome relaxation at the end of a hard season, whilst there was also the considerable bonus that professionals received extra payment.

Then there was the social scene. Leveson-Gower observed that during his career: *One of the factors that has added something to the success of the Scarborough Festivals has been the Grand Hotel where a good number of visitors taking part usually stay. The managers have always looked after our comfort and everyone who has been asked to take part on these occasions has enjoyed that part of the nine days or so spent 'off the field' just as much as the play itself.*

It must be remembered that Scarborough Cricket Festival was essentially the product of upper-class initiatives. The Grand Hotel, designed by Cuthbert Broderick of Leeds, was opened in 1867 and quickly became the social centre for the gentry. The amateurs playing in the Festival traditionally stayed at the Grand, where the hospitality was lavish.

Rather than allow cricketing guests to be pestered at dinner, the hotel manager agreed with C.I.Thornton that a room should be set aside for the cricketers' exclusive use. This became known as the Cricketers' Room and was situated close to the main staircase and beside the main dining-room. Here the traditional dinner given by the teams' organiser was held each year and gradually the walls became lined with portraits of all the great amateur players who had graced the Festival over the years.

Much to the regret of all who enjoyed the privilege of dining in the famous room on such occasions, the Cricketers' Room was closed on 11 January 1979.

Not only was the Cricketers' Room a feature of The Grand Hotel's affinity with the Festival, for in the immediate post-war period of the 1940s, players often took tea on the field at

Don Bradman giving a Press conference in the Festival marquee in 1948. A little light refreshment is available.

North Marine Road, rather than in the Pavilion. Tea was then served in some style on silver trays by the head waiter and his staff from The Grand Hotel. And from the bandstand the sound of appropriate melodies drifted in the air.

The professionals did not stay at The Grand Hotel. They stayed at the guest houses which surround the ground at North Marine Road. Landladies in the vicinity were not slow to exploit the advantages to their trade of such a situation and, with careful wording, advertised the importance of cricket and the Scarborough Cricket Festival to an enjoyable holiday. This irritated a succession of honorary treasurers of the Scarborough Cricket Club, who felt that some acknowledgement of the value of cricket to increased private profits should somehow be reflected in the club's coffers. Needless to say, their pleas were seldom heeded.

The more obvious demarcations between amateurs and professionals were usually less rigrously enforced at the Festival, at least on the field of play. When, however, the relax-

ations seemed likely to impinge on the social side, they were quickly rectified.

In 1931 . . .the question of entertaining during the Festival was considered. The President decided to revert to the old custom, that he will entertain the Amateurs and the Professionals will be catered for in the Pavilion.

Scarborough Cricket Festival began when class consciousness was highly developed. It also coincided with a period of cricket dominated by W.G.Grace, a time when the amateur gentleman overshadowed the professional player, both off the field and on. This on-the-field domination was a reversal of the pattern earlier in the century and was a consequence of the rise of the public schools.

The public schools ethos claimed that games, particularly cricket, embodied the values of courage, manliness and honour, which Victorians desired in life itself. The values of games and life were thought to be intertwined and so the phrase 'it's not cricket' took on a wider meaning than being confined to cricket itself. Such values were also absorbed

Women's cricket. The Rest of England XI which met Miss Molly Hide's England XI at Scarborough at the 1950 Festival.

The 1950 West Indians at Scarborough. From left to right: K.T.Ramadhin, E.D.Weekes, C.B. Williams, R.J.Christiani, A.F.Rae, G.E.Gomez, A.L.Valentine, J.B. Stollmeyer, H.H.Johnson, C . L . W a l c o t t , R.E.Marshall.

into social class distinctions and although the Gentlemen v Players fixture at Scarborough was more relaxed than the corresponding fixture at Lord's, occasionally a bit of 'needle' crept in with social class undertones.

When the distinction between amateur and professional was abolished in 1963 and everyone became 'players', a tradition of cricket since its inception was finally laid to rest. At the first match in 1885, W.G.Grace compiled 174 for the amateur Gentlemen. At the last match in 1962, Ken Barrington, the epitome of the professional Player, made 100 and the Players won, perhaps appropriately, by seven wickets. The captains were M.J.K.Smith and Fred Trueman.

The balance of power had changed completely, on the field and off. No longer was it necessary to make distinction between cricketers by means of separate entrance gates to the pitch, separate changing-rooms, initials before or after surnames and all the other nuances to reinforce class barriers. The jibe that amateurs batted and professionals bowled, a historical nicety originating in the days when squires employed labourers to 'play' for them and continued as groundstaff boys, at Lord's

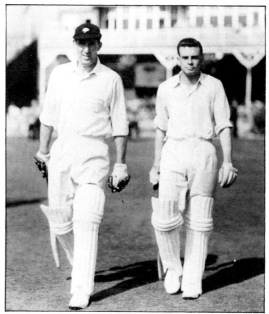

Bottom left: *Australia's Jim de Courcey (left) and Ian Craig going out to bat against T.N.Pearce's XI in 1953. Right (from top to bottom): Vic Wilson (left), of Scarborough CC and Yorkshire, goes out to bat with a young Dickie Bird at the Festival in the late 1950s; Brian Close (left) and Frank Lowson at the 1954 Festival; crowd pleasers both. Tom Graveney (left) and Denis Compton make their way to the wicket in the 1950s.*

and at county grounds around the country, slaved away bowling to members, began to wear a little thin. The year 1962 marked the end of an era in cricket and in social history.

The 1960s proved also to be a turning point in the history of Scarborough Cricket Club. The Festival prospered financially, which may have led to a false sense of prosperity. In the meantime, a number of factors were beginning to combine to affect the traditional three-day

The 1962 Festival Committee. Back row (left to right): J.Midgley (secretary), F.B.Swift, G.H.Smith, H.Wilson (treasurer). Front: L.Rollett, W.A.Wood (chairman), His Grace the Duke of Norfolk (president), T.N. Pearce, Alderman F.C.Chapman.

The 1965 Festival Committee. Back row (left to right): T.W.Baker, L.Rollett, G.H.Smith, H.Wilson, F.B.Swift, J.Midgley (secretary). Front: W.A.Wood (chairman), A.B.Sellers (president), T.N.Pearce.

game of cricket and the repercussions of those were to have a considerable impact on the Festival. These factors could be broadly divided into three categories, namely structural, financial and social.

Structural changes to cricket in the 1960s saw the coming of one-day limited overs competitions like the Gillette Cup, the playing of Sunday cricket, increases in the number of Test matches at home and abroad and the extending of the season later into September, all of which placed severe restrictions on the availability of teams and players for the Festival.

The structural changes in cricket were brought about primarily through the increasing financial problems affecting county clubs. Costs began to mount and rising inflation

The England XI in jovial mood at the 1965 Festival as they take the field against the Rest of the World XI in one of the first sponsored matches at Scarborough. Left to right: Barry Knight, David White, Fred Rumsey, Peter Parfitt, Bob Barber, Colin Cowdrey, John Murray, Fred Titmus, Ken Barrington, Mike Smith (captain), John Edrich.

Wilfred Rhodes (centre) visits the president's tent. The BBC's Peter West is extreme right.

started to take its toll. Projects concerned with ground development and maintenance came under pressure and became deferred.

The Packer Affair in the 1970s resulted in a general rise in payment to players and presenting cricket became an increasingly expensive business. Compounded by declining attendances at traditional three-day county cricket, the financial problems began to threaten the very existence of county clubs and the authorities were obliged to look for alternative forms of income, if necessary outside the game itself.

The Gillette Cup showed the way. In 1963, the sponsorship by Gillette of a new 60 overs-a-side knock-out competition made sponsorship of cricket respectable. Other limited-overs competitions followed, such as the John Player Sunday League in 1969 and the Bensons and Hedges Cup in 1972. Prudential and Cornhill Assurance Companies later sponsored the game at Test Match level and cricket and the commercial world were quickly joined.

Social changes in the 1960s affected everything, cricket included. Changing patterns of leisure were promoted by technological advances in mass communications. Television became a major leisure activity and spelt the beginning of the decline in attendances at ordinary sporting events. Car ownership became more widespread and that influenced holiday arrangements considerably. Nowhere was this more noticeable than at seaside resorts like Scarborough.

In the late 1960s and 1970s, the long established landladies' guest houses and small hotels began to be converted into self-catering flats. The motor-car and the day-tripper replaced the train and the weekly lodger as a main contributor to Scarborough's tourist industry. Road by-passes were planned at Tadcaster and Malton; car-parking became a political hot potato. 'Business' became even more the business of Scarborough, so much so that the gentry of Victorian and Edwardian Scarborough would have been appalled at the naked commercialism exhibited along the promenade of South Bay. Amusement arcades, fish and chip shops, ice-cream parlours and trinket shops proliferated in the 1960s, reflecting a faster moving, coarser and cruder Scarborough.

A modern Lord Londesborough would be horrified to discover that in 1982, The Grand Hotel, all style and Victorian elegance, was sold to Butlin's; the privileged Cricketers' Room is no more. Even more galling to his lordship would be the knowledge that all

Peter May (left) and Ted Dexter going out to bat at North Marine Road.

players in modern times, from whatever social background, invariably stay together at the same hotel.

Despite the problems, Scarborough Cricket Club and the Festival survived through astute management and a willingness to adapt to and initiate change, exemplified by an approach made to Rothmans of Pall Mall to sponsor an invitation team at the Festival in 1965. Rothmans had already underwritten several private overseas tours, as well as sponsoring matches for charity. Their teams were known as Rothmans Cavaliers. The outcome of the Scarborough initiative was that a match was arranged to take place at the Festival between An England XI and A World XI, with the World XI being sponsored by Rothmans.

A further enlightened twist to this venture was that the World XI was selected by public ballot in 'Radio Times', the result being featured on television in the BBC 'Sportsview' programme, which gained Scarborough much publicity.

The teams for the Festival's first sponsored match in 1965 were

England XI	Rest of the World XI
1. J.H.Edrich (Surrey)	C.C.Hunte (West Indies)
2. R.W.Barber (Warwicks)	E.J.Barlow (South Africa)
3. P.H.Parfitt (Middlesex)	R.B.Kanhai (West Indies)
4. K.F.Barrington (Surrey)	G.S.Sobers (West Indies)
5. M.C.Cowdrey (Kent)	K.C.Bland (South Africa)
6. M.J.K.Smith capt (Warwicks)	Hanif Mohammed (Pakistan)
7. B.R.Knight (Essex)	J.R.Reid capt (New Zealand)
8. J.T.Murray (Middlesex)	W.Grout (Australia)
9. F.J.Titmus (Middlesex)	C.C.Griffith (West Indies)
10. F.E.Rumsey (Somerset)	W.W.Hall (West Indies)
11. D.W.White (Hampshire)	L.R.Gibbs (West Indies)

E.J.Barlow and the Nawab of Pataudi replaced N.O'Neill and R.B.Simpson in the 12 names selected by 'Radio Times' readers.

Another first for the Scarborough club on this occasion was that the match was covered by 'live' television, although much to everyone's disappointment rain forced an abandonment of the match. The full Festival programme in 1965 was T.N.Pearce's XI v West Indies; An England XI v Rest of the World XI; MCC v Yorkshire and the format was repeated in 1966 with the Pakistan tourists replacing West Indies.

The club's Annual Report in 1966 was fulsome. *The first week of the Festival was blessed with weather to match the occasion. Large crowds flocked to see the wonderful array of talent assembled at North Marine Road and went away happy in the knowledge that they had seen the game's skills performed before them by masters of the craft.*

The Rothmans sponsorship ended in 1969

Top to bottom: *Geoff Boycott receives the Fenner Trophy from Festival president Sidney Hainsworth in 1972. Left to right: Sir Leonard Hutton, Lady Hutton, Sidney Hainsworth, Geoff Boycott, Tom Pearce, Jackie Bond, Waid Wood and Mrs Hainsworth; Herbert Sutcliffe, president of Scarborough CC, and Mrs Sutcliffe outside the president's tent at the 1968 Festival. John Midgley (secretary) is on the left, Waid Wood (chairman) on the right; HRH the Duchess of Kent, president of Scarborough CC in 1976, meets West Indian all-rounder Bernard Julien at the Festival; Somerset at the 1978 Festival with Ian Botham third from left on the back row.*

Top: *Two great supporters of the Festival, Bob Taylor and Godfrey Evans.*
Bottom: *Sir Leonard Hutton chats to spectators in the Trafalgar Square Enclosure during the 1973 Festival.*

and other ideas were needed. A Carling single-wicket competition, later transferred to Lord's was staged; a Women's Test Match between England and Australia took place; and an England XI v An England Under-25s XI provided some competitive cricket.

All these efforts brought short-term benefits, yet despite the cricketing successes and very good gate receipts, membership of the club throughout the 1960s was falling — 4,527 in 1961 to 3,109 in 1970 — despite only a minimal increase of 5s (25p) in the most popular categories of membership.

The reasons for the fall in membership are complex. The cricket was attractive and daily attendances were, at times, excellent. But the repeated uncertainty about the following season's programme must have had an effect on traditional Festival watchers. Over many years, Festival followers had become accustomed to the habitual Festival format and programme. They booked their seats a year ahead because they were content with the status quo and it was decline in advanced bookings which was the sign that all was not well.

Old habits die hard and as Kilburn remarked: *Much of the charm of the Festival lies in repetition. Though details may differ, one year is very like another in essentials, with the same spectators to be seen pursuing the same line of conduct . . .routine cricket is strict.*

In 1968 and 1969, the Annual Report was forced to carry 'match to be announced' notices in the 'Cricket Attractions' section for the following year's Festival. This contrasted sharply with the procedure of the previous twenty years or more and it was clear that a more stable programme was desirable as the 1960s came to a close.

Those members who travelled considerable distances and those from outside the county were most likely to be unhappy with changes which disturbed the continuity of the past. Yet the club really had little alternative in its attempts to deal with the problems of the 1960s. What was certain was that the traditional three-day matches could no longer sustain the Festival against the advances of the new limited overs cricket which was attracting a younger, more vibrant audience. The old had to be married to the new.

In 1970 there was an attempt to do so. A sponsorship agreement was concluded with Messrs J.H.Fenner & Co Ltd of Hull, and the Fenner Trophy was introduced to the Scarborough Cricket Festival. The concept was for a 60-overs-per-side knock-out tournament spread over three days, consisting of two semi-finals and a Final. The four first-class counties to take part were to be Yorkshire, on a permanent basis, and the three major trophy winners from the previous season — the County Champions, the Gillette Cup holders and John Player League winners.

The instituting of the Fenner Trophy was a most significant change. The club announced: *We are pleased to report that*

Messrs J.H.Fenner & Co Ltd of Hull, have agreed to sponsor this event, which replaces the fixture between Yorkshire and MCC. Both Yorkshire and MCC have agreed to cancel their fixture in order that the knock-out competition could take place and our thanks are due to them for their co-operation.

This brief statement and curt severance of the match between Yorkshire and MCC at the Scarborough Cricket Festival, brought to an end, somewhat abruptly, a tradition which had been the cornerstone of the Festival for nearly a hundred years. The famous match in 1871 between Lord Londesborough's XI and C.I. Thornton's XI, which was the springboard and forerunner of the Festival, was really Yorkshire v MCC in disguise and it seems a pity that the fixture was allowed to die without more acknowledgement of its contribution to the club's history.

The Fenner Trophy quickly became a success. Receipts in the first year were £5,045 compared to £901 for the previous year's Yorkshire v MCC match.

The 1971 Annual Report was enthusiastic: *There is no doubt that the outstanding feature of the 1971 Festival was the Fenner Trophy Knock-Out Competition. The three games certainly captured the imagination of the*

India and Pakistan met in a warm-up match at Scarborough before the 1979 World Cup. Skippers Venkata-raghavan (India) and Majid Khan (Pakistan) inspect the wicket.

public and gave the Festival a much needed shot in the arm.

By 1975, receipts from the three days of the Fenner Trophy had risen to £7,716, whilst membership continued to fall, to 2,948. Quite clearly, a major task facing the club in the 1970s was to find a balance within the Festival between the new one-day, limited overs, 'instant' cricket, with its obvious attractions to the casual watcher and the traditional three-day cricket upon which the Festival had always been based and which retained a hard core of

Bob Woolmer (left) and Mike Proctor look pleased as they receive £500 each for winning the first double-wicket tournament in 1980. The cheques are presented by Tom Pearce.

In 1980 the first floodlit Festival cricket match was played at Scarborough FC's Athletic Ground on Seamer Road. Dennis Lillee, playing for D.B.Close's International XI, was a little too quick for Scarborough CC and a crowd of some 2,000 saw the International XI win by 26 runs.

faithful adherents amongst the long-standing members of the club, many of whom travelled considerable distances to watch cricket at Scarborough.

Other problems for the Festival continued to mount. In 1977 the cricket world was shaken to its foundations by the activities of Kerry Packer and the establishing of a 'cricket circus' for the benefit of Channel 9 Television in Australia.

Cricket circuses were not new. William Clarke's travelling band of professionals, known as the All-England XI, travelled the country in the mid-nineteenth century, but the effect of Packer was to revolutionise thinking about cricket, especially in the matter of the game being recognised and used as a tool for commercial exploitation. Players quickly recognised their greater earning potential, both inside and outside the game.

Expenditure rose so that by the end of the 1970s, the costs of staging the Festival were in a different scale to what had been the case ever before. Added to that was the additional factor of inflation, which rose by 26 per cent between 1973 and 1980.

Festival	Income (£)	Expenditure (£) (players, officials, band, marquees)
1975	12,556	4,262
1980	9,288	14,019

The continuing encroachment of the cricket season later into September did not help. Increasingly difficult became the task of persuading and cajoling players into making the trip to Scarborough, at a time when many were involved with their counties in competitions like the closing stages of the Sunday League and the Gillette Cup Final. The coming of the Bensons & Hedges Cup competition in 1972 also had the effect of pushing the fixture list further into September and, when a twin tour programme was arranged, six Test Matches became the norm.

Due to the proliferation of Test matches around the world, the time between Test Matches was reduced so that the availability of top players was further restricted, with a good example being in 1978 when Pakistan began a Test series against India a little more than a week after leaving England.

Although financial pressures were at the root of the structural changes in cricket, for Scarborough Cricket Festival and the club's officials, a related, but more subtle problem became apparent.

The difficulty was that as financial matters became a more open topic of discussion among cricket followers, the requirement to play hard, competitive cricket at all times was considered to be more important, necessary and desired in the minds of spectators. Value for money became associated with obtaining results. Limited-overs cricket automatically produced a 'result' as opposed to a draw. Winning became a major pre-occupation of the media and became projected as being all-important.

The new cricket-watching public, brought up on an increasing diet of one-day, limited-overs cricket, were not inclined to tolerate cricketers who were not perceived as playing 'competitively'. Kilburn's view of what constituted the 'Festival Spirit' became challenged by the mood of the times and the spectator of the late 1970s, whose outlook was more pragmatic, less romantic than before and for whom risking defeat was anathema. Yet Festival cricket had always been of a different order.

It does not matter greatly who wins a Festival match; it is much more important that somebody should win and by the smallest possible margin at the closest call of time . . .Neither in Festival cricket nor in any other kind of cricket can there be forgiveness for deliberate acceptance of defeat, but in Festival cricket at least there is grace in risking defeat to provide a stirring finish.

The objectives outlined by Kilburn have always needed to be finely balanced. From the spectator's point of view that *the element of earnestness must at all costs be preserved.* Throughout the history of the Festival, it was accepted that there had been occasions when the balance of play on the field had tilted towards the frivolous; letters to the 'Yorkshire Post' newspaper usually followed.

The situation was normally rectified at the following Festival by the president, or either 'Buns' Thornton or Tom Pearce, reminding players of he requirements of Festival play, after which the matter usually lay dormant for a further period. 'Earnestness' was restored.

The essential difference in the 1970s was that the changed structure of first-class cricket had produced many players whose understanding, attitude and approach to the Festival was different to that of players in previous times. An invitation to the Festival which before had been considered an honour had, in some players' minds, become a chore and that was reflected in the manner in which some of the cricket was played. This was especially true in the three-day matches, where prize money was not as substantial, or as immediate, as in the one-day game. Players were betraying the Festival spirit.

Festival cricket, then, its cricket played . . .for its intrinsic purpose, but with an awareness of obligation towards those who pay to see . . .When a player engages himself to take part in Festival cricket he contracts to

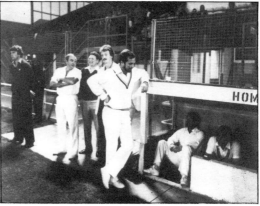

Top to bottom: *Floodlit cricket at Seamer Road in 1981. Yorkshire's Ray Illingworth makes a point during the game against Scarborough; the Scarborough team take the field. Yorkshire won by 25 runs on a chilly September evening; 1981 and the last Fenner Trophy Dinner with seven former England captains in attendance. Back row (left to right): Ray Illingworth, Brian Close, F.G.Mann, Keith Fletcher. Front: Peter May, Norman Yardley (Scarborough CC president), S.B. Hainsworth (chairman of Fenner & Co), Sir Leonard Hutton.*

provide the best within him in the best of spirits.

As a philosophy for taking part in sport, Kilburn's ideal is unsurpassed, but there is no doubt that much of that quality was being lost in the 1970s as economic pressures tightened their grip on the Festival.

Economic pressures also forced J.H.Fenner & Co Ltd to give up sponsorship of the Fenner Trophy in 1981. The competition had been an inspired concept and became the main contributor to gate receipts at the Festival. The club recognised the debt it owed to Sidney Hainsworth and Arnold Silvester, in establishing the credibility of the competition in its early years and Hainsworth, chairman of Fenner's, was elected president of Scarborough Cricket Club in 1972 and 1973.

Old friends share a joke. Neil Harvey (left) and Ray Lindwall at the Centenary Festival in 1986.

D.B.Close's International XI and New Zealand in 1986. In this match, Ken Rutherford of New Zealand made 317 in only 230 minutes. It was the fastest-ever triple century, the fourth by a New Zealander, and contained eight 6s and forty-five 4s, coming off 245 balls. The match ended in a draw.

Neither was it a disadvantage to cricket that Sir Leonard Hutton was a member of the board of directors at Fenners. After being president in 1975, it was a fitting and immensely popular choice that Sir Leonard was again elected for the Centenary Festival in 1986.

The Centenary Festival was the 100th staged at North Marine Road, yet the celebrations for such an historic event were somewhat muted. It was generally felt that the Festival was in decline. Membership, a reliable guide to cricket followers' optimism, had fallen dramatically by nearly one-third in the 1980s, from 3,067 in 1980 to 2,135 in 1985.

Despite Asda Stores taking over sponsorship of the knock-out competition from the Fenner company in 1982, and the Scarborough Building Society sponsoring the three-day traditional fixture against the Tourists — the invitation team carrying the name D.B.Close's XI — it appeared as though the Festival was 'marking time'.

What was really needed was an injection of vitality and energy to set the wheels of expectation spinning again in the minds of Festival die-hards and casual watchers alike. Then, as always in the history of Scarborough Cricket Club, the right man appeared, at the right time. That man was Don Robinson.

Don Robinson had lived as a boy near the cricket ground. For many years he had been one of Scarborough's most prominent businessmen and entrepreneurs in the entertainment and tourist industry. The restoration of the Opera House Theatre was one of his ventures, as was the establishing of the Marineland Funfair and Water World attractions on Scarborough's North Bay.

As chairman of Scarborough Football Club, he had been instrumental in putting that club on stable financial footing, from which base the club succeeded in reaching the FA Trophy Final at Wembley on four occasions in the 1970s, which nicely complemented the three successful visits to Lord's by Scarborough Cricket Club in the same decade.

The town certainly had outstanding publicity from its sporting successes in that era, although Robinson's attempt to interest the cricket club in a ground-sharing scheme at North Marine Road in 1979 was more a publicity venture than a practical reality. By the time Scarborough Football Club were promoted to the Football League in 1987, Robinson had moved on to become a director and chariman of Hull City Football Club, setting about the task on Humberside in the same vigorous manner that characterised his approach to his business affairs. An inspired committee decision meant that Robinson was invited to become president of Scarborough Cricket Club in 1988.

The invitation to Don Robinson was presented by Fred Robson, who had succeeded

Guests at the 1988 Festival Dinner. From left to right: Don Robinson (president of Scarborough CC), Gilbert Gray QC (speaker), Micheal Parkinson, David Kendall (speaker), Lord Mountgarret (president of Yorkshire CCC), Councillor G. Allinson (mayor of Scarborough).

Lord Mountgarret and Tim Rice discuss happenings at the 1988 Festival.

Sachin Tendulkar drives for India against the World XI during the 1990 Scarborough Cricket Festival. David Bairstow is the wicket-keeper, Roger Harper the bowler. In 1992, Tendulkar became Yorkshire's first overseas player.

In memory of Sir Leonard Hutton. The Yorkshire (left) and Derbyshire teams observe a minute's silence at Scarborough during the 1990 Championship match that was played at the end of the Festival.

Left: *Keith Fletcher is served by Christine Goodall in the Festival marquee in 1988. Team managers do not have to bat or field after lunch.*

Right: *On the gate. Two stalwarts Les Clegg (left) and Ted Walker have admitted — and barred — spectators at North Marine Road for many years.*

Geoffrey Smith as chairman of Scarborough Cricket Club in the previous year. Smith, a former accountant, had been chairman of the club for seven years, having joined the committee in 1954 after being a playing member. He was another of the long-serving committee members so characteristic of the club's history and was also a member of the Yorkshire committee for several years. With his quiet, diplomatic and sometimes whimsical approach, he did much to continue the good relationship between the two clubs.

Fred Robson, too, is experienced in the ways of Scarborough Cricket Club. A Durham man and a useful club cricketer, he had played for Scarborough since 1963, joined the committee in 1968, was elected vice chairman in 1980, chairman in 1987 and had witnessed the changing face of Festival cricket and of Festival finances. More specifically, he recognised the necessity for the club to keep pace with modern developments in the entertainment and business worlds. It was from that perspective that Don Robinson was approached to become president of the club.

The list of past presidents of Scarborough Cricket Club is an imposing one. In modern times it features titled aristocracy like HRH The Duke of Edinburgh (1961), His Grace The Duke of Norfolk (1963), HRH The Duchess of Kent (1976), to set alongside cricket notables like Brain Sellers (1965), Herbert Sutcliffe (1968) and Sir Leonard Hutton (1975, 1986).

With due respect to those worthy individuals, it is unlikely that any of them had as much impact on the club as Don Robinson.

Robinson made it abundantly clear from the outset that he was going to be a 'hands-on' president and not simply a figurehead; and was as good as his word. By making use of a vast number of associates in the business and entertainment industries, he jolted any suspicion of complacency out of the Scarborough Cricket Club system and created a 'buzz' reminiscent of the arrival of 'Alfie' Rutherford forty years before.

The Festival woke up with a start. A sense of expectation filled the air. An 'atmosphere' was rekindled. People were talking again with optimism. In modern marketing language, the realisation that the Festival was an entertainment product to be sold in a competitive outside world market, was brought forcefully to the attention of anyone remotely connected with the club.

Not that tradition was abandoned, or even overlooked. It was skilfully adapted to the present requirements, as Robinson resurrected one of the major social occasions of yesteryear, the Festival Banquet. Major civic and sporting dignitaries were invited to what proved to be a substantial fund-raising affair. Thanks to Robinson's organising abilities, a splendid dinner-dance was held in the Festival marquees to the accompaniment of a monster firework display on the ground, whilst as a real echo of times past, the London Stock Exchange played a match against a Yorkshire League XI as a curtain raiser to the 1988 Festival.

Not only that, but Robinson reinstituted the tradition led by C.I.Thornton, H.D.G.Leveson-Gower, T.N.Pearce and latterly D.B.Close, of the invitation team for the three-day match carrying the name of a team organiser and so Michael Parkinson's World XI took the field against MCC in 1988 and 1989 and against India in 1990.

Don Robinson clearly had a major role to play in the areas of sponsorship, advertising and the media. He was quickly able to secure the agreement of Tesco Stores Ltd to sponsor a three-day international match at the Festival and for Ward's Buildings to take over the sponsorship of the four counties knock-out tournament, originally the Fenner Trophy, which had been continued by Asda Stores Ltd and was the centrepiece of the modern Festival, at least as far as gate receipts were concerned.

Other major sponsors like Joshua Tetley and McCain Foods (GB) Ltd were attracted, joining longer-established local sponsors like Plaxtons and the Scarborough Building Society in being associated with the Scarborough Cricket Festival. Boundary-board advertising suddenly became in greater demand as Yorkshire Television was persuaded to cover extensively not only the Festival but also Yorkshire matches at North Marine Road. The television company also sponsored the Festival Banquet and few days were allowed to pass without some items of news about the Festival appearing in different branches of the media.

Such items ranged from team news and ticket prices, to the state of the wicket and the installation of new seats in the North Stand for the greater comfort of spectators. As in the days of Robert Baker, W.W.Leadbeater and 'Alfie' Rutherford, Don Robinson had command of the details.

The Robinson effect was far more than the stiff breezes and bracing climate for which Scarborough is noted. It was a whole gale force which produced a stimulating and confidence-building response in committee, members and

public alike. The only requirement for presidents in the past had been to make at least one appearance at the Festival, but Robinson's involvement was year long and practical.

Expectations were heightened as the quality of teams to play at the Festival were announced and major sponsors obtained. From a surplus figure of £7,510 in 1987, profits rocketed to £28,270 in 1988.

Only twice since World War Two has the president of Scarborough Cricket Club been invited to serve a second successive term of office, but is unlikely that many voices were raised in objection when the committee invited Don Robinson to continue in 1989. The financial results were just as impressive as the previous year, with income up to £144,516 and profits at £28,068. In 1990, Robinson was elected a vice president of the club.

The 1980s had finished with a bang and another high profile figure became president in 1990. Michael Parkinson, invited by Robinson to front the invitation team at the Festival, presided over another financially successful year as profits of £30,914 accrued in a period of general recession.

When income from the Jack Knowles Deceased Trust is added, Scarborough Cricket Club is able to look forward to the 1990s with much greater optimism than had been the case even five years earlier. In 1991 the policy of an actively involved president was continued as Charles McCarthy, deputy chairman of McCain Foods (GB) Ltd, attended three-quarters of scheduled committee meetings, a commitment well beyond the call of duty for earlier presidents.

The present administration of Scarborough Cricket Club is well aware that it has much to do if the Festival and the club are to prosper in the twenty-first century. Scarborough Cricket Festival is an accepted part of cricket and has given great pleasure to a vast number of people. Those people who have contributed over the years, in the words of Jim Kilburn *have painted a corner on the canvas of a nation's life, and added their mite to the sum of human happiness.*

Scarborough Views — Reminiscences

FESTIVAL cricket at Scarborough, according to J.M.Kilburn, has always been 'cricket on holiday'. Few would argue with that assessment and as is the way with holidays, memories remain. Those memories lie dormant waiting to be rekindled by a photograph, a conversation, or sometimes an old scorecard, which bring to the mind's eye those experiences of pleasure, occasionally pain, on which cricket lore thrives. In this chapter, writers, players and celebrities reminisce about cricket at Scarborough.

A few weeks before he died, John Arlott, a friend of cricketers, remembered:

Some thirty years of reporting the Scarborough Festival for radio was as pleasant a job as a man could wish. The atmosphere was always marvellous, with the accent on people achieving rather than stopping others. That and, of course, the hospitality. For those who rate cricket festivals by their liquid refreshment, Scarborough was always a delight. Whoever picked the wines — in this writer's time at least — knew what he was doing and repeated it for other people's pleasure. Of all festivals, it is, perhaps, consistently the highest in its level of play. For those thirty-odd years it was possible to see the best players in the world — most of them more than once — and invariably — as is not always true of first-class cricketers — enjoying themselves. Indeed, it might be said that no other festival ranked quite with Scarborough for performance, pleasure, and refreshment; and, my word, what a delight it always was.

Great players, too, have their memories. On a lovely late summer's day at Queen's Park, Chesterfield, itself one of the most beautiful grounds in all of England, I asked Geoffrey Boycott about playing cricket at Scarborough, including the first time he played there.

I played for Barnsley there in the Yorkshire League. Everybody looked forward to the Scarborough fixture. Barnsley usually had the Whitsuntide and Bank Holiday and alternated home and away. There were some good characters playing for Barnsley, one of the top sides. We had Dickie Bird playing, who was a top batsman in the Yorkshire League at that time, Eddie Legard, Eric Butcher, a tall, gangly fast bowler, a professional called Graham Pearce from Hull and two Yorkshire schoolboys in Peter Myers and myself.

I was about fifteen or sixteen. I can't remember whether I got any runs. I'll have to look at the scorebook . . .no, no, I can't remember, really! It was such an event, you know. You went on the Sunday and you stayed overnight in bed and breakfast lodgings, because you just liked Scarborough and it was

John Arlott, doyen of cricket broadcasters.

Geoff Boycott shares a joke with Arnie Sidebottom and Ray Illingworth in front of the Pavilion at North Marine Road during Yorkshire's County Championship match against Sussex in 1982.

a day out by the seaside. And then you played in this lovely atmosphere, lovely ground.

The best two leagues were the Bradford League and the Yorkshire League so you knew you were playing in one of the best leagues. Scarborough always had, about that time in the late Fifties, early Sixties, a top side. Ted Lester played for them, a wonderful player; Harry Halliday played. They had the fast bowler Bill Foord . . .they had a good bowler in Geoff Dennis, a good league bowler. They always had a good side, they always had some ex-second team, ex-first team players. They were a tough side. They had a left-hander called Stockwell, a tall . . .ooh, my word, he used to beat the living daylights out of everybody. Crikey . . .oh aye, wherever you bowled. I mean, in the leagues, he scored runs like shelling peas!

Stockwell and Ted Lester together. They used to bat so quickly as well that, at times, instead of batting the forty-seven overs, as it

was in those days, they'd bat forty-two and declare, leaving five extra overs to bowl you out. That's how confident they were. Oh boy, playing against them was an experience for a youngster. They were regarded as the top side, no question.

Sir Donald Bradman played at Scarborough in three Festivals. He was injured in the Test at The Oval in 1938 and did not play in that year, but his memories of his other visits are very clear. He wrote the following:

I have been asked by Ian Hall to pen a short piece on my memories of the Scarborough Cricket Festival and this I do with pleasure. Obviously, my first direct association was in 1930, that being the year of my first tour of England. But strangely there was still talk even then about the way C.I.Thornton's XI had beaten the all-conquering 1921 Australians and we were warned to look out for a hard game at Scarborough.

The match was badly interrupted by rain and ended in a draw, but for me its greatest significance was that it saw the final appearance in a first-class match of Wilfred Rhodes.

He was a giant in the game and had indeed taken over 2,000 wickets before I was born. It was an honour and privilege to play against him.

On my next tour, 1934, I had been quite ill during the early part of the trip and was only able to produce good form in the closing stages. In fact at Scarborough I played what was probably my most satisfying match of the season.

Australia batted first and opened with Ponsford and Brown. The latter was bowled by Farnes for three, after which I went in and I was out before lunch, having made 132 (one six and twenty-four 4's) in ninety minutes against Farnes, Bowes, Verity and Nicholls. I felt the stumping decision against me was highly questionable, but nevertheless returned to the dressing-room feeling somewhat elated. Imagine my surprise when I was accosted by our captain with the greeting, "What did you want to throw your innings away for?" It was the only uncharitable remark ever made to me by Billy Woodfull and totally out of character.

I think there had been a somewhat acrimonious exchange between Woodfull and Leveson-Gower before the match, the latter being accused of trying to turn the match into a Sixth Test rather than a Festival game and Woodfull was anxious not to lose.

My next English tour ended disastrously when I broke my ankle in a Test at The Oval and therefore couldn't play at Scarborough, which was a great disappointment, but 1948 saw one of the great milestones of my career.

Not only did I captain Australia, but made top score of the match, 153, and when was accorded the remarkable tribute of being made a Life Member of Yorkshire County Cricket Club.

The ceremony was performed by the then Yorkshire president, Mr J.P.Taylor, who at the same time handed me a lovely silver salver endorsed by an appropriate inscription — and the inlaid white rose of Yorkshire in enamel.

I proudly display the salver in my living room in Adelaide and I am equally proud to have a BBC recording of the speeches.

Although not completely sure of my ground I believe I am still the only 'foreigner' to have been made a Life Member of Yorkshire CCC and that is something to cherish.

As my own innings in the game of life draws to its close I derive great solace from the knowledge of my close affinity with Yorkshire

Don Bradman and R.W.V.Robins going out to toss at Scarborough in 1948.

(particularly Scarborough and that other favourite hunting ground, Leeds), but even more than that, the deep and lasting friendships with people who have made Yorkshire great — happily some still able to make a worthy contribution.

Sadly, of course, others like the incomparable Sir Leonard, have gone to higher service where hopefully one day I'll catch up again with Hirst, Rhodes, Hutton, Verity et al.

One of the players Geoffrey Boycott men-

tioned as being a top batsmen in the Yorkshire League in the 1950s, went on to become an even better umpire. Harold 'Dickie' Bird's memories of Scarborough go back a long way:

I have many fond memories of Scarborough cricket ground, both as a player and as an umpire. I think way back to 1948 when I first played there as a fifteen-year-old for Barnsley against Scarborough in the Yorkshire League. It seems like only yesterday; can it be forty-three years ago?

Looking back over the years, one memory will always stand out. That was in the 1959 Scarborough Festival, which I think is one of the best of cricket festivals.

If you remember, Yorkshire had just won the County Championship for the first time in ten years, by beating Sussex at Hove on the previous day. We came up to Scarborough full of high spirits and thrilled to have brought the Championship back to Yorkshire again. On arriving late that night amidst celebrations, we went to bed to get ready for the match, Yorkshire v MCC.

The next morning we could not get near the ground, because there were thousands of well-wishers congratulating us on our Championship win. When we did get through to the ground, the match was a little late in starting. I have a photograph on the wall at home, taken before the match started and already the clock on the Pavilion shows

11.30am which was the starting time. It was a day I shall always remember and those memories money can't buy.

I am delighted to be able to say a few words about Scarborough Cricket Club which, in my opinion, is one of the best clubs in the world. Of the Yorkshire crowds, too, who take their holidays especially for the Yorkshire matches and those at the Festival. They really appreciate good cricket. I hope they will for many years to come.

Dickie Bird's recollection of the thrill of finishing a Yorkshire season at Scarborough is echoed by David Hopps of 'The Guardian'. He remembers a different occasion and why cricket at Scarborough has a special appeal for followers of the first-class game:

The appeal of Scarborough? It must be its vitality. Take the 1987 Benson and Hedges Cup Final. As memorable as Yorkshire's triumph at Lord's, was the aftermath less than twenty-four hours later, as the admiring and grateful throng assembled at North Marine Road to applaud their heroes home.

As the Yorkshire side walked down the concourse to the Pavilion nearly two hours before the start of their Sunday League match against Middlesex, they were moved by the sight of several thousand spectators already in the ground to sound the first ovation of many.

Every Yorkshireman received a special

tribute that day. Phil Carrick doffed his cap to the crowd in salute; David Bairstow nearly burst his shirt buttons with pride as he bustled on to the field; Jim Love, the match-winner, glanced behind him for a second in that bemused way of his. "There was so much applause I thought Boycs must be walking in behind me," he joked afterwards.

Victory against Northants had been achieved in the most palpitating fashion, by virtue of losing fewer wickets. If Lord's had been enemy territory, a place to feel pride, gratitude and, for many, vindication, it was at Scarborough where Yorkshire cricket folk are traditionally at their most relaxed and lighthearted that emotions were allowed to run free.

Ashley Metcalfe played an innings that day to sum up Yorkshire's delight. In another age they would have called it 'gay'. It was delightfully irresponsible, a brief outburst of stroke play by a batsman still on a high. He eventually skied a catch and never stopped running until he reached the Pavilion, where a queasy stomach caught up with him. John Emburey, Middlesex's England spinner, had been all agog at Metcalfe's antics. "Thank heavens for that," he said as the catch was held. "Now perhaps we can all get on with the game."

Scarborough is Yorkshire cricket's great place of reunion: a meeting point where a grand and proud county allows itself to smile. Familiar faces reassemble at a time when the

gifts, or otherwise, bestowed by another season have all but been revealed. Old stories are retold with gusto, new stories vie with them for attention, Cricket chat spreads outwards from the ground into the pubs and hotels in the town like nowhere in England.

These days the pitches, alas, are too slow, although the Test and County Cricket Baord do not share my view. But nothing can surpass the vitality of Scarborough when the air is fresh, the skies are blue, the conversation is bright, and the cricket is enterprising. Call me blessed, because there is no better view from any Press box in the country, but if there was justice in the world here is where every Yorkshire season should rightly finish until the end of time.

One of the great traditional matches at Scarborough was the Gentleman v Players match, which was a central feature of the Scarborough Cricket Festival for nearly eighty years. In the first match, in 1885, W.G.Grace made 174 and in the final match, in 1962, Ken Barrington made 100. Somehow it seems appropriate that an amateur made the first century in the series and a professional the last. The matches were usually played in a competitive spirit, even after allowances were made for the amount of spirits consumed by certain amateurs who stayed at the Grand Hotel. The professionals booked in at favourite 'digs' near to the ground, or at the Balmoral Hotel in

Phil Carrick holds aloft the Benson and Hedges Cup on the balcony of the Pavilion at North Marine Road in 1987. Yorkshire had won the trophy at Lord's the previous day, thus ensuring a heroes' welcome for the side before the Sunday League game against Middlesex at Scarborough.

Tony Lewis at Scarborough in 1962, the last season of Gentlemen and Players. This photograph was taken for the Cricketers' Room at the Grand Hotel.

Huntriss Row in the middle of town. They tended to drink beer.

Tony Lewis played several times for the Gentlemen, including that final match in 1962. He has fond memories of what was a delightfully idiosyncratic sporting occasion:

My first memories of the Scarborough Festival are gloriously crusted in the old traditions of the amateurs residing at the Grand Hotel and the professionals at the Balmoral.

For a young amateur it was black tie for dinner each evening. The Grand Hotel buzzed with cricket conversation. Indeed the cricket teams for all matches were posted outside the hotel and cricket-lovers came in to drink in the bars or simply to sip away at a table in the Palm Court area at the bottom of the large central staircase, listen to the piano trio and wait for the amateur cricketers, the ladies and guests to troop down to the Cricketers' Room for dinner.

The Cricketers' Room was an intimate treasure trove of photographs. Every amateur who had ever played in the Festival had his photograph on the wall. Every possible formality was observed until the very last drop

of port was nudged to the left and the second part of the evening was about to begin.

This meant partying and the start was always at the Balmoral, known as the Immoral, where dancing was already underway. Possibly we would have left behind Major Leveson-Gower, who would be busy informing some pretty lady inquirer how she might travel by train from Scarborough to Weston-super-Mare on a Sunday. His twin bibles were Bradshaw and Wisden in that order.

The cricket was fun when played competitively. There was still sherry before lunch and wine to follow. The Scarborough brass band got many a valve clogged up with spittle but generally they made a harmonious background to the day's contest. Close of play was at 6pm, signalled by the playing of God Save The Queen *which had us standing to attention wherever we were fielding or batting and pressing the thumb and forefinger straight down the sides of the trousers. Most of us had done our National Service.*

The standards of everyone's play dropped if they were in residence for the whole Festival. I recall the last Gentlemen v Players match in 1962 and playing quite well. I got 35 in the first innings and then nicked Trueman to Geoff Millman without scoring in the second. My last innings as an amateur after seven seasons dating back to my debut for Glamorgan in 1955. We would all be simply cricketers from 1963 on.

Anyway, at Scarborough, getting out early was never a problem because you could always nip out of the ground to one of the many fish shops and have some kippers sent to a long-lost aunt.

There was a Scarborough spirit that communicated itself to the big crowds. Of another world, maybe, but quite unforgettable.

The captain of the professional players in that final match versus the amateur Gentlemen at the Scarborough Cricket Festival was Fred Trueman. He had also captained the Players in the corresponding fixture at Lord's earlier in the season. He makes the point that because the Festival was played at the end of the season, some players had poignant memories of Scarborough as the Festival really marked the end of their careers. Bradman, Hassett and Trueman himself had that experience. Nevertheless, Freddie Trueman enjoyed the Festival, at least as it was played in the Fifties and Sixties.

The Scarborough Cricket Festival was a date that every top-class cricketer entered in his diary with the hope that he would be one of the chosen few to be invited.

It was considered at the time to be the climax

Fred Trueman, skipper of the Players at Scarborough in 1962, in the match that marked the end of the distinction between amateurs and professionals. Henceforward they would all be known as 'cricketers'.

of the season involving a very enjoyable social scene in a most relaxed atmosphere. It could also be a time of sadness as many players made their last appearance in first-class cricket as I did myself.

The opening game was usually Yorkshire v MCC followed by Gentlemen v Players and then President's XI v The Touring Side. Sadly times have changed and these titles have now disappeared. The last twice I have attended the Festival, the humourous atmosphere that existed has also seemed to have vanished.

Lots of milestones were reached on the Festival occasion, players arriving to take part needing three or four wickets to complete their hundred for the season or probably fifty or sixty runs to complete their thousand for the year.

The best one I ever remember was the Indian touring team, when one of their players informed us he would like to complete the double — a hundred wickets and a thousand runs! In the one game he needed, as far as

I can remember, something like twelve wickets and 160 runs. Of course he did not achieve his ambition. After being clean bowled in single figures in the first innings he proceeded to belt the stumps with his bat, much to the amusement of the players.

Another instance that stands out in my mind took place after lunch, which was always served in the grand marquee in the presence of the president, Lord Mayor and the visiting dignitaries. It was in the Gents and Players match and the great man Len Hutton was still at the crease. The crowd was settling down when my friend Trevor Bailey ran up to deliver the first ball to begin the afternoon's play. Known only to a few people at the time, from his full run up, he delivered a rosey-red apple which Leonard hit in the middle of the bat bursting the apple into a thousand pieces all over the pitch. The crowd loved it as the clearing up operation took place before the game could continue.

T.N.(Tom)Pearce, who filled almost every role in the game.

People came from all over the British Isles to join the fun and atmosphere the Festival generated, booking their holidays a year in advance to ensure they did not miss out on seeing great cricket and rubbing shoulders with the stars of the day.

There are many more instances I could write about but we neither have the time or space, just memories I was pleased to be involved in.

During the period in the Fifties and Sixties described so eloquently by Tony Lewis and Fred Trueman, the man charged with the responsibility of organising the teams and obtaining players to appear at the Festival was T.N. (Tom) Pearce. Few men can have had as much all-round experience of cricket and cricket administration as Tom Pearce, having filled the posts of captain, chairman and president of Essex, besides being a Test selector and an international rugby referee. Before Tom Pearce took over the role, C.I.Thornton and H.D.G.Leveson-Gower had been the principal organizers of teams, assisted by Lord Hawke — the London Committee. Thornton's association with the Festival lasted fifty-three years and Leveson-Gower's fifty-two years. With Tom Pearce's thirty-five years service, continuity was maintained and the club owed a great debt to them, as did the town, a fact recognized by each having the Freedom of the Borough of Scarborough conferred upon them, T.N.Pearce writes:

My involvement with the Scarborough Cricket Festival began in 1946 when I was invited by H.D.G.Leveson-Gower to play for the MCC and the Gentlemen in the Festival and so began an attachment which extended to 1980.

When I handed over the responsibility of selecting teams it was because I felt that owing to the extension of the County Championship into September, I was unable to have sufficient outstanding players which I thought suitable for such a high class festival.

In fact, I did organise the teams playing under Mr Leveson-Gower's name in 1948 and 1949, before they played under my name from 1950 to 1980. During that period all the great players of the time appeared in the teams playing in the Festival.

The first years were quite straight-forward as the matches were MCC v Yorkshire, Gentlemen v Players and my XI v The Tourists, but this arrangement ended with the passing of the amateur status.

Whilst this arrangement was in force, the amateurs and their wives stayed at the Grand Hotel and dined every night in the Cricketers' Room, more or less on parade, after which everybody was free to do their own thing.

The Cricketer's Room was a great institution and was a very good way of returning hospitality to the Mayor and the committee of Scarborough Cricket Club.

As I was the Hon Secretary of the British Sportsman's Club of which HRH The Duke of Edinburgh is president and the late Duke of Norfolk was chairman, I was able to persuade them to honour the Scarborough Cricket Club by being its president for a year, HRH in 1961 and the Duke in 1962. To keep the whole thing in perspective, I was elected president in 1971 and honoured with the Freedom of the Borough of Scarborough in 1974. Oh, happy times.

One of the outstanding Scarborough players mentioned by Geoffrey Boycott was Ted Lester. Lester progressed from Scarborough to become an aggressive middle-order batsman for Yorkshire in 228 matches between 1945 and 1956, playing firstly as an amateur and then as a professional after 1948. On retiring from first-class cricket, Lester returned to Scarborough to break Yorkshire League batting records and help establish the club's formidable reputation at the time Boycott's cricketing career was just beginning. Ted Lester eventually became Yorkshire scorer — one of the most respected on the county circuit — and his early memories of cricket at Scarborough

SCARBOROUGH VIEWS — REMINISCENCES

A Yorkshire team containing three Scarborough products, Ted Lester, Vic Wilson and Bill Foord. Harry Halliday played for Scarborough after his county career ended. The full line-up (left to right): Coxon, Wardle, Brennan, Smailes, Yardley, Sellers (captain), Lester, Hutton, Halliday, Wilson and Foord.

are intriguingly associated with that occupation:

I was born within the proverbial stone's throw of the ground. From an upstairs window I could see a part of the playing area and from the front gate I could watch the revolving rollers of the main scoreboard. Provided I knew who was batting, I could easily follow the progress of the game and, before being allowed to actually visit the ground, spent many happy hours just watching the scoreboard.

Another early memory was of the special treat during the Festival when I was taken across the road to family friends and deposited in a bedroom where, from a window situated behind the Festival tents, I could watch the cricketing greats of yesteryear and listen to the band which in those days played throughout the day. Never in my wildest dreams did I imagine that twenty years later I would be playing in the Festival and sharing a dressing-room with most of the great post-war players.

At the age of seven, I became a junior member of the club — for the princely sum of 7s 6d! I certainly obtained my money's worth, as I rarely missed a match, when there was no match I attended nets, initially as an outfielder for the four or five nets in operation and then, after two years 'apprenticeship, ' I became an eager participant in the 'junior' net.

Alf Fattorini was the groundsman. A big man in every way. he seemed to spend every hour from dawn to dusk looking after his beloved ground. I can see him now, between the shafts of the heavy roller, cajoling and encouraging us youngsters to help him push it up and down the square, which had been specially treated with a 'secret' receipe and produced some of the fastest wickets in the

country. He spent almost as much time preparing his net pitches, which were better than many first-class wickets today and any success I might have had in the game was due in no small measure to being able to practise under such favourable conditions.

Alf smoked thick, black twist in a large pipe and, after becoming a pipe smoker myself, he gave me a fill of this obnoxious mixture and after that I was absent from the cricketing scene for a considerable length of time!

I did recover and was a spectator when Ces Pepper drove a ball over the houses in Trafalgar Square — the biggest hit I ever saw on a cricket ground. It must have given him enormous pleasure. Probably nearly as much as mine when I pulled a ball over the West Stand and shattered the window of a householder, who many years before had regularly stopped us playing football outside his house.

The Scarborough ground has many memories. I scored my maiden first-class century there against Derbyshire in 1947 and made my highest score in the Championship against Warwickshire in 1949. In 1954, when playing for T.N.Pearce's XI v Pakistan, I made my last first-class hundred on my home ground. One of the most pleasant of all the county grounds, it is unquestionably and, not surprisingly, my favourite.

Alf Fattorini built up a formidable reputation as a groundsman able to prepare wickets with a bit of pace in them, no doubt due to the 'secret recipe, if not the thick, black twist. On the subject of wickets, few people are as qualified to pass an opinion as Geoffrey Boycott. He spent a considerable amount of time on the Scarborough wicket and recalls it well:

It's always been conducive to scoring runs, even when its turned a little or seamed a bit. I've even played against Mike Hendrick in a sea fret when the pitch was as flat as anything, quite a good batting pitch, I mean not necessarily the best ever, but a very good batting pitch. Nice day, good crowd and then we went into bat one evening against Derbyshire and the tide was coming in and soon there were great big green marks — about two inches long — and the thing was seaming all over! We kept looking at the pitch thinking there was snakes in it. And it really was flat. And dry, and straw coloured. No green grass on it. But then, suddenly, these great, sort of, greenish, reddish marks appeared. It was amazing. It was like a sea fret coming in . . .

Some people don't believe it. I would have found difficulty in believing it, except that I have experienced it. To say Mike Hendrick was a handful is an understatement . . .ha, ha, ha. Put it that way . . .I wasn't looking to score any runs. I was just looking to lay a bat on the ball and watching the hands of the clock go round, hoping an umpire would call time. I mean, that was one of the few occasions in my life when I was watching the clock and thinking, 'Crikey, I wish it'd hurry up and get round there'.

. . .I've never had that happen before so much. I've played there occasionally when the tide is coming in and its swung a little bit, but I just played that once when I couldn't believe it could change so dramatically. There was this sea fret that sort of came in and seemed to hang about.

We went on to talk about how the rapidly changing weather conditions at Scarborough can sometimes influence the course of a three or four-day match and can occasionally trap the unwary.

I've gone on some mornings and played at Scarborough and its been, sort of, well, overcast, greyish, darkish and you've thought, crikey if you were in Bradford you'd think it was going to chuck it down with rain. And by eleven o'clock, the sun is out cracking the flags and you couldn't wish to be anywhere else in Yorkshire. Gorgeous day . . .

If you had tossed up too early sometimes at Scarborough, too early, picked your side, looked at the overcast atmosphere and you had people like Les Jackson bowling, you'd have thought, 'I'd better have a little bowl here, might get a wicket or two', And you would have been very much mistaken, because by eleven o'clock, its cracking the flags, the sun is out and, as any batsman knows, there is no better time to bat than on a good pitch when

the sun is out and ball isn't doing anything. You could have made a real mess of the toss, so you didn't want to be caught out tossing-up too early at Scarborough.

Most people realise the importance of having a good wicket as far as batting is concerned, but many cricket followers are unaware of the importance of the outfield to batsmen, particularly when the bowler is getting a bit of assistance from the wicket and the batsman is relying on good timing and placement to beat an attacking field. Boycott continues:

The best pitches to bat on at Scarborough were a few years ago. Nowadays they are so flat, so good, they are too easy. They are really not good cricket pitches, they are just flat batting pitches where moderate players get runs. That has happened in the last five or six years and that is bad for cricket.

Because the outfield is so good, the ball just runs away. Gorgeous, keeps on running away from you . . .that is why, when we used to play on the pitches at Scarborough where there was a little bit in it in the morning and with the new ball you could make it do a little bit and it used to turn a bit as well, they were good cricket pitches. And so, even if you had a little deviation, lateral movement — seamer, spinner — throughout the game, that was good for cricket; it tested your technique.

The one thing you always knew was that if you pushed the ball — played a shot — you got full value for it, because the outfield took it away. You weren't on some kind of slow pudding, where the ball never ran and it was just a nightmare, not only trying to play the ball, but getting the thing to run. At least at Scarborough you had a contest between bat and ball — a very good contest — and you never felt totally threatened or static. You could play. If you could push the ball, play your shots, you were alright. And they were better cricket pitches and better cricket was played. If you could make 280, it was a decent score and even if you made 300, it would still turn, you could get batsmen out when they first came in because it turned, or seamed, a bit and if a guy got in he could get some runs, no problem.

Some people probably think its gone forward, but its actually gone backwards. They think forward means a better batting surface, but actually, just a flat batting surface makes it easy for batting. It nullifies the best bowlers and it makes moderate batsmen look good when they are not. It doesn't do a lot for the game.

In 1948, J.M.Kilburn the cricket correspondent of the 'Yorkshire Post', wrote a delightful book called 'The Scarborough Cricket Festi-val'. Just eighty-six pages in length, it captures the mood and spirit of the Festival in the years when the traditional Festival was at its zenith. Years when class distinctions were reflected in the cricket and in the social activity which was an integral part of the event. Years when despite such demarcation lines, the Festival aura was of relaxation, enjoyment, humour and, importantly, purposeful cricket. Such qualities combined to make the Scarborough Cricket Festival quite special. Jim Kilburn understood the Festival and had a close affinity with the Scarborough club for several reasons. In the following letter he explains why:

My father played for Scarborough Cricket Club in the early years of this century and through the cricket club originated a life-long friendship with W.S.Robinson (Robin) who subsequently captained the team for fifteen years and was chairman for thirty-seven years. We joined families with my marriage to Miss Robinson.

In my boyhood, my father let me go to Scarborough during the school holidays. There I came to know W.W.Leadbeater, the long-serving secretary, George Herbert Hirst, who was match professional and David Hunter.

At that time there was both afternoon and evening practice and in the afternoon a net was set aside for junior members, of whom I was one. There we were coached by David Hunter, who took the bowling without pads or gloves and murmured, "Well bowled honey," or "Good shot". On red letter days when the men's net finished early, George Hirst would come across and play with us. I mean 'play with us' because he never commanded, but always suggested. "Try it this way," he would say when making a correction.

Our family holidays were nearly always taken at Festival times so I can recall nearly every Festival from 1919 to my retirement from cricket writing.

I do not write now because I have lost my eyesight and, in any case, I have written so much about the Festival in my various books and in periodicals that I should only be repeating myself if I wrote any more.

Jim Kilburn, now in his eighties, lives close by the St George's Ground at Harrogate. Yorkshire play a fixture there each season and two seats are permanently reserved in the stand for one of cricket's best-loved writers and his wife, Mary. It really was a great pleasure to accept an invitation to visit Harrogate and talk to Jim Kilburn. His memories and reminis-cences about cricket at Scarborough are as sharp and clear as ever and it made fascinating listening.

Top to bottom: *George Hirst pauses to sign an autograph before going out to umpire a Festival match in the 1930s; David Hunter demon-strates the art of wick-etkeeping to eager onlookers at North Marine Road in the 1920s; Wilfred Rhodes pictured in front of the Pavilion at Scar-borough.*

In Goodall's day they were 'dragey' about the receipts at the Festival. They would never make an estimate of the crowd, you see, because in those days the Inland Revenue wanted some of the money according to the gate money. So the Press, of whom I was one, would like to say, well, the crowd was 8,000, or whatever it was, you see. But Goodall would never give us the figures. So we said "Well why not?" and of course he hummed and hahd and said it was nothing to do with the public. So we said "Oh well, in that case . . ."

The next day the estimated attendance was 23,500 and something! Well, of course, this fetched him round to the Press box straight away. "Where did you get these figures from?" "Oh well, we just estimated them. There was no official guidance given of any kind." Well this went on for three days before it dawned on the committee and after that it wasn't so bad.

We talked about Festival crowds and the people who flocked to the Festival in the post-war period.

The biggest crowd they ever had was when the 1948 Australians came and then they were sitting on every window still and every wall and five or six deep on the grass. On that occasion, particularly, they were sitting two deep in front of the enclosure railings. It must have been impossible to see, or anything like that, because they were almost below the level of the pitch, especially where it slopes away towards the president's tent.

A big proportion of the crowds came from the North-East, because that was their only chance of seeing most of the prominent players of the year all at once, so to speak. They couldn't follow them down to Surrey and Hampshire and all over and if you had taken away the first-class status, the Festival would have gone down in no time.

Throughout all the Festivals he remembers at Scarborough, Bradman's 132 before lunch in 1934 would rank as the best innings Jim Kilburn saw, but the player who consistently gave him the most pleasure was Patsy Hendren, someone who, for Jim Kilburn, encapsulated the essential spirit of the Festival. Finally, he talked about George Hirst:

After he finished, Yorkshire didn't lose him in any way. He still remained very much the great man of Yorkshire cricket knowledge, so to speak. If they wanted an opinion, they asked George.

He was tremendous character you know. He had a wonderful talent for extracting the best out of you. Bill Bowes has often said to me that he never went away from a Yorkshire net without feeling himself a better player. And if he was no use at all, he wouldn't get that

impression out of George. He would say, "Well now then, you go away and try, old boy. And then come back again".

Entirely different from Wilfred, you see. If Wilfred was coaching you, he would try to bowl you out. He wouldn't tell you why, or what to do about it. He would say, "That's no good." And so did 'Ticker' (Mitchell) in the same way. And 'Ticker' could frighten people off. It's all right telling someone it's wrong, but if you keep telling them it's wrong they'll think they will never do it right. George gave everyone the impression they would get better.

Bill Bowes wrote in his book, "I never hope to meet a better coach, or a better man."

The last thoughts in this chapter about cricket at Scarborough go to Geoffrey Boycott. I asked him which was the best innings he played at Scarborough. There was a long thoughtful pause

I'll have to think about that. I don't know. It goes back over such a long time . . .a long, long time . . .so many memories.

Several minutes elapsed.

Probably . . .The best I played there was against Northants, who beat us comfortably on uncovered pitches. We had lovely sunny weather, but it rained overnight. When we went into bat, it was a real 'sticky dog', jumping and turning. Bishen Bedi bowled and I think I made twenty-odd before getting out and I, well, it was a good old 'sticky dog' and you didn't get many of those. Hot sunshine like this after overnight rain and the bloody thing jumped and turned everywhere.

A flat pitch, anyone gets runs. I mean, this is a flat pitch today. Phil Carrick's got 43 not out and he's played just the same as Kellett who got 111. If you walked in now, you wouldn't tell a lot of difference. With uncovered pitches and a little rain overnight like its been, you wouldn't let a number seven like Phil Carrick come in and plunder runs like that, you'd be able to do summat with the ball.

We talked about innings at Scarborough by other players.

One of the finest innings I ever saw was by young Graham Stevenson who, playing in his first game against Middlesex on one of those pitches, a three-day match, ah, but it turned. Low scoring game and in the second innings I think we only needed 190 to win and Titmus and Edmonds were bowling us out on a turner. When he went in, it must have been eight or nine wickets down, we still needed fifty to win. We were in trouble and he was a very young lad then, a very young lad. And he made forty, I think. Nearly won the game, he just got out. He kept hitting Titmus for fours and sixes, with the crowd shouting and jumping up and down, it was very tense.

Crikey, we were only 150-8 when he went in, they were bowling us out. And he kept lobbing him here, lobbing him there. If someone had told him it was Freddie Titmus, he'd have got out second ball! 'Cos nobody dared tell him. He was a young lad and a big hitter and nobody told him. I remember coming off and . . .oh, aye, it was wonderful. It's things like that that stick in my mind. He kept peppering that little slate roof, not the Pavilion end, the other end, kept peppering them on there. He'd have gone white as a sheet if you'd have told him it was Freddie Titmus. Yes, I remember that. 'Cos he nearly won the game, it was exciting, he had the crowd on their feet, which was real cricket, you know, in a low-scoring game.

I mean, you've had a match here with Sri Lanka. Two innings in four days, that's cricket? It's much more exciting in low-scoring matches. I mean, four runs off the edge were priceless weren't they? I don't mean pitches that jump up in your face, but Scarborough never did that. It turned, it seamed a bit on overcast days, seamed quite a bit, but you could always score your runs if you could bat. You could play the lateral movement, you had the skill and even if you weren't a technique player, but you were a guy who liked to hit, or battled, you could get runs either way.

Guys would come in and, if it turned a bit, they weren't good players, but the ball came on, nice bounce, and they'd wack it! So either way that was good for the crowd, they either wacked it or got out, you know, one way or the other. But if you get a flat 'nothingness' pitch and a very moderate player, you can't get him out. You can't get him out and he can't dictate to you either way. Its just stalemate.

As usually happens in conversations about

cricket at Scarborough, the question of whether a ball actually was hit over the houses into Trafalgar Square cropped up. Boycott agreed that it was possible; a freak occurence like Bob Beaman's long jump, when everything in the action came together just right and so he did not rule out the possibility. He also thought that one or two hits might have gone through the gap in the houses and so the tale got better with the telling, but he was prepared to believe that a ball could genuinely be hit 'over the top'.

Our last thoughts turned towards the Scarborough Cricket Festival in modern times and Geoff Boycott, as ever, returned to the basics.

I think the atmosphere and everything is good and the way they have improved it. Don Robinson has been the man about that, no doubts at all. You need somebody, an entrepreneural spirit and what have you, and he's been brilliant for that, absolutely brilliant. A bit of a showman, people can say what they want, but there are far more plusses in what he's done than any minuses.

I think the biggest problem the Festival had, in the Seventies, was it got that the cricket was benefit match cricket; there was no competitive element.

The idea of having Festivals is good at places which people enjoy going to, like Scarborough, with a nice atmosphere, the band playing and everything. But, the fundamental thing is that if you don't have a competitive element to a degree, you defraud the public. The cricket, the standard, has to be reasonably high, there has to be a competitive element. If there isn't, what you have is 'joke' cricket. That is the main thing they have to keep abreast of, for whatever else they do, if the cricket is not of a reasonable standard, they will lose the support.

Glory, Glory, Roads to Lord's

IN THE 1930s, Yorkshire County Cricket Club dominated English first-class cricket. Between 1930 and 1939, the county of the broad acres won the County Championship seven times in ten years. As well as the great players who became household names — Sutcliffe, Verity, Leyland, Bowes, Hutton and others — many more quality players were produced who found employment with other counties. Other very good players had to be content with club cricket, such was the measure of competition to get into the Yorkshire side.

By the 1950s, however, the balance of cricket power in the first-class game had swung towards the South of England. Surrey was the new force in the game. Their powerful bowling attack of Bedser, Loader, Laker and Lock, led by a dynamic and inspirational skipper in Stuart Surridge, was instrumental in bringing eight Championships in ten years to The Oval. North versus South rivalry was never greater than in the late 1940s and 1950s and boys of all ages identified closely with their sporting heroes.

Len Hutton and Dennis Compton became the key figures in the North versus South cricket debate and partisan northerners thought it was no accident that Denis Compton appeared only once at Scarborough. The period was one of booming attendances and the faithful who flocked to Park Avenue, Bradford, and especially Bramall Lane, Sheffield, to sit on the concrete football terraces, were fierce taskmasters. The Yorkshire tradition demanded success.

As always in sport, the pendulum swung again. Through the 1960s, Yorkshire regained the initiative. Seven times the Championship Pennant flew at Headingley in the ten years from 1959 to 1968. That was the era of Trueman, Close, Illingworth, Binks, Boycott, Stott, Taylor, Sharpe, Padgett, Hampshire, Nicholson, Birkinshaw, and Ryan. All were products of the league systems in the county, which most people in the North firmly believed underpinned the pre-war Yorkshire success story.

Yet the southern challenge in the 1950s had shaken Yorkshire confidence in the supremacy of Yorkshire cricket. Voices were raised about the previously unquestioned value of league cricket in the production of young players. How had Surrey, for example, been so successful without a league system? Stories began to filter through to northern ears of the strength of some clubs in the south who only played 'friendly' cricket. Was there indeed such a thing as 'friendly' cricket? For players born and bred into league cricket the concept that 'friendlies' could produce players of equal ability was laughable.

Yet there was no opportunity for testing the proposition that, apart from a few areas around Birmingham and in Staffordshire, the best club cricket was played in the northern leagues. Despite pre-emminence in the first-class game, Yorkshire club cricketers in the 1960s had no national stage on which to parade their talents.

The problem was solved in 1969. A national cricket club knock-out competition was established, sponsored by 'The Cricketer' magazine and called The Cricketer Cup. Scarborough Cricket Club entered the competition, eagerly. Supporters licked their lips in anticipation of proving that their team was good enough to take on the whole country. Incredibly and in bizarre circumstances, Scarborough fell at the first hurdle.

The first-round match was scheduled to be played against the quaintly-named Pocklington Pixies. The Pixies were a side based on the public school at Pocklington, near Beverley, whose headmaster, Guy Willatt, a former captain of Derbyshire, was still playing at fifty-one years of age. The Pixies played friendly matches and were coached by Mike Stevenson, a schoolteacher who became a respected journalist for the 'Daily Telegraph'. Stevenson's tongue-in-cheek claim to be a player of international repute, was based on having played for Ireland and Denbighshire, as well as gaining a Blue at Cambridge and appearing in three matches for Derbyshire. Despite these credentials to boost morale in Pixieland, Scarborough expected a comfortable victory.

Rain, however, took a decisive hand; not a ball was bowled. Furthermore, due to the inclement weather and despite other attempts, the match could not be concluded within the stipulated time for the completion of the round. Indeed, the sides had not even bothered to assemble at Pocklington on the last possible date because the ground was so wet. But the rules of the competition were quite clear, the result had to be decided by the toss of a coin. What happened next has been a topic of conversation ever since. Geoff Dennis, the Scarborough captain at the time, takes up the amazing 'tale of the coin'.

Well, Mike Stevenson, Pixies' skipper, it was his suggestion; I think I rang up John Midgley (secretary, Scarborough Cricket Club), but I think the rules were there. If you couldn't do it by this time, it had to be the toss of a coin . . . there was no other way. I cannot remember whether John cleared it with anybody, but we didn't do it on our own. The unusual thing about it was, we ended up doing it over the phone! . . .before we moved here, down in the other house. You'd better ask Margaret, she tossed the coin . . .!

Margaret: *Yes, I tossed the coin when we lost.*

Geoff: *Margaret's expression! You see, I couldn't say, 'Well I'm sorry' because he (Stevenson) already knew by then . . .we rang John Midgley then.*

Margaret: *It was a awful feeling looking at that coin. I couldn't believe it. That we had lost and were out after all that, just for the toss of a coin.*

Geoff: *I mean, we could have told Mike Stevenson, you know, 'Bad luck chum' that sort of thing, but . . .*

Margaret: *. . .but even if we had won, if we had won by the toss of a coin, I wonder if he would have ever believed that we had won, you know? You do think that, don't you? . . .We all supported Pocklington Pixies after that!*

J.M.Kilburn once said, *Cricket days remembered are coloured by the weather'* . . .Geoff and Margaret Dennis probably support that perceptive observation. More so when Pocklington Pixies went on to reach the Final at Lord's and lost to Hampstead by only 14 runs.

After the traumas of 1969, the Scarborough challenge got under way again the following year, but was halted in the fourth round by Steetley, a Bassetlaw League side from Nottinghamshire. The margin of defeat was just one run, with Bill Foord run out off the last ball of the match.

It was all very frustrating. At least the Scarborough players were beginning to come to terms with the format of the competition; the lessons, although painful, were being learned.

According to Geoff Dennis, the emotion generated in the knock-out trophy matches was far greater than anything encountered in league games, even championship deciders at the end of the season. The game at Steetley was a case in point for apart from a really highly-charged ending and the drama of the last ball, a number of wickets had been lost in the final few overs. The captain's recollection that *one or two were a bit upset* is probably a massive understatement.

Despite the disappointments, progress was being made and in 1971, the team reached the semi-final stage before bowing out to London side, Ealing. This relative success brought greater confidence in the knowledge that the players were beginning to be more familiar with the conditions of the competition. Amongst these was the requirement that no bowler should bowl more than eight overs. This meant that a minimum of six bowlers were needed to bowl the required 45 overs. In later years, this was altered to allow a maximum allocation of nine overs per bowler and so a minimum of five bowlers was needed.

Scarborough, however, were always fortunate in having several genuine all-rounders, with sometimes as many as nine players capable of bowling. This gave the captain a lot of flexibility and proved to be a great asset. Despite all this, it was felt that the side had thrown away a winning position against Ealing. Even Malcolm Heath, usually a mild-mannered giant of a man, packed his bags and left the ground early, convinced that his chance of going to Lord's had disappeared.

The year 1972 was Geoff Dennis' last as captain. Unusually for a captain, he was an opening bowler and for many years had spearheaded the Scarborough attack with Bill Foord, who had taken over a hundred wickets for Yorkshire whilst playing as an amateur, before declining professional terms and settling for a teaching career.

Dennis and Foord were feared throughout the Yorkshire League and had much to do with Scarborough successes in the period they played together. Unfortunately, Bill Foord was not destined to play a part in the campaign of 1972, which proved to be an outstanding finale to Dennis' career, with Scarborough winning the national knock-out competition for the first time.

'The Derrick Robins Trophy' travelled north, but it was not all plain sailing.

The first round nearly proved disastrous again. Visitors Guisborough were dismissed easily enough for 86, but at 46-6, Scarborough were staring defeat in the face. Geoff Dennis then played a match-winning innings of 32 not out in 25 minutes, including two sixes. Fortune on this occasion favoured the brave, perhaps even the desperate! At least the spectre

Geoff Dennis receives the Derrick Robins Trophy from F.R. Brown at Lord's in 1972 after Scarborough's six-wicket victory over Brentham.

of the tossed coin had been exorcised. Or had it?

Low and behold, after a routine win against Stockton, Scarborough were once again drawn, this time at home, against the dreaded Pixies from Pocklington. The team were very determined. And there was no mistake. The Pixies were put firmly in their place as Bill Mustoe played a decisive part, making 100 not out in the Scarborough total of 229-8 and then taking 3-26 as the Pixies subsided to 104-7.

Came the fourth round. Retford could only make 67, in reply to Scarborough's 178 all out. The wicket was poor and Ray Bloom's 76 in the Scarborough innings was rated by Tony Moor as the best knock he saw in all his years in the competition. High praise indeed, particularly as Ken Stockwell produced a blistering 76 not out off only 34 balls to see off Edinburgh Academicals in the fifth round.

The Academicals had travelled from Scotland with high hopes, but by being bowled out for 92, they merely prepared the way for a vintage display by Stockwell. The innings was all the more remarkable by being played in a sea fret that made most things invisible. Despite that, it included three sixes and 14 fours — 74 out of 76 in boundaries — made out

of Scarborough's total of 94-2. All the people who could see it remembered it.

Few players in Scarborough's history were able to savage a bowling attack as devastatingly as the left-handed Ken Stockwell, whose long reach and powerful driving, particularly off the front foot, was ideally suited to the good batting wickets at North Marine Road. In all, Stockwell played for Scarborough for thirty-two years produced some outstanding performances, some of which remain in the young Geoff Boycott's memory, but perhaps none was more memorable than his innings against Edinburgh Academicals. Once again Scarborough had reached the semi-final stage. Hopes were high, tension mounted.

The semi-final was against the Essex side, Hornsey, and, like most semi-finals, it proved to be a tight and competitive affair. Hornsey batted first and made the challenging score of 210-4 and, although the Scarborough bowlers did a reasonable containing job, they were not able to take wickets in the same way as in previous rounds. Scarborough's reply owed a great deal to the talented, but sometimes unpredictable batting of the young, left-handed Brian Rennard, who made 80 not out and steered Scarborough home with two overs

The winning team of 1972. Back row (left to right): J.Midgley (secretary), C.W.Kirby, W.Pincher, P.Hart, K.C.Stockwell, M.B.Heath, M.Kirkland, W.Mustoe, G.R.Bloom, W.A.Wood (chairman), C.W.Foord. Front: A.Jack (scorer), B.Rennard, J.Hutton, G.H.Dennis (captain), A.J.Moor (vice-captain), C.Oxtoby.

left. The Final at Lord's beckoned. The opponents were Brentham.

The joy at reaching the Final was tempered with a certain amount of relief that expectations had finally been fulfilled. Even so, it was not allowed to interfere with the main objective; that of bringing the trophy back to Scarborough. The players were quietly confident, for although the frustrating experiences of the previous three years had made them more cautious, they felt that having played London sides, Ealing and Hornsey, they were more familiar with what southern teams had to offer.

As so often happens, the Final did not produce the drama of some of the previous matches. This was due partly to Scarborough's comfortable six-wicket victory, yet as in many mundane matches, there were some memorable incidents. No incident has since been talked about more than Colin Oxtoby's dismissal of danger man James shortly before lunch. The wicketkeeper, generally reckoned to have been one of Scarborough's best ever, caught the batsman out and removed the bails in the same action, to bring an identical and immediate response from both umpires, 'Lofty' Herman and Bill Alley. The magical moment was captured on film and is highlighted in a collage of photographs in the Scarborough pavilion clubroom, which records the first trophy victory.

The course of the match itself was decided in the period after lunch, as everything that could possibly go right did so, at least as far as Scarborough were concerned. All the bowling changes worked, great catches were taken, run-outs effected and Brentham were dismissed for 129. The advantage was not thrown away. Stockwell and Bloom put on a

good stand for the first wicket, after which the result was a formality, Bill Mustoe rounding things off with a flourish by making 37 not out, including a six over the Tavern. On his first visit to Lord's, Geoff Dennis lifted the trophy.

It all ended well, but it might not have done so. A more sensational story nearly hit the headlines. The team stayed at the Clive Hotel in north-west London, not too far from St John's Wood. Ray Bloom had gone down a few days earlier and, having been to Lord's to savour the atmosphere, was sure he knew the way to the ground from the hotel. It was agreed that the coach should follow Bloom's car on the morning of the game. It did so, but on the fourth trip past Swiss Cottage and with the 11am starting time approaching fast, nerves, already taut, began to jangle.

When the coach then got stuck facing the wrong way up a cul-de-sac, most players and a distraught captain thought that their hour of glory was about to become a nightmare. Eventually, the coach did arrive at the Grace Gates, to the relief of anxious supporters, but there was precious little time to spare. There is surely truth in the adage that there is more to a game than playing it!

After the euphoria of the victory in 1972, Scarborough had to wait another four years before success was tasted again. In that time the side underwent a period of reconstruction. Younger players began to make their mark as long-serving members bowed to the inevitable passages of time. The main effect of these changes was felt in the bowling department. Geoff Dennis and Bill Foord, so long the scourge of Yorkshire League opening batsmen, retired; Bill Pincher, a dangerous support

The 1972 Cricketer Cup Final	
At Lord's. Scarborough won by 6 wickets	
Brentham CC	**Scarborough**
M.James c Oxtoby b Pincher 38	K.C.Stockwell c Holley b Wilmore 36
R.Kingdom b Heath 2	W.R.Bloom lbw b Holley 25
G.D.Barlow c Bloom b Dennis 5	J.Hutton lbw b Reid 9
J.Hopkins c Moor b Kirby 42	B.Rennard lbw b Holley 1
D.Vincent b Kirby 18	W.Mustoe not out 37
D.W.Bloomfield c Moor b Pincher 3	A.J.Moor not out 14
R.A.James b Pincher 7	Extras 10
B.J.Reid b Kirby 0	Total (4 wickets) 132
J.L.Swann not out 0	Did not bat: W.Pincher, C.Oxtoby,
A.D.Holley run out 0	C.W.Kirby, G.H.Dennis, M.Heath
A.Wilmore lbw b Pincher 0	Bowling: Reid 8-0-33-1; Holley 8-2-18-2;
Extras 14	Swann 8-5-7-0; James 3-1-16-0; Wilmore
Total (all out) 129	4-4-0-35-1; Kingdom 2-0-11-0
Bowling: Heath 8-3-18-1; Dennis 8-1-23-1;	
Stockwell 8-3-24-0; Pincher 7-3-10-4; Mustoe	
2-0-10-0; Moor 5-1-13-0; Kirby 4-1-17-3	

bowler and aggressive batsman, left to try his luck as a professional in the North Yorkshire & South Durham League.

On the day Scarborough Cricket Club set off for their 1976 Final at Lord's, only four players — Tony Moor, Ken Stockwell, Brian Rennard and Malcolm Heath — were left from the team of 1972.

The competition now had a new sponsor, whisky giants John Haig & Co Ltd. The new brew certainly agreed with Scarborough Cricket Club because, in the seven years of competition for the Haig Trophy, Scarborough were winners no less than four times and semi-finalists on another occasion. The team also won the Yorkshire League title four times and were runners-up in the other three years. Seasons 1976 to 1982 were vintage years for Scarborough Cricket Club.

At the heart of the success was Tony Moor, the man who took over the captaincy from Geoff Dennis. Born overlooking the ground at North Marine Road, Moor came from a strong sporting family. He became a professional footballer, making over 300 appearances in goal for York City and Darlington between 1962 and 1971, and that grounding in professional sport was put to good effect in Moor's handling of affairs both on and off the field. Few players were left in much doubt as to what was expected of them as representatives of Scarborough Cricket Club. Moor led from the front and was probably the most successful captain in Scarborough's history.

Not that things were easy in 1976. Scarborough were drawn away in every round and the advantage of the intimidating effect that the North Marine Road arena often had on visiting sides was never a factor. Once again, it was the ability to take wickets in limited-overs cricket, as well as contain, that proved to be the key to success.

A score of 131-9 did not look enough against Sheffield Collegiate, who were then bowled out for 101. In the regional Final against fierce local rivals York, 209-6 was thought to be hardly an adequate total, but York made only 171-9. Pickering (78) and Steetley (131-9) were disposed of comfortably, but in the sixth round, the Northumberland side, Benwell, were made of sterner stuff. Scarborough made a moderate 168-9 and Benwell, making 165-8, lost by only three runs in an extremely tight finish.

With the bit now between their teeth, Scarborough swept away the paltry challenge of London side Southgate in the semi-final, bowling the home side out for 91 after having made 167-7. Supporters made plans for another visit to Lord's.

Although the side of 1976 was different to that of 1972, many of the principles were similar. As in 1972, seven bowlers were used at Lord's, to restrict Dulwich to 136-9 in the required 45 overs. The bowling, too, had variety. Malcolm Heath, a 6ft 6ins opening bowler, who took 143 first-class wickets in his career with Hampshire, including 126 at an average of 16.42 in 1958, brought his medium-paced seamers down from a considerable height. Martin Shepherdson, Ken Stockwell and Tony Moor were steady swing bowlers, whilst Steven Glaves, the quickest of the attack and often used at the end of the innings was a dangerous if sometimes erratic, left-arm over-the-wicket seamer.

They were backed up by what became arguably the best spin bowling combination in league cricket. Chris Clifford, off-spin and Phil Hart, left-arm spin, were both good enough to play in the first-class game. Clifford

Scarborough at Lord's in 1976, celebrating victory in the Haig Trophy Final. Back row (left to right): P.Woodliffe, M. Davison, B.Rennard, M. Heath, A.J.Moor (captain), K.C.Stockwell, C.C.Clifford, M. Shepherdson. Front: S.P.Glaves, P.Hart, R.C.Sherwood, D.Kneeshaw.

played eleven matches for Yorkshire and, later in his career, thirty-six matches for Warwickshire, taking a total of 126 wickets at an average of 37.6 at first-class level. He then resumed his teaching career, going on to join Bill Foord as the only two players to take 1,000 wickets for Scarborough Cricket Club in first-team matches, although Robert Baker, back in the nineteenth century, probably accomplished the same feat, but records are incomplete.

Hart, born in the village of Seamer just outside Scarborough, to his great delight and immense personal satisfaction, realised a Tyke's lifetime ambition by being selected for Yorkshire for three matches at the age of thirty. Hart could claim to be man-of-the-match in the Final of 1976, for not only did he bowl his eight overs for 18 runs, he also produced a vigorous 29 not out to support Brian Rennard's 55 not out, which saw Scarborough make 140-5 and get home by five wickets.

One week later, the Championship of the Yorkshire League was duly won and, in the following winter indoor season, Scarborough

---

The 1976 Haig Trophy Final

At Lord's. Scarborough won by 5 wickets

Dulwich CC

G.Murray run out 55
S.Courtney b Heath 0
A.Chadwick b Shepherdson 4
G.Stagg c Kneeshaw b Heath 0
P.Rice c Sherwood b Stockwell 6
N.Ahmed c Kneeshaw b Stockwell 31
D.Williams c Kneeshaw b Stockwell 2
D.Woods b Glaves 5
K.Lewis run out. 6
J.Fortune not out. 5
R.Walsh not out 4
Extras 18
Total (9 wickets). 136
Bowling: Heath 8-4-11-2; Shepherdson 8-4-19-1; Hart 8-2-18-0; Stockwell 6-2-13-2; Clifford 3-0-7-0; Moor 5-0-28-0; Glaves 7-0-31-0

Scarborough

K.C.Stockwell b Williams 12
D.Kneeshaw b Williams 0
B.Rennard not out 55
A.J.Moor c Walsh b Woods 15
R.C.Sherwood b Lewis 13
P.Woodliffe b Nisar Ahmed 0
P.Hart not out 29
Extras 7
Total (5 wickets) 140
Did not bat: M.Shepherdson, C.Clifford, S.Glaves, M.Heath
Bowling: Fortune 7-2-10-0; Williams 7-1-17-2; Lewis 8-1-33-1; Stagg 4-0-23-0; Nisar Ahmed 8-3-14-1; Woods 7-0-36-1

completed a hat-trick of successes by winning the Wrigley Indoor National Club Six-a-Side Championship. 1976 really was an outstanding year.

Three years later came the hat-trick of Trophy wins. Quite remarkably, in the Scarborough side of 1979, there featured an aggressive 48-year-old left-handed batsmen and right-arm bowler of cunning variations, whose enthusiasm and competitive spirit burned as fiercely as it did when he made his debut for Yorkshire as an 18-year-old protégé. Thirty years on, Brian Close relished the prospect of a Cup Final at Lord's.

Close had been recruited by local business-man and entrepreneur, Don Robinson, to promote Scarborough Football Club's ambi-tion to gain admittance to the Football League. Robinson was chairman of Scarborough FC at the time and Close was an England Test selector. Scarborough Cricket Club became involved when Close expressed a desire to continue playing league cricket and the arrangement was confirmed in the bar of the Opera House Theatre, owned by Robinson.

There is very little to say that has not already been said about a man who became known at various times as 'Mr Cricket', 'Captain Courageous', and a few other things besides. Suffice to say that in the two seasons Brian Close played for Scarborough, his commitment to the team and the club was every bit as great as if he were still at the height of his career. He drove thousands of miles from all parts of the country to play in matches and, providing he had a pot of tea and the 'Sporting Life', he was as content as the most junior member of the team. Amazingly, in 1980, together with Phil Hart, he took part in a sponsored parachute jump from an air balloon to raise money for club funds. After much speculation, the intrepid pair eventually jumped from umpteen thousand feet, landed safely and raised £800. It was rumoured that only Phil Hart wore a parachute!

Close was not outstandingly successful with either bat or ball in his playing time at Scarborough, but his presence was consider-able and, at times his experience and sugges-tions were valuable additions to what was already a very strong outfit. Brian Rennard, who succeeded Tony Moor as captain for the Trophy victories in 1981 and 1982, is unstint-ing in his praise for the former Yorkshire and England captain's advice and help, for what was a difficult task in taking over from the redoubtable and staggeringly successful Moor.

The 1979 Final, against Reading, was in many ways the most satisfying of the five Finals that Moor took part in. Victory was achieved in the last over of what was a fine match, full of twists and turns, and the spirit between the teams was excellent, something which could not be said about all the Finals played at Lord's. By this time Scarborough were becoming 'old hands' and supporters, too, were perhaps a little over-confident, although for players like Chris Stephenson, Mel Brown, John Precious and Simon Dennis, who were making their first appearances in the Final, it was a new and nerve-wracking affair. Nevertheless, Scarborough had the experience. They were expected to win.

The build-up to the 1979 Final was bigger than had been the case before. The national media were becoming more aware of the competition, thanks to the promotional efforts of Haig & Co Ltd, and the National Cricket Assocation, through the efforts of their indefatigable secretary, Brian Aspital and his assistant, Philip August. The media, naturally, seized on the presence of Brian Close in the Scarborough ranks and with national radio interviews and Fleet Street curiosity, the expectation of victory and the pressure on the favourites increased.

Reading totalled 190-4 in their 45 overs. It was the highest made against Scarborough in any Lord's Final, despite the efforts of spinners Hart and Close, who conceded only 50 runs in 16 overs at a time when Reading were batting well. In reply, the Scarborough innings began disastrously with prolific openers Stephenson and Moor being dismissed quickly with only six runs on the board.

The middle order then partly recovered the situation, with important contributions from Rennard (27), Woodliffe (54), Close (20), Sherwood (44) and Precious (12), but time was running out and with six overs left, Scarbo-rough still needed a run per ball to win. The hero of the hour was 18-year-old left-arm pace bowler Simon Dennis, who made a bold 23 not out.

Dennis, a nephew of Sir Leonard Hutton and the son of the 1972 Scarborough trophy-winning skipper, Geoff Dennis, went on to gain a Yorkshire cap and take over 250 wickets in first-class cricket for Yorkshire and Glam-organ, but is likely to remember those last few overs at Lord's in 1979 with every bit as much pleasure. So too is Phil Hart. Tony Moor explains:

It got to the start of the last over. I think we wanted four to win. We were in the dressing-room right behind the bowler's arm (the home team dressing-room in the south tower). Mel Brown hit a two and then he skied one and it sent Simon Dennis down to the striking end. Mel Brown was out and I was kneeling on a little settee, looking out through a side window, with Phil Hart next to me and he

was in next. And I looked round . . .and I could see him go . . .He just went white.

And he's sat there and I said, "Come on, you're in," because, as you know, it's a long way down. And he goes "Huh," and then he's walking out. I said "You want your bat!" And he says "Oh yes," came back, picked his bat up and walked out. Simon Dennis had come across as he was walking out to the middle. We wanted two to win and there were two balls left and he (Simon) had gone up to Harty, who had played for a few years and Simon was only seventeen or eighteen, playing his first season and Simon said "What do you think I should do?"

And Harty says, "You make your own decisions and whatever you decide, don't involve me!" . . .Simon did well . . .he danced up the wicket, had a big hoick and squirted one through for four!

Later that evening, both teams were dining in separate parts of the Westmoreland Hotel. The meal was over and Waid Wood, the chairman of Scarborough Cricket Club, was saying a few words. The door of the room opened and all the Reading players came in. They stood in the middle of the room and clapped the Scarborough team, thanked them for a great game, then turned and walked out. In the circumstances of losing by such a close

The 1979 Haig Trophy Final
At Lord's. Scarborough won by 2 wickets.

Reading

D.Johnston c Shewood b Close 33
M.Tutty b Hart 29
M.Head c Brown b Hart 11
A.Walder b Moor 28
M.Simmons not out 39
D.Gorman not out 19
Extras 31
Total (4 wickets). 190
Bowling: Dennis 8-1-29-0; Glaves 7-1-34-0; Sherwood 5-0-20-0; Moor 8-0-20-0; Hart 8-4-17-2; Close 8-0-33-1; Woodliffe 1-0-6-0

Scarborough

A.J.Moor run out 1
C.Stephenson b Jones. 1
B.Rennard c Jones b Amjas. 27
P.Woodliffe c Head b Jones 54
D.B.Close c Gorman b Laitt 20
R.Sherwood run out 44
S.J.Dennis not out 23
J.Precious c Child b New 12
M.Brown c Gorman b Jones 2
P.Hart not out 0
Extras 9
Total (8 wickets) 193
Did not bat: S.Glaves
Bowling: Jones 7.4-2-30-3; New 8-1-29-1; Tutty 5-1-31-0; Laitt 8-1-38-1; Amjad 8-0-30-1; Simmons 8-2-26-0

margin in a really tremendous match it was, as Tony Moor put it, *Quite something.*

It looked very much as though Scarborough were on their way to Lord's again in 1980. Brian Rennard had taken over the captaincy from Tony Moor, who felt that he wanted to concentrate on playing, without the added responsibility he had enjoyed and endured for eight years.

Scarborough's opponents in the semi-final were Moseley, a Birmingham League side, who faced a score of 196-8 and were on the brink of defeat at 137-5 with overs running out. There then followed an incredible display by wicket-keeper Taylor, who, in a once-in-a-lifetime innings, wrenched the match from Scarborough's grasp. Martin Shepherdson was the bowler to suffer as Taylor, batting at the pavilion end, lashed the bowling of the bewildered Shepherdson for five sixes and a single for 31 runs in an over, to follow the six his partner had hit off the last ball of Shepherdson's previous over.

Brian Rennard remembers it well:

We thought it was impossible for them to win. Then this guy came in, wicketkeeper, Jack somebody or other. Shep was bowling and I probably froze with it being my first year. Closey got a bit ratty and unfortunately he (Shepherdson) went for six sixes in seven balls ...obviously we just blew it.

Martin Shepherdson, was one of Scarborough's very competent and sometimes underrated players. He appeared in two Lord's Finals bowling a total of 16 overs for a miserly 18 runs. Few people will remember that, but no one will forget Moseley.

It could be said that Scarborough were lucky to be in the semi-final at all. They had actually lost to Brighouse earlier in the competition, but the Bradford League club were found guilty of fielding an ineligible player and so Scarborough survived. In the third round, against Appleby Frodingham, Stephenson and Moor put together an opening partnership of 254, a Haigh Trophy record, but overall Scarborough had to be content with winning the Yorkshire League title for a second successive season and supporters and players hoped for better things the following year at national level.

They were not to be disappointed. Putting the setback of 1980 behind them like true champions, Scarborough went from strength to strength. The Haigh Trophy was won at Lord's in consecutive years in 1981 and 1982. The Yorkshire League was won again in 1981, to record a second Haig Trophy-Yorkshire League 'double'. The team was also runners-up in the Yorkshire League in 1982, narrowly missing a further double triumph.

The reasons for the success were threefold. The experience gained in previous years had been put to good effect. The fielding, both in ability and in organisation, was a key element in pressuring the opposition and added to that was the all-round bowling strength, which had been a cornerstone of previous teams. Now the batting had become more consistent. Much of that was due to the opening pair, Moor and Stephenson. They were supported admirably by the more experienced Rennard and new-comers Adrian Dalby, a batsman of real quality who gained a winners' medal in each of his only two years at Scarborough; and the extremely promising David Byas. Bill Pincher returned from his spell as a league professional and added all-round power to the side, but the contribution of the openers was of fundamental importance.

In each season, 1980-81-82, Moor made over 1,000 runs in club cricket. Chris Stephenson narrowly failed to do the same, being only a few runs short in 1982. Stephenson's best year was in 1981, when he broke Alan Richardson's 42-year-old record by scoring 1,462 runs in the season, whilst in the run to the Final in 1981, Stephenson set a new Haig Trophy competition record aggregate of 553 runs at an average of 110.6.

The stocky right-handed farmer from Beverley proved an ideal foil to the taller, left-hander Moor and century opening partnerships became a regular feature of the Scarborough innings in their eight years together. Stephenson, an accumulator of runs, rather than an outstanding stroke-player, had a compact style, great powers of concentration

Tony Moor (leftt) and Chris Stephenson in front of the scoreboard which bears testament to their mammoth first-wicket stand in the 1980 Haig Trophy game against Appleby Frodingham.

The 1981 Haigh Trophy Final	
At Lord's. Scarborough won by 57 runs.	
Scarborough	**Blackheath**
A.J.Moor c Shepherd b Hooper 27	P.Wallace lbw b Ellis 0
C.H.Stephenson c Kilbee b Hill 0	P.A.Humm b Moor 2
A.Dalby run out 42	C.Swadkin c Stephenson b Ellis 1
B.Rennard c and b Rice 12	J.R.Kilbee b Moor 9
W.Pincer lbw b Olton 15	O.T.Price run out 2
D.Byas c Rice b Shepherd 3	J.S.Fowler not out 44
R.C.Sherwood run out 11	M.F.Olton b Moor 6
M.Brown run out 1	J.E.Shepherd b Clifford 9
M.Shepherdson c Price b Shepherd 11	R.Rice run out .10
C.C.Clifford not out 3	A.J.Hooper c Pincher b Sherwood 0
P.Ellis run out 2	R.K.Hill not out 2
Extras 30	Extras 15
Total (all out) 157	Total (9 wickets) 100
Bowling: Rice 8-1-23-1; Hill 7-1-17-1; She-pherd 7-1-24-2; Swadkin 8-1-15-0; Hooper 8-2-22-1; Olton 7-0-26-1	Bowling Ellis 8-5-4-2; Shepherdson 8-5-8-0; Moor 8-4-10-3; Pincher 8-1-22-1; Clifford 8-2-21-1; Sherwood 3-1-14-1; Dalby 2-0-6-0.

and made maximum use of his abilities. Temperamentally they were ideally suited. Ironically, for such a successful player, Stephenson never succeeded in three trophy Finals, his total of 13 runs at Lord's scarcely did him justice, even though his scores in earlier rounds were often crucial.

The campaign of 1981 opened against Amaranth with Stephenson (125) and Dalby (127) thrashing the bowling in a mammoth Scarborough total of 327-2 made in 30 overs. From then on, the opposition was brushed aside, as Scarborough made untroubled progress to a semi-final contest against Aberdeenshire and a trip to Scotland. It proved to be the match of the season.

The Scottish champions made 183-7. Scarborough's reply, on a slow wicket, became somewhat bogged down. Eventually the scores were level with one ball to go. A four was hit and Scarborough were through by six wickets. Chris Stephenson finished with 90 not out and batted throughout the innings. Not for the first time, the opener had demonstrated patience and responsibility when the temperature was rising, but it had been a near thing. On to Lord's again.

Blackheath were the other Finalists and, despite Scarborough's record in the competition, the Londoners were confident enough to have a professional video made anticipating victory. And when Scarborough were bowled out for 157, it looked as though the Blackheath confidence was not misplaced.

In the event, however, Scarborough recorded the easiest of their trophy victories at Lord's. The margin was a comfortable 57 runs, as Blackheath were pinned down to 100-9 in 45 overs. The bowling figures at the start of the Blackheath innings were outstanding for a

limited-overs game. Martin Shepherdson, fully recovered from his mauling in the previous year's semi-final, bowled eight overs for only eight runs. Paul Ellis did even better with eight overs for four runs and two wickets. Tony Moor conceded only ten runs in his eight overs and took three wickets. The batsmen became thoroughly demoralised. Blackheath were never a threat.

Ten years after their first victory in the national club knock-out competition, Scarborough were back at Lord's again in 1982, looking for their fifth victory. The batting was now the strongest part of the side, with Moor and Stephenson able to rely on Dalby, Rennard, Pincher and the emerging David Byas to hammer home the usual sound starts. The bowling, less penetrative in the seam department than in the days of Foord, Heath and Dennis, nevertheless was tight and usually

The victors with the spoils. Scarborough's players are all smiles after their 1981 victory over Blackheath.

gave little away in the early stages and with spinners of the quality of Clifford and Hart, the attack was exceedingly well balanced.

As always, the Scarborough fielding was consistently sound and the experience gathered in a decade of success was a distinct advantage when matches got close.

Matches certainly did not come any closer than in the sixth-round contest against old rivals, Harrogate, at North Marine Road. Scarborough had progressed to this stage of the competition with a series of comfortable victories, including one by six wickets over Percy Main in the regional Final, but Harrogate were a very consistent Yorkshire League side and there had been some close battles between the two clubs in the recent past. Scarborough players prepared for a close contest and they were not disappointed.

Tony Moor contributed 65 in Scarborough's total of 209-7, but it was thought that 220 was more the score required to have any confidence of victory. The Harrogate reply revolved around Peter Chadwick, one of the best post-war Yorkshire League cricketers, who had played six matches for Yorkshire in the early 1960s, when competition to get into the Yorkshire side was particularly fierce. He was in commanding form and it looked as though Scarborough would be defeated, but a controversial run out left Harrogate on 209-9 and the scores level. Scarborough, having lost fewer wickets, were the narrowest of winners.

There was to be no relaxation. The match against Old Hill in the semi-final turned out to be just as nerve-racking as the Harrogate affair. Again it was played at North Marine Road and, as against Harrogate, Scarborough batted first and were restricted to 173-9. Only Adrian Dalby (52) was able to prosper against the Birmingham League side's attack and it was left to the Scarborough bowlers to defend what was really an inadequate target. Once more they rose to the occasion, aided by some superb fielding.

The highlight was a diving catch by Moor in front of the Tea Room on the Popular Bank side of the ground, but that, too, produced some controversy. The boundary was marked by a rope which itself was clear enough, but a few feet inside the rope there was a line remaining from an earlier match. Moor completed the catch over the line, but inside the rope. Some Old Hill players did not entirely see it that way and were somewhat disgruntled. Their concentration may have slipped; the overs ran out with Old Hill nine wickets down and three runs short, Scarborough were off to Lord's for the second year in succession and a third visit in four years.

The 1982 Final was a dramatic affair.

Certainly it was the toughest Final Scarborough played in, as Finchley were in control for most of the match. The feeling between the sides was not particularly good and with the atmosphere tense, the mood was combative. Fifteen wickets fell in the day. Eight men were run out; the edginess of the two sides was very apparent. Once again at Lord's, the scores were low and Bill Pincher, returning for a third Final ten years after his first, was firstly the Scarborough villain, then the hero.

Tony Moor remembers, with feeling:

I think he (Pincher) had a black-out or something when he came into bat. I'd got about 30 and I pushed one into the covers, between cover and extra cover and called for one. I just set off and was three-quarters on the way — and he was just leaning on his bat and never moved! So I turned round and got, sort of three-quarters way back, but I was run out. Then he ran Brian Rennard out. He stayed in and somebody else (Byas) was run out . . .We were just over 100 with either two or three overs left and we finished with 150 . . .He just whacked it everywhere in the last two overs did Pinch . . .As I said, it was a good job he did, 'cos I'd have thrown him off the balcony!

Brian Rennard remembers too:

When Pinch went in the occasion got to him. I put him in number four. At the time it was wrong, but in the end it paid dividends. He ran Tony out, I had to separate them, I think at lunch time . . .to keep it quiet, which they did, which showed the team spirit at Scarborough. So Tony got run out. Then he (Pincher) ran me out . . .! Some of the shots Byas played then, off drives, cover drives, square cuts, he looked a class player then . . .

Scarborough's score of 150 looked totally inadequate at tea time when Finchley had made between 80 and 90 without loss, although the scoring rate was fairly slow. A video of the match showed scenes inside the Finchley dressing-room at the tea interval and a loser's cheque, made payable to Scarborough Cricket Club, is clearly visible. Even so, Brian Rennard, in his fifth Final, knew that an early wicket after tea would make the task of making five-per-over less than straightforward, especially for new batsmen coming in for the first time at Lord's.

So it proved. A wicket fell in the first over after tea, a catch by Moor off Clifford accounting for opener Milton for 39. Another batsman was run out for 10. Pincher dismissed Selwood, the other opener, for 49. The tide turned. No other batsman reached double-figures as Finchley, including four run outs, crashed to 146-8. Scarborough were winners again, by four runs.

Had there been a man-of-the-match award,

The 1982 Haigh Trophy Final

At Lord's. Scarborough won by 4 runs.

Scarborough		Finchley	
A.J.Moor run out	30	T.Selwood lbw b Pincher	49
C.H.Stephenson run out	12	M.E.Milton c Moor b Clifford	39
A.Dalby c Johns b Selwood	2	P.Halstead run out	10
W.Pincher not out	61	D.Foskett lbw b Pincher	0
B.Rennard run out	0	R.Edrupt not out	1
D.Byas run out	23	W.Puri run out	8
J.Precious c Milton b Alldis	8	J.S.Alldis run out	7
M.Brown b Alldis	2	K.Bharadia b Dalby	0
C.C.Clifford not out	2	W.Jordan not out	3
Extras	10	Extras	24
Total (7 wickets)	150	Total (8 wickets)	146

Did not bat: N.West, P.Ellis
Bowling: Herbert 9-0-19-0; Edrupt 9-4-12-0; Selwood 9-3-20-1; Milton 9-3-22-0; Alldis 8-0-53-2; Bharadia 1-0-14-0

Bowling: Ellis 9-1-35-0; West 9-5-13-0; Moor 5-1-14-0; Clifford 9-0-36-1; Pincher 9-0-16-2; Dalby 4-1-8-1.

Bill Pincher, despite his abberrations, would have been a strong candidate. A score of 61 not out and two wickets for 16 runs off nine overs was a fine all-round effort. Having played in the first Final in 1972, Pincher left the club to play as a professional in the North Yorkshire & South Durham League and returned in 1981. He played in the 1981 Final, by which time he had been appointed head groundsman at North Marine Road, following in the footsteps of his father-in-law, Bernard Pearson, who retired after thirty-three years tending the ground.

It was a hard act to follow. Pearson was one of the 'old school' groundsman, who was devoted to his profession and, along with his wife Anne, put far more into Scarborough Cricket Club than ever they took out. From his flat overlooking the ground, very little escaped Bernard Pearson's eagle eye, including the small boys who played in the alleyway which runs behind the high wall of the

Victorious Scarborough players and supporters after the 1982 win over Finchley, when victory was earned by the narrow margin of four runs.

Trafalgar Square enclosure, separating the ground from the backyards of the guest houses.

Unbeknown to those budding players, the old fox had left a small hole in the wire netting which ran along the top of the wall and so, thinking they had beaten the system, they were able to sneak through to retrieve the ball which occasionally went astray on to Bernard's hallowed turf. Sometimes Bernard allowed them time to loiter on the outfield, to play a few shots as small boys do, imagination working overtime. If, however, they outstayed their welcome, his presence soon became apparent and a rapid retreat, like rabbits down a hole, was the end result.

Pincher stayed for three years, before being succeeded by Mike Corley and then returned again to play for one season in 1988. Despite the altercation at Lord's, Tony Moor appreciated Pincher's ability:

He was a good cricketer was Pinch . . .He never used to move the ball; straight up and down and a very short run, very whippy action and he used to come through a lot quicker than people used to think. He hit the ball very hard when he was in and he got a lot of valuable runs...But he wasn't easy to handle. He always wanted to be bowling; didn't like taking off and he was sometimes a bit of a problem like that.

If anything is certain in sport, it is that the wheel turns. After five triumphs in ten years in the national club cricket knock-out competitions, Scarborough have not contested the Final since 1982. They did reach the semi-final in 1984, before losing to former rivals Old Hill. In that year, the Yorkshire League title was secured for the third time in five years, but with quality players like Moor, Stephenson and Rennard retiring in quick succession, the task of maintaining the tremendously high standard of the trophy winning years has proved too difficult, at least for the time being.

Some of the views of the three captains over that decade of unparalleled success are worth noting. Geoff Dennis, who led the way in 1972, still very obviously gets a tremendous thrill from recalling the first Final at Lord's and his first visit to the famous ground. The rush to the match. Being late for the briefing from D.H.Robins. The dressing-rooms. He has forgotten who won the toss. But remembers how his wife, Margaret, missed the tour of the Long Room, because he was tied up with 'one thing and another' after the game. Then the banquet at the hotel and back home in the early hours. The 1972 side paved the way and there is always something special about that.

In Geoff Dennis' opinion, having at least six regular bowlers available gave Scarborough a distinct advantage in the competition against sides who often had to use an 'occasional' bowler. His big problem in the ordinary Saturday League matches was to keep all the bowlers happy. Understandably, he feels that the tension was greater in the knock-out competition than in League matches. Especially when tossing-up was required and hobgoblins and Pixies were involved!

Tony Moor's experience in professional football was invaluable in coping with the occasions at Lord's. Not one for facts and figues, his recollection of important incidents in specific matches is still sharp and his overall view of the fifteen years he played in the competition is perceptive.

When I first started at Scarborough there was no Sunday cricket, there was nothing played on North Marine Road . . .and then, when this started, it was new and it had tremendous enthusiasm. In the early years it was a super competition and I made a lot of friends playing in it, but in the latter years it got very 'professional' if you like to call it that and a lot of chatting when you were batting and it lost its charm a little bit.

*I think at that stage (*around 1980*) our fielding was probably one of the prime parts of the side. We used to go down there (to North Marine Road ground) probably twice a week and work at it and so many of the games we won from losing positions was through taking a good catch and getting on top again.*

We always knew that no matter what score we got, we had the bowling and a good fielding side and if we only got 150, we could get sides out for less . . .At that time, we lost so few matches, the confidence was so high that we never felt, or the idea of losing never seemed to come into it . . .When we brought a youngster into the side, he very soon got the same confidence as we had . . .A lot of sides were in awe of us and sides who used to get into winning positions against us, couldn't follow it through.

Brian Rennard was a 21-year-old when he went to Lord's in 1972. He thought then that it would be the one and only visit. Little did he know that he was to play a further four Finals and captain the side in successive winning years. Rennard made his first-team debut at sixteen years of age and developed into an excellent Yorkshire League cricketer, with on occasions, real flair.

If slightly loose in technique, he was capable of playing excellent shots. Like Geoff Dennis, he had never been to Lord's before that first trip and, although he was determined to enjoy the experience, he admits to being somewhat overawed by the ground, the facilities, the atmosphere and the occasion. He had made a match-winning 80 not out in the semi-final

Trophy cabinet in the
Members' Bar in the
North Marine Road
Pavilion.

and was disappointed to score only one run in the Final, but his time was to come and in 1976 he became one of only three Scarborough players to make a fifty at Lord's, Phil Woodliffe and Bill Pincher being the others.

Rennard agreed that having several bowlers was a great advantage but, contrary to the opinion expressed by Geoff Dennis, Rennard did not feel under greater pressure in the knockout than in league matches. He felt that the early rounds were often mere formalities and that the area Final was the first game of real consequence.

I can remember, I think Preston came one year and they scored, well they didn't scare us, but they were down at ten o'clock training, doing press-ups, batting and all that. We were used to turning up an hour before the game and have a good half-hour knock-up, then have a sit down. They really thought they could play cricket; they got about 80. We got 240 and they got 80 . . .the hardest games were the area Finals, then the quarter-finals and semis.

Rennard agreed with Moor that teams visiting North Marine Road often had difficulty coping with the size of the ground compared to normal club grounds and the increased speed of the ball over the outfield. First-class wickets also are firmer and the pace quicker. Rennard also made the point that as matches usually took place on one side or other of the square, correct positioning on the longer boundary was extremely important to save runs in limited overs matches. Likewise the necessity of having the right fielders in the right places was paramount.

More than anything, though, Rennard attributed the success to a good team spirit, but is realistic enough to acknowledge that it is easier to develop good team spirit in a winning team. In the years 1972 to 1982, Scarborough Cricket Club was certainly that. For players and supporters on their way to Lord's in that period, they were indeed 'the glory years'.

Yorkshire Relish — Scarborough in the Leagues

IN the days of Hambledon, the idea that cricket would one day be played in competitive leagues would have been the figment of a vivid imagination. The very concept was alien to the social and cultural setting of the eighteenth century and so it was not until the first developments in mass communications at the close of the nineteenth century, that such an idea gained any credence whatsoever.

Professionals had long been important members of the cricket scene in the early part of nineteenth century. In cricket, William Clarke's itinerant band, which he called An All-England XI, was the arch group of professional players, but the general acceptance of professionalism in other sports was slower to materialise.

In football, for example, professionalism did not come about until 1885, largely as a result of agitation by clubs in the cotton-mill towns of Lancashire, but The Football Association itself had been formed much earlier, in 1863, and when the FA Cup was introduced in 1871, the Wanderers beat the Royal Engineers 1-0 at The Oval cricket ground. The Wanderers

Scarborough Cricket Club in 1895. Back row (left to right): J.King, J.Baines, F.Allison, W.W.Leadbeater (scorer). Second row: E.Moore, W.Peacock, H.Hovington, W.Moore. Seated: T.Walker, S.F.Yeoman (captain), W.Fox. On ground: W.Langdale, R.Bland.

Players pictured before the opening game of the 1904 when the 'First Fifteen' met the 'Next Twenty-four'.

went on to win the trophy a further four times, beating teams like Oxford University and Old Etonians in the process, and during this period the FA Cup was entirely an amateur affair.

With the advent of professionalism, however, names like Blackburn Rovers, West Bromwich Albion, Preston North End, Aston Villa and Wolverhampton Wanderers began to appear on the trophy and in 1888 the Football League was formed consisting of twelve clubs. All were from the industrial regions of the Midlands and the North of England where professionalism was rooted.

With football embracing the mantle of league competition, cricket too began to respond to the idea. Again, the local leagues formed were in the industrial regions, especially in Yorkshire and Lancashire. In 1899, the Yorkshire Cricket Council came into being, with a competition designed to improve club cricket throughout the whole of Yorkshire. Twenty-four of the principal clubs in the county were approached to join and twenty two did so.

Despite the stated aim, the Yorkshire Cricket Council was primarily based around Leeds and Bradford and was really an amalgamation of the existing West Riding and West Yorkshire Leagues, despite clubs from further afield, such as Harrogate, Hull, Rotherham and Sheffield United being founder members. The Yorkshire

Cricket Council soon became established and in 1903 Scarborough Cricket Club successfully applied for membership.

After World War One, the Scarborough club did not rejoin the Yorkshire Cricket Council immediately and it was not until 1922 that membership was resumed, by which time the League numbered more than seventy clubs.

The problem of deciding the championship of such a vast organisation led periodically to various suggestions of how the League should be structured, as clearly all clubs could not play against each other. Clubs were free to arrange matches against whoever they chose and the method of scoring results was based on a percentage of points obtained against points possible; a minimum of twenty completed matches being required to qualify for the championship.

A committee set up in 1922 to investigate the championship problem, proposed that the top four clubs in the table on 26 August should play two semi-finals and a Final for the title, but the proposition was defeated by 27 votes to 23.

The structuring of the Yorkshire Cricket Council was a matter destined to run and run, with possible regionalisation and various methods of deciding the championship being the major issues.

In fact, the recommendation of the 1922

The Scarborough first team about to take the field in 1924. George Hirst is on the extreme left.

committee was adopted in 1924 and a four club play off was introduced which lasted until 1933. After that the semi-finals were abolished and the top two teams competed in a championship final. The agreement lasted only until 1936, however, as back into the mixture came the top four play-off idea. Throughout this period the Yorkshire Council was growing in size and eighty-three teams were in the competition in 1935.

That year was to be a turning point, as a number of clubs who had been in at the formation of the Council seceded to form the Yorkshire League, followed later in the year by the withdrawal of twelve other clubs to form the Wharfedale & Airedale League. Dissatisfaction with the cumbersome nature of the Yorkshire Council, allied to travel problems, were the primary reasons for the withdrawals, which immediately reduced the Yorkshire Council to fifty-five clubs.

Scarborough benefited immediately from this turn of events and made an appearance in the play-offs in 1936, only to lose to Heckmondwike by a massive 216 runs as Heckmondwike punished the Scarborough bowlers to the tune of 335 runs. In reply, Scarborough's 'big two', Alan Richardson and Jack Pearson, managed only 11 runs each and Scarborough subsided to 119 all out.

The tables were turned in 1937. Scarborough and Heckmondwike again met in the play-offs and this time Scarborough were successful as they bowled their opponents out for 109, with Eric Bowker and Alan Richardson each taking four wickets. Jack Pearson's 67 not out then steered Scarborough home. The Final was a low-scoring affair. Only Pearson (40), Goward (21) and Richardson (19) reached double-figures and Scarborough's 94 all out looked totally inadequate against a strong Firbeck Main batting line-up. Eric Bowker, with 6-23 had other ideas and Firbeck Main collapsed to 64 all out. Scarborough were champions.

They were champions again in 1939, when Alan Richardson showed his quality in the Final against Bullcroft Main. He made 127 not out as Scarborough, 178-1, won by nine wickets and a young Vic Wilson, later to become Yorkshire captain, made 16 not out.

Other successes in the 1930s included the winning by the First XI of the East Yorkshire Challenge Cup competition in successive seasons 1929-30-31. This league competition founded in 1924, initially consisted of just four teams — York, Hull, Driffield and Scarborough — but eventually expanded to feature teams along the coast from Whitby to Hull and was the competition in which Scarborough 'A' team (Second XI) came to compete successfully after 1932, being champions in 1937-38.

Before moving into the East Yorkshire Cup competition, the 'A' team had played in the Pickering and District Beckett League, with the 'Reserves' (Third XI) taking part in the

Scarborough & District Beckett League. A 'Possibles' team (Fourth XI) also played friendly matches during the 1920s and, at various times, an 'Occasionals' (Fifth XI) took the field to play a few matches.

In 1930, Scarborough Cricket Club teams played a total of ninety-two matches, increasing to ninety-eight by 1939, which when added to the Festival and County Championship matches played on the ground, illustrates the provision made for cricket by the Scarborough club. A verse which appeared in the Annual Report of 1930 epitomised the feeling for the game of cricket during the period.
England has played at many a game,
And ever her toy was a ball;
But the meadow game with the beautiful name
Is king and lord of them all
— Begbie.

In the post-World War Two era, Scarborough Cricket Club continued to flourish in the leagues. Champions of the Yorkshire Cricket Council in 1953, the First XI moved into the Yorkshire League in 1954, which by this time consisted of a group of twelve senior clubs whose grounds and facilities were of a

high standard. They still operated under the umbrella of the Yorkshire Cricket Council, which by that time consisted of a number of 'inner' leagues, including the Central Yorkshire League, South Riding League, Pontefract Section and Yorkshire League along with Non-Section Members.

The championship of the Yorkshire Cricket Council involved a play-off between the leading teams in those 'inner' leagues.

In 1957, Scarborough won both the Yorkshire League and Council championship titles and did the 'double' on four more occasions until, in 1972, the Yorkshire League became autonomous from the Yorkshire Cricket Council. The catalogue of success for the club included twenty-eight seasons between 1957 and 1984 when Scarborough were Yorkshire League champions on thirteen occasions and runners-up five times.

Since 1984, however, the championship pennant has not flown at North Marine Road and the club is anxious to restore the balance. Other 'doubles' included the championship and Haig Trophy years of 1976 and 1981. In that golden twelve-year period of the 1970s and

Scarborough's First XI in 1938. Back row (left to right): J.Meads, J.Allan, G.Dennis, F.Temple, J.Knowles, V.Wilson, H.Huggan. Front: E.Bowker, F.S.Brooker, J.A.Richardson (captain), J.Johnson, F.H.Stephenson.

Scarborough's First XI in 1966. Back row (left to right): H.Halliday (coach), M.Kirkland, C.C.Clifford, R.Coward, G.H.Dennis, C.Kirby, B.C.Moor, C.W.Foord, M.Heath. Front: K.A.Calvert, K.C.Stockwell, J.B.Mitchell, J.Hutton, G.R.Bloom.

early 1980s, the National Club Knock-out Trophy was secured on five occasions together with six Yorkshire League championships. As early ambassadors, Scarborough Cricket Club brought the strength of cricket in the north, particularly the Yorkshire League, to the forefront of national club cricket and did much to stimulate interest in the National Cricket Association's efforts to establish a national knock-out competition.

The First XI were not the only successful team at North Marine Road at this time. In the 1950s, the 'A' team were a dominant force in the East Yorkshire Competition, being winners in five out of seven seasons. A celebration dinner to mark the 'double' success of the first and second teams in 1953, was held at The Grand Hotel, although by 1957, when the feat was repeated, the celebration dinner was held at the cricket pavilion at North Marine Road. Perhaps the committee, ever mindful of the accounts, was concerned that the pattern might become too regular to warrant the expense of the full-scale hospitality of The Grand Hotel.

Since those times, championship victories have been rarer, but another first was achieved in 1986 when both Second XIs won their respective leagues. This unusual situation was due to the Ridings League being instituted in 1972 for the Second XIs of Yorkshire League clubs. As Scarborough's Second XI — the 'A' team — had been members of the East Yorkshire Cup Competition since the early

1930s, the decision to join the Ridings League was deferred.

Eventually, in 1981, the club entered the Ridings League with a very young side under the captaincy of former First XI stalwart John Hutton, whilst the 'A' team under the newly-appointed captain Malcolm Davison, remained in the East Yorkshire Cup Competition. This arrangement has proved to be a success and both teams have more than held their own in the respective leagues, with the Ridings XI winning the League Knock-Out Cup in 1988 and lifting the championship title for the second time in 1989.

The captaincy of a club the size of Scarborough Cricket Club can be a mixed blessing. Being captain of the First XI is not an easy job; being captain of a Second XI has even more problems. It is often stated that the health and strength of a club, be it football or cricket, lies in the contribution made by the reserve players. Not for them the glory of appearing at Lord's Finals and basking in the spotlight. Theirs is a less glamorous and sometimes undervalued role.

Before he retired at the end of the 1981 season, Colin Hurd was captain of the 'A' team for five seasons, having played East Yorkshire Cup cricket for fourteen years, as well as making around fifty appearances in the First XI. He outlines the problems of being a Second XI — 'A' team — captain.

We were always playing against first teams

The 1977 First XI. Back row (left to right): T.Jack (scorer), M.Shepherdson, M.Davison, C.Clifford, S.Glaves, K.C.Stockwell, M.Brown. Front: B. Rennard, P.Woodliffe, A.J.Moor (captain), C.Stephenson, R.Sherwood.

Scarborough Juniors, winners of the 1987 Bright Bowl. This knockout competition is for under-18 teams with the Final staged at North Marine Road each year.

of other clubs. We were a second team and we were there not necessarily to win. There is a conflict between winning and producing first-team players and sometimes the two don't mix. Some players — I mean one of our loyal men, Gordon Downes — well, he appreciated it, but didn't agree with not trying to win and

I can understand that. My view was slightly opposite. That we still tried to win, but not at all costs.

The problem was that you were up against your Pickerings who, in my day, were the top club. They were a very strong side and would have probably taken on a lot of the Yorkshire

League sides, the lower sides, and possibly beaten some of them. There was Hull Zingari, again a first team. I think of some of the people who made up these better sides and if you go to Pickering well, you know who we are going to talk about now — Dave Cowton. He was a law unto himself and a very good player.

Another problem for Second XIs was that of change:

You went down to Pickering and saw the same eleven people for ten years or whatever. As a second team we were bringing up third-teamers. You were getting both the outcasts from the first team coming down and young lads coming up. There were also people like myself, a steady number, who was there nearly twenty years. First teams and changing players, they were the main differences.

I think the other difference was the umpires and the grounds. Some grounds in the competition were pretty poor, although there were some good ones too. The umpires, I think, were a bit more parochial than in the Yorkshire League and the higher Leagues. I don't think they were biased, it's just that there were many who were not as good. And you were at a certain disadvantage coming from Scarborough. If say, Ken Stockwell had been in the 'A' team for very long, they'd have done him, no doubt.

I asked Colin if he felt that there was a general feeling against Scarborough Cricket Club because of the club's status.

Mainly the umpires. Not from the players. I think it was a very friendly, but competitive league.

Naturally some people were envious, but we got over that, I certainly was not aware of any sort of problem, probably because of Gordon Downes and myself, as we got on with most people and we tried to keep the image of the club up.

We then discussed the reaction of teams coming to play at North Marine Road:

They only played there once a year. We played eleven or twelve times and for the poorer teams in the East Yorkshire Cup it was an awe-inspiring thing. Better wickets, faster wickets. I think you have to play regularly on that type of ground to know what it is about. It worked a little bit against us when we went away.

Going back to players, Zingari had Trevor Markham, a first-class all-rounder at that level and again, he could probably have played better cricket. There was always one person who stands out in each team. Bridlington had Jim, Jim Wood, who was a bit of a character, but a good player. He also told you he was a good player as well, every week, every time he saw you! Each side, I mean even Hymer's, the sort of lower club sides, had a chap called Barry Loughton, who was their opening bowler over many years. Hornsea had a lad called Rob Charlton, who was a character and a good player.

They all had probably one good player and ten average ones, whereas if you went into the First XI, you had a few more good players and that's the difference. Its the same at whatever standard you are and in the Yorkshire League its the same sort of thing, but there's more

The Scarborough team which won the 1989 Ridings League championship. Back row (left to right): S.Hardy, M.Cowell, A.Wood, D.Bowes, M.Dobson, J.Riley. Front: S.Branton, J.Precious, W.Mustoe (captain), P.Ellis, M.North.

of it. *This is where the difference between the East Yorkshire Cup and the Yorkshire League is quite a big jump. I found that. Whereas I was quite an adequate player in East Yorkshire Cup, I was not quite so adequate in Yorkshire League.*

We considered players who had come through the ranks at Scarborough from the East Yorkshire Cup side and, if one of the aims of the 'A' team was to produce players for the First XI, whether it was successful in doing so.

I'm not sure that it was, to be honest. There were people like Chris Kirby, who was a village lad from Weaverthorpe. He came through from the Reserves, our third team, then East Yorkshire Cup and succeeded quite well in the first team. He played in one of the games at Lord's and he was quite a good player in his own way.

I'm trying to think of some who started from school, Malcolm Kirkland was one. He came through the 'A' team into the first team. 'Mally' Davison eventually ended up in the first team and was a useful player in that company. I'm not sure we put it into operation — Shepherdson, Rennard — but it wasn't really a grounding school. We used to get people like Chris Stephenson, who'd come in from, like Beverley, and they would come in from outside and go straight in. They were good players. We used to ask players if they would like to come to Scarborough, rather than expect to be brought through. It has been a good system up to these last few years. But we've not been getting those players from outside quite so regularly.

The success of the Scarborough Cricket Club

First XI over the years has posed particular problems for players who were successful enough in the 'A' team to warrant a chance at Yorkshire League level. Players who were not outstanding players, but on the fringe of the first team. Colin Hurd considered that problem carefully as he had been in that position.

We've got this danger of making people not being wanted in the second team if we're not careful, because if you were a second teamer and looking at the first team, all you were really there for was to field, to be honest. Unless you were very lucky. If you were opening the batting in the second team, you could be number ten, nine, in the first team. You sort of went fielding for half a season and never had a bat in the hand.

I'm not complaining. We had the Stockwells, Moors, Blooms, all this lot, who were extremely good players. Some might even have been county players; in fact Ray Bloom was. The others may have been had they gone that route. They played so well, others didn't get a chance very much. I suppose I was unlucky to be there at that time, the wrong time for me. You just never know.

For young players coming from the surrounding rural areas to play for the premier club there were additional cultural factors to consider.

This is I think the problem with bringing young village lads in. They are leaving probably Division 'A' of the Beckett League, which is locally a good standard, and they've come into the East Yorkshire Cup. It is a better standard, though not all that much, but you're travelling to Hull and York and all over the

The First XI of 1990. Back row (left to right): C.Clifford, S.Hardy, A.Wood, M.Cowell, T.Watts, C.Hugill, T.Jack (scorer). Front: S.Paget, D.Greenlay, P.Hart (captain), N.Cowton, S.Gormley.

place, whereas they're used to being straight home with their mates and they're quite happy to play at that level.

Its not easy to step out of your own environment, from a village. I did it from a village, but its not easy. To start with, I was dropped from the first, second, third teams in three consecutive weeks and never had a bat in my hand! These are the problems. We all have selectoral problems, we all don't agree, but its no use taking your bat home and saying 'Sorry I'm not playing any more,' but that's what some used to do.

And I disagree with that policy. If you go down to play at Scarborough, you're a Scarborough player. You don't go and play for Scarborough 'A' or first team, the selectors decide that, That's how I and Gordon Downes looked at it. The East Yorkshire Cup is a good league, its a good competition. I enjoyed it.

Once it was decided to field two Second XIs in 1981, the future of Scarborough Reserves was at risk. It became increasingly difficult during the 1980s to recruit sufficent players to make up a full compliment of four senior teams. In contrast, interest in junior cricket was increasing. In 1982, the Reserve XI finished bottom of the Beckett League Division 'B', having fielded forty-one players, but with only five players playing in more than ten games.

Nevertheless, there were signs that amongst the younger members there was enough talent and sufficient numbers to justify fielding a junior team in a league competition. Thus the decision was taken to disband the Reserve team and enter a team in the Derwent Valley Junior League in the 1983 season. In many ways it was sad that the 'Reserves' had to be sacrificed, as they had operated as the club's Third XI for more than seventy years and many who became some of the club's best players, began their careers in the 'Reserves'.

The decision has been vindicated, as the change in structure has resulted in a very successful and thriving junior section of the club, with the junior team winning the Derwent Valley Junior League in 1985-86-87-88-90 and the Knock-out Cup in 1985-86-90. The junior players, being under fifteen years old at the start of the season, have a limited career at that level, so in 1990 a fourth team, made up largely of players under eighteen years of age, was entered in the Derwent Valley Cricket League (Division 'B'). This team plays at Hackness and bridges the gap between junior cricket and the senior East Yorkshire Cup and Ridings League teams.

League cricket has been the lifeblood of Yorkshire cricket for more than a century and few clubs in Yorkshire can match Scarborough Cricket Club's involvement, or record of

success, in all the leagues in which the club has competed. Cumulative results since the Yorkshire League was formed in 1935 put Scarborough comfortably at the head of the table. East Yorkshire Cup records show Scarborough 'A' as always a force to be reckoned with and in every league in which the club has been represented, Scarborough has been the team every other team wants to beat.

As times change, not as many regular spectators now make their way to North Marine Road on a Saturday afternoon to watch one of the league teams in action. Very few players attend practice and that contrasts sharply with the buzzing hive of activity when either George Hirst presided over five nets in the 1920s, or the young Ted Lester waited anxiously for a brief chance to bat after fielding out in the 1930s.

After the war, Harry Halliday too had a lot on his plate to satisfy the desires of all those who wanted to take advantage of 'nets' on Tuesday and Thursday evenings, whilst when Tony Moor was captain in the 1970s, few dared risk too many absences if they wanted to retain the selectors' favour.

Yet Scarborough Cricket Club provides as much opportunity for playing cricket as ever it did, with four senior teams and one junior team playing no less than ninety-seven league matches in 1991, together with several more cup and friendly games. Local evening cricket leagues provide opportunities to play rather than to practise and many Scarborough players take advantage of that situation.

Despite such competitive involvement, Scarborough Cricket Club's level of success in the leagues is declining, especially at 1st team level, where the Yorkshire League title has been won just once in the last ten years. The 1991 Annual Report confirmed the club's awareness and concern at the neglect of the maxim that 'practice makes perfect'.

The all-weather practice wickets were laid during the spring, but sadly neither these nor the grass practice wickets were greatly used. It is hoped to re-establish specific evenings for practice and the committee is looking at this whole area of coaching and practice and will endeavour to make the best provision possible in anticipation that the players will avail themselves of the facilities which should ensure greater success on the field of play.

As presented in previous chapters, Scarborough Cricket Club is a club with two identities. In the last decade, the club has been successful in dealing with the financial problems presented by changing circumstances of the late 1980s and recession in the early 1990s and the Festival is thriving again. Success in the leagues is proving to be more elusive.

Scarborough's Finest

THE relationship between Scarborough Cricket Club and Yorkshire County Cricket Club has always been close and usually cordial. During its history, Scarborough CC has provided Yorkshire with some excellent players who have given the county long service, whilst others have played for Yorkshire without being able to break into the first-class game on a regular basis. The flow of players has been both ways. Some of the great names of Yorkshire and English cricket have been pleased to bring their playing days to an end by playing for Scarborough Cricket Club at North Marine Road. John Found writes about the careers of 'Scarborough's Finest'.

DAVID BYAS born 26 August 1963
Fewer players in recent years have had as big an impact on the game locally as David Byas. Son of a Wolds farmer, this former Scarborough College boy set new pinnacles of batsmanship for a Scarborough player.
His batting achievements in the 1984 season can be summarised as follows:
Most runs for Scarborough CC in one season — 2,140
Most runs in the Yorkshire League in one season — 1,394

Yorkshire League's highest score — 200 not out
With Tim Watts he recorded the League's highest second-wicket partnership — 244

David Byas has all the attributes of a natural athlete; he is tall, powerfully built, possessing a good eye and temperament and above all, natural ability. As a left-hander, a brilliant fielder and with a farming background, there is an uncanny resemblence to Vic Wilson, the former Yorkshire captain who also played for Scarborough. Similarly, he hits the ball extremely hard, standing up to his full height to hit the ball straight down the ground.

He joined Scarborough Cricket Club as a player at the age of sixteen and his progress was steady if unspectacular until 1983, when he started to show the tremendous form which local people knew that he possessed. He scored his first century at nineteen and scored 504 runs in the season. From 1984 onwards, he topped the batting averages and underlined the widespread belief that he was county material.

In 1985, he was appointed captain of the club, being one of the youngest ever to hold the position. He set about the captaincy with the single-minded dedication that had earlier stamped his batsmanship.

Eventually, he attracted the attention of the

David Byas swings to leg whilst playing for Yorkshire v The Yorkshiremen in the 1990 Festival.

county selectors, making his mark, initially in the Second XI and regularly from 1988 onwards the Yorkshire First XI. His outstanding fielding and his usefulness, as an occasional bowler, particularly in one-day cricket, helped secure him a regular spot.

His potential was at last realised in the 1991 season when he secured the number-three spot with such success, that he was awarded his county cap.

His loyalty to Scarborough persists and on occasions when the county are without a match, David Byas turns out for the club. His modesty and general good humour have made him one of Scarborough's most popular players.

J.W.(JIM) CAMMISH – (1921-1975)

Jimmy Cammish was one of that rare breed of cricketer, a leg spinner who turned out for the county. He was born in Scarborough and played for the club in 1948 and 1949. In those two seasons he captured 111 wickets, finishing top and third in the bowling averages respectively. Then, for two seasons, he played his cricket in New Zealand, representing Auckland. He was back in Scarborough for the 1953 season, this time taking 43 wickets. His chance for the county came in 1953 but he played in only two matches and his three wickets cost 155 runs. He then emigrated to New Zealand where he lived until his untimely death in 1975.

It is said of Jimmy Cammish that he used to carry a cricket ball about with him and would spend hours spinning it in his hand. He gave the Scarborough attack variety.

C.C.(CHRIS) CLIFFORD – born 5 July 1942
P.R.(PHIL) HART – born 12 January 1947

Yorkshire cricket is strewn with the names of pairs of cricketers who are inexorably linked with each other. Names such as Hirst and Rhodes, Holmes and Sutcliffe, Wilson and Illingworth have a significant place in cricketing lore. So, in the annals of Scarborough cricket the names of Clifford and Hart are no less revered. For over twenty years these two have performed wonders for the club, each in his very different way.

Scarborough has been uniquely fortunate to have together two such talented spin bowlers, Clifford orthodox right-arm off-spin and Hart, left-arm. It seems appropriate, then to consider them in tandem. They have played together since 1970 and between them they represent something like fifty years of cricket.

Chris Clifford came into the Scarborough side in 1963 and he soon made himself an automatic choice with his accurate and often penetrating spin bowling. He has just completed twenty-six seasons with the club and

shows no sign of losing his zest for the game of cricket.

In that time he has taken 1,080 wickets in all matches for Scarborough and he could well become the leading wicket-taker of all time if he continues to maintain his form. In half of those twenty-six seasons he has been the leading wicket-taker and he has headed the averages on five occasions. In 1984 he had a haul of 93 wickets in the season. In 1976 he achieved the distinction of taking nine York wickets in a Yorkshire League match. He and Hart seem to reserve their best performances for the matches against York, having turned in match-winning performances on countless occasions. Indeed, one York supporter was heard to remark on one such occasion that if Scarborough brought two cardboard replicas of the pair and put them at each end of the pitch, the York batsmen would soon get themselves out!

Phil Hart is the cricket enthusiast par excellence whose appetite for the game has remained undiminished despite injuries to his person which would have daunted lesser mortals. He has played a leading part in eighteen seasons with the club, reserving some of his best performances for national knock-out matches. In all, he has taken 531 wickets for Scarborough at an average of 17.7, heading

Phil Hart, cricket enthusiast par excellence.

One thousand wickets each. Phil Carrick (Yorkshire, left), Bill Foord and Chris Clifford (Scarborough) celebrate after Carrick and Clifford reach the coveted milestone.

the averages of three occasions. He has taken over fifty wickets in a season on three occasions.

Both players attracted the attention of the county, although neither played more than a handful of games for Yorkshire. Chris Clifford played for Yorkshire in 1972, playing eleven matches and taking 26 wickets in the season, with a best performance of 5 for 70. In 1979 and 1980 he played 36 matches for Warwickshire. In 47 matches in first-class cricket, he took 126 wickets at an average of 37.61. Phil Hart played for Yorkshire, at the age of 34, as a replacement for Phil Carrick, who was suffering an acute loss of form. He played three matches.

Both Hart and Clifford have made valuable runs for their side and have scored fifties on several occasions. Chris Clifford had a top score of 86 in 1975 and Phil Hart one of 77 not out in 1986, when in that season he scored 427 runs. It was Hart's batting in the John Haig

Trophy Final at Lord's in 1976 which gave a much needed impetus to the innings and did much to bring victory.

D. BRIAN CLOSE – born 24 February 1931

Arguably the best all-rounder produced by Yorkshire since the war was Brian Close. A bowler, batsman, outstanding fielder, close-to-the-wicket or in the outfield, Brian captained his county and England with great distinction. His records here are not for this volume and are well catalogued elsewhere.

After he retired from first-class cricket, Brian's business ventures occasionally brought him to Scarborough. As eager as ever to play the game to which he had given so much, it was entirely logical that he should play for Scarborough CC.

For two seasons he turned out for Scarborough when his commitments would allow.

A young Brian Close walking out to bat at Scarborough.

Although he never captained the side his influence was considerable and his presence on the field always gave the side a head-start over other teams. His performances were seldom spectacular for of course he was nearing his fifties, but he scored runs and bowled effectively when the circumstances arose.

In his first season, 1979, Scarborough won through to the Haig Cup Final at Lord's and it was a spurt from Brian Close soon after the Scarborough innings got into difficulties, which helped the Club maintain its 100 per cent record at Headquarters.

Brian Close fully entered into the spirit of things at his new club and, amongst other things, he will perhaps be remembered for his efforts to raise money for Scarborough Cricket Club by volunteering with Phil Hart to take part in a sponsored parachute jump — successfully!

After the retirement of T.N.Pearce as Teams Organiser, D.B.Close's International XI played in the Festival from 1982-1986.

FRANK DENNIS – born 11 June 1907

Frank Dennis is often regarded as a Scarborough man, partly because of his family connections in the town, although as far as cricket is concerned, he only had one full season with the Scarborough club.

A fast right-arm bowler, he was also a hard-hitting left-hand batsman — unlike his brother, Geoff, a former Scarborough captain who bowled left-arm and was a right-hand batsman. Frank played for the club in the 1931 season and met with a good deal of success, topping the bowling averages and coming second in the batting. He took 39 wickets and had a batting average of 38.3 with a top score of 86. The following season he turned out for Hull.

Frank Dennis played his first county match in 1928 when he had a successful debut. The following season he showed even greater promise, taking over 80 wickets for Yorkshire at an average of 21.82. He was also awarded his county cap. This promise, unfortunately, was not to last for his bowling at times, though quite hostile, was often wayward and inaccurate. He captured 163 wickets at a cost of 29.26 in 90 matches for Yorkshire, playing on and off until 1933.

After the war, he emigrated to New Zealand to take up farming. He still takes a keen interest in Scarborough and Yorkshire cricket.

S.J.(SIMON) DENNIS – born 18 October 1960

Simon Dennis possesses excellent credentials for a cricketer. He is the son of a former Scarborough captain (Geoff Dennis), he is the nephew of two former Yorkshire cricketers, Sir Len Hutton and Frank Dennis and as a teenager he was considered good enough to play for the English Schools. Like his father, Simon bowls fast left-arm and bats right-handed.

As a youngster he came up through the ranks of his school, Scarborough College, and Scarborough Reserves and the East Yorkshire Cup side. He progressed to the club First XI at the age of seventeen and played for the team, albeit irregularly for the next seven seasons. He played in the Haig Trophy winning side of 1979, when he scored the winning run.

Eventually, he did well enough to attract the attention of the Yorkshire selectors who were desperately seeking an opening bowler. He made a handful of appearances in the early 1980s, until, in 1983, he took 52 wickets in the season and was awarded his county cap.

Dennis' progress was not to be maintained for illness, in the form of a rare blood disorder, intervened and he never really recovered the form of 1983. At times he looked a very fine bowler but the county finally released him in

1988. Thereafter he played for Glamorgan until his retirement from first-class cricket in 1991.

He took 173 wickets for Yorkshire at an average of 32 runs per wicket; his best performance being 5 for 35. He scored 338 runs for an average of just under nine. His top score was 53.

C.W.(BILL) FOORD – born 11 June 1924

If you were to ask regular Scarborough supporters who was the most popular club player or who had done most to further the cause of local cricket, more often than not the answer would be Bill Foord, the former schoolmaster who turned out in club colours for almost forty years. When he was not playing he would be coaching men and boys in the nets at North Marine Road.

As player, coach, spectator or committee man, he has played a fundamental part in the history of the club since the war. Foord started his bowling career with Scarborough as a seventeen-year-old in the early 1940s in the friendly matches that were able to be played during the war years.

However, his career started in earnest in 1947, when he took 55 wickets for Scarborough and earned a trial with Yorkshire. From that time onwards he was the automatic choice to take the new ball.

As a bowler, he was a model for youngsters to copy. He had a high, easy action that was so economical he gave the impression that he could bowl all afternoon. In fact he often did! His pace was a brisk fast-medium that seemed to make the ball hurry off the pitch and he had the ability to move the ball both ways through the air and off the wicket.

His career with the county was an on/off affair and certainly he was not given the opportunity to secure a regular place. When he did play, he met with reasonable success, as 126 wickets at a cost of just 27 runs will demonstrate. His best figures were 6 for 63 and he took five wickets in an innings on five occasions. Foord's ability unquestionably improved as he grew older and with such a marvellous action, he did not suffer the decline in his thirties which afflicts most fast bowlers. His best seasons for the club were in the 1960s, when he topped the bowling averages on three occasions, but he took 50 wickets or more in a season on nine occasions (74 in 1964).

He is one of only three cricketers to have taken 1,000 wickets for the club, the other two being Chris Clifford and (probably) Robert Baker in the nineteenth century, but the records here are incomplete.

He last played regularly for Scarborough's First XI in 1971 at the age of 47, but instead of hanging up his large boots, he performed sterling service for the lower sides, especially the Reserves, for whom he was captain and mentor for another ten yers.

Bill is still a regular attender at all the club's home matches and he has served on the cricket club committee since 1968.

ROBERT FRANK – born 29 May 1864, died 9 September 1950

One of the giants of local cricket during the early years of this century was undoubtedly Robert W.Frank of Pickering. 'Roberty' Frank was cousin to Joseph Frank who rose to fame when he broke the hand of the legendary Spofforth, bowling for Scarborough & District against the Australians in 1880. The Frank family have produced many notable cricketers down the years.

Robert Frank was a fine all-round cricketer. He was a slow bowler and a forceful right-handed batsman who could hit the ball very hard indeed. He played a number of games for Scarborough between 1886 and 1888, showing reasonable promise but in 1889 he headed the batting averages, performing so well that he caught the eye of the county selectors. He played nineteen games for the county between 1889 and 1903, on one occasion making a score of 92. However, an injury to his hand and a disagreement with the county committee, a luxury Frank could not afford, cut short what might have been a successful career.

Meanwhile, for Scarborough Cricket Club he was the leading batsman throughout the 1890s and well into the new century. He topped the batting averages no fewer than eight times but his social activities prevented him playing as regularly as he might have liked! In 1900 he scored four successive hundreds for Scarborough, 167, 104, 109 and 187. In fifteen innings he made 780 runs for an average of 60.

From 1900 he led the Yorkshire Second XI side until the outbreak of World War One, where his own ability, his qualities of leadership and his insistence on high standards of fielding did much to ensure that the county was supplied with a steady supply of fine cricketers. He became a member of the Yorkshire Committee, a vice president of the county and of the Scarborough Club.

He is one of the many people of the day who fell foul of the foibles of the Scarborough secretary, Robert Baker. Preferring to play for a representative side on one occasion, rather than turn out for Scarborough, Baker vowed that he would never play for the club again. Shortly after this contretemps, Scarborough were to host a match between themselves and Middlesbrough. Frank offered his services to the visitors who were delighted to accept. The result was one of the most devastating innings ever seen in local cricket. In three and a half hours, Robert Frank scored 309 out of the Middlesbrough total of 382; he hit nine sixes and 37 fours, breaking three bats on the way. It was one of the greatest feats of controlled hitting ever witnessed at North Marine Road. Onlookers described how one six hit a house outside the ground and came back first bounce to the far wicket!

In later years, Robert Frank was a familiar figure at matches at Scarborough and in his home town of Pickering. He attended the Scarborough Cricket Festival for 64 years without fail up to the year before his death in 1950.

HARRY HALLIDAY - born 9 February 1920, died 27 August 1967

After retiring from first-class cricket in 1953, Harry Halliday became a hotelier in Scarborough. In view of his known abilities he was appointed coach to the Scarborough Club in 1960.

Harry was to prove one of the best-loved characters ever to step out on to the North Marine Road turf. His value to the club was inestimable both as a player and as a coach. He introduced group coaching with that other Scarborough legend, Bill Foord and his depth of knowledge and an avuncular air made him an instant success wth cricketing schoolboys.

In 1961, Harry topped the Scarborough batting averages (63.1) as well as winning the Yorkshire League batting prize. The following year he was first again with an average of 57.6, despite being well into his forties. In 1963 he scored the only century by a first-team player. However, tendon problems prevented him playing again on a regular basis, although he continued his coaching duties until 1966. His untimely death in 1967 robbed the club of a fine coach and a loyal and devoted servant.

GEORGE 'SHOEY' HARRISON – born 11 February 1862, died 14 September 1940

Few cricketers can have had as meteoric a career as George Puckrin Harrison. He was born in Scarborough but as a teenager, he went to the little village of Ganton, some nine miles distant, to learn the trade of cobbler — hence his nickname 'Shoey'. He played village cricket on the excellent little ground in Ganton where he soon came to the notice of Sir Charles Ledgard and of the Revd R.P.Bainbridge, both supporters of the Scarborough club.

The latter introduced him to Robert Baker and for the last month of 1881 he played for Scarborough as a professional. The following season, he topped the Scarborough bowling averages, taking 31 wickets at an average of

9.4. He also played for Sir Charles Ledgard's XI in Ganton and it was Sir Charles who first recommended him to Yorkshire.

The county brought him into their side the following season and he was an instant success, so much so that he headed the Yorkshire bowling averages with 88 wickets. He had had some sensational figures to his name, including 9-14 for the Colts of the North v the Colts of the South. In that match he took six wickets in seven balls. He was picked to play for the Players side versus the Gentleman in that same season, an almost unprecedented selection for someone in his first full season. Despite an onslaught on his bowling, in particular by W.G.Grace who was out to teach this young upstart a lesson, Shoey bowled 52 overs in the day, taking 3 for 108. He took 100 wickets at 13.26 in that debut season of 1883.

In a match against Gloucestershire, Harrison was asked to field as a substitute for a Gloucestershire player who was late arriving. Throwing a ball in from the boundary, he tore muscles in his right arm. This proved to be a devastating blow, for he was never to bowl as fast or as well again. He did return to something like his old form in 1890 and 1891. He played a few games for Scarborough in 1890, when his form was such that he returned to the county side and headed the averages. He was similarly successful in 1891, when he took 38 wickets. His over-all first-class record was 249 wickets at an average of 15.7.

He then dropped out of county cricket entirely, going on to play for Bowling Old Lane, where he had previously had a successful career. He took over 1,000 wickets for that club.

M.B.(MALCOLM) HEATH

There are relatively few records of Scarborough players who represented counties other than Yorkshire. One notable exception to this was the former Hampshire fast-medium bowler, Malcolm Heath.

When he retired from first-class cricket because of injury in 1962, Malcolm's business interests brought him to the Scarbrough area. As his disability was not too serious, he was able to turn out for the club on a weekend.

His career with Hampshire had been a distinguished one and, although he didn't always fulfil the promise of his first season (1954), when he headed the southern county's bowling averages, he nevertheless performed yeoman service. He captured 527 first-class wickets in nine seasons, at an average of 25.11. In 1958 he took 126 wickets at 16.42, coming second in the county averages and versus Derbyshire at Burton upon Trent, on a rain-affected wicket, took 13 for 87 in a day. Incredibly, Hampshire lost the match by 103 runs, being bowled out for 23 and 55 in reply to Derbyshire's 74 and 107. In 1961, he played a part in Hampshire's County Championship-winning performances with 68 valuable wickets.

His performances with Scarborough were never spectacular, as he was never able to achieve maximum fitness, but his experience and ability to bowl tight made him a valuable addition to the squad. He was happy to play second-team as well as first-team cricket, where he bowled with a cheerfulness and skill that made him an inspiration to younger players.

In 1976, he played in the Haig Cup Final at Lords, where his opening spell with Martin Shepherdson did much to set Scarborough on the winning path. For Scarborough, he had eight seasons in the First XI and his 175 wickets cost only 18 runs each.

GEORGE HIRST – born 7 September 1871, died 10 May 1954

After his retirement from first-class cricket, which he announced in an emotional speech from the Pavilion balcony at North Marine Road in 1921, George Hirst took up duties as a coach at Eton College. The short summer term at Eton enabled him to play for the Scarborough club during the months of July and August from 1923 onwards. He also took part in some of the Festival matches as an umpire.

His deeds for the county are legendary: 36,356 runs at 34.13 average; 2,742 wickets 18.73; and the only player ever to make 2,000 runs and take 200 wickets in the same season. However, it is interesting to examine how he faired in the cut and thrust of league cricket as a man in his fifties. In reality, he played the game for Scarborough as he had done for Yorkshire, that is with great spirit and to the best of his ability. Indeed, George Hirst would know no other way.

His presence at Scarborough aroused a great deal of public interest, not only in the town but at grounds where Scarborough were scheduled to play. For instance, posters in Hull announced that 'G.H.Hirst will play!' to the great benefit of the gate receipts. Crowds at Scarborough were well in excess of 2,000 when Hirst played. A local Press account asserted that Hirst 'is a bigger favourite than ever he was when he played for his county'.

In the seven part-seasons when he turned out for the club, he topped the batting averages six times, scoring 2,682 runs at an average of 58.3. His average in 1926 was 117.2 and two years later at nearly fifty-seven years of age, his average was 108 and he hit a top score of 124.

His bowling successes were equally impres-

George Herbert Hirst, who announced his retirement from the Pavilion balcony at Scarborough.

sive, for he topped the bowling table three times and was second once, in 1929. In 1924, when he took 45 wickets at a cost of less than 8 runs per wicket, his striking rate was one wicket every four overs, exceptional returns by any standards. In all, in his seven years with Scarborough he captured 182 wickets at an average cost of 13.1 runs.

George Hirst gave a lot back to the game he loved and as a coach at North Marine Road, many youngsters who became notable cricketers in their own right, have cause to thank George Hirst, one of the greatest cricketers of all time.

DAVID HUNTER – born 23 February 1860, died 11 January 1927

It is well over sixty years since the death of David Hunter, yet he is still remembered with affection bordering on reverence by older members of Scarborough's cricketing fraternity. The town has produced many gifted cricketers but none has achieved the pre-eminence of 'our David'. The local 'Illustrated Monthly Magazine', writing about him in May 1897, described him as *the most talked of man in Scarborough*.

David Hunter was the youngest of five brothers, sons of a local builder, three of whom showed a great natural aptitude for the game of cricket, and for wicket-keeping in particular. David succeeded his brother, Joe, as Scarborough's wicketkeeper when the latter took over from the great George Pinder behind the stumps for Yorkshire. He played for the club with conspicuous success, achieving local fame as a batsman as well as keeper. In one match he batted throughout an entire innings for 75 not out and in another, at Hovingham Hall, he set a Scarborough record by catching the first five batsmen.

When Joe retired from first-class cricket, due to failing health and injuries to his hands, several aspirants for the post of stumper were tried but with little success. Louis Hall recommended David Hunter. His first match was against Cheshire at Bradford in 1888 but prior engagements prevented him being

available regularly. However, he played in the cricket Festival of that year against the might of MCC, taking three catches in the match and being Yorkshire's second top scorer in the second innings: 21, lbw to W.G.Grace.

The following season he made the position of Yorkshire wicketkeeper his own, claiming 55 victims and scoring 157 dogged runs. He seldom made big scores for the county but he always proved a difficult customer to dislodge and there were many instances when his tail-end batting helped saved the day.

In 1897, he was granted a benefit match, selecting the Roses match at Bradford on 19, 20 and 21 July. His part in the match was undistinguished until the second Yorkshire innings when eight wickets tumbled for 38, leaving Hunter as the last man in (Bobby Peel being absent ill) to help save the match. For 35 minutes he and Schofield Haigh defied the Lancashire attack, adding 28 priceless runs before he was out. It proved the salvation of the match for there was then insufficient time left for Lancashire to get the 56 runs required for victory. His benefit realised nearly £2,000 and a large crowd cheered his arrival back at Scarborough railway station.

Hunter played for many more seasons with conspicuous reliability and success. An England place, however, eluded him, even though he was rated by many the best wicketkeeper in the country. It would appear that his batting was to keep him out of the national side. His Yorkshire captain, Lord Hawke, however, regarded him highly as a batsman and in 1898, Hunter and he put on 148 for the last wicket against Kent at Sheffield. This stood as a Yorkshire record until 1982, when Boycott and Stevenson scored 149.

In 1908, Lord Hawke played few games for Yorkshire, his mantle as skipper being worn by Hunter, still fit and active at 48. For the record, Yorkshire were county champions that year!

For the county, he set a wicketkeeping record that has never been equalled — 863 victims caught and 327 stumped. Writing in his book, 'Yorkshire Cricketers 1839-1939', Peter Thomas says: *After 21 years with the county, facing some of the most varied and powerful bowling of all time and scorning the use of rubber finger tips in his gloves, Hunter's hands were as sound and undamaged as they had been the day he started keeping wicket for Scarborough.*

When he retired in 1909, he was presented with an illuminated address and £500 by the Yorkshire committee. The framed illuminated address has pride of place in the Pavilion at North Marine Road. In all, he played in 521 matches for Yorkshire and his first-class victims totalled 1,265 (914 caught and 351 stumped).

David Hunter resumed his connections with the Scarborough Club, both as an occasional player and as a highly respected coach. In the 1920s, Scarborough could boast Hunter and the immortal George Hirst on their coaching staff, with over forty years of county experience between them. When Hunter died in 1927, a crowd of several thousand lined the streets to pay their last respects to one of the town's great cricketing sons.

JOSEPH HUNTER – born 3 August 1855, died 4 January 1891

Joseph Hunter played for Scarborough during the 1870s, frequently opening the batting. However, it was his prowess behind the stumps which caught the attention of the Yorkshire committee when they were looking for a replacement for George Pinder. He was given his chance in 1878, when Pinder was injured and in all he played in ten games that season.

It was another three years before he secured a regular place and he remained the first choice wicketkeeper for another seven years. Finally, recurring illness and injuries to his hands caused him to retire. Recalling his career, 'Cricket Magazine' in 1892, said of him that at one time he had no superior behind the stumps. This was underlined when he was chosen to tour Australia in 1884-5. He played

in all five Tests with some success. He averaged over 18 with the bat and made three stumpings and took eight catches behind the wicket. He thus became the only Scarborough-born player ever to play in Test cricket. Lord Hawke, in his reminiscences, recalled that Hunter was offered less-favourable terms to tour Australia than some of the other players. Hawke advised him to hold out for more or refuse to go. This advice he followed and he gained an increase in remuneration.

For nearly a hundred years, Joe Hunter held the record number of dismissals in a match for the county, catching out nine of Gloucestershire in 1887. He also held the record for the most dismissals in an innings, six all caught. This was not beaten until David Bairstow created a new record of seven catches in an innings, eleven in the match, in 1982. Interestingly this feat was performed at North Marine Road, Scarborough.

After retiring from county cricket Joseph played a few more games for his home club. Unlike his more famous younger brother, he was a headstrong batsman, but was probably the more talented of the two in this department. He scored nearly 1,200 runs for Scarborough, with a top score of 60 not out.

His recurring ill-health shortened his life and he died in 1891 at the age of thirty five.

JOE JOHNSON – born 16 May 1916

Joe Johnson was a little left-arm bowler who was allocated to Scarborough by Yorkshire in the years immediately prior to World War Two. He also spent one season, that of 1947, after the war, when, in addition to his duties as a professional cricketer he did much valuable work on the ground.

His county experience was limited to three matches between 1936 and 1939, mainly being as a reserve replacement for Hedley Verity, when the latter was called up for Test duty. His big chance did not arise until 1939, when he turned in a match-winning performance for Yorkshire against Leicestershire, taking 5 for 16 in Leicestershire's second innings. Sadly, war interrupted any ambitions he may have harboured of being a county cricketer, and in 1946 Yorkshire looked elsewhere for their spin bowler.

Johnson was a remarkably good fielder, having played football for Doncaster Rovers and quite a useful bat. He turned in some excellent performances for Scarborough, twice topping the bowling averages with over 50 wickets in the 1938 and 1939 seasons. In 1939, he demolished the Heckmondwike side with a haul of 9 for 43.

He was clearly one of those unlucky players whose careers were seriously interrupted by the onset of hostilities. By 1946 he was no longer young enough to regain his earlier skills.

E.I.(TED) LESTER – born 18 February 1923
One of the most exciting batsmen to come on to the Yorkshire scene after the war ended was Ted Lester. He was a free-scoring batsman with a range of strokes all round the wicket; his late cutting was a joy to see. He was quite different from the usual mould of Yorkshire batsmen of the 1930-40 era, being somewhat unorthodox and always anxious to score quickly.

Whatever reservations the county committee may have held regarding his methods, it was impossible for them to ignore his record with the very successful Scarborough side, nor his achievements when he came into the Yorkshire side on a regular basis in 1947. It was a hot summer and the conditions suited his style of play. He finished the season with an average of 73, in one prolific spell hitting three

Ted Lester, certainly Scarborough CC's most successful product in first-class cricket. He was a Yorkshire regular from 1945 to 1956.

centuries in successive innings (two in a match versus Northamptonshire).

His best season was 1949 when he scored over 1,800 runs and was even tipped for international honours in some cricketing journals. In all he scored 10,616 runs for Yorkshire in 228 matches at an average of 34.02 but increasing foot problems meant that the pressures of three-day cricket were eventually too much for him.

In 1956 he returned to league cricket with Scarborough where he played as match professional until 1961. He also captained the Yorkshire Colts side with great success. Ted Lester first played in Scarborough colours in 1936, at the age of thirteen, turning out on a few occasions for the Possibles side. By the age of sixteen he was smashing all the records that Jack Pearson had set at Scarborough Boys' High School. He was then eager to take up a career as a cricketer and when he came into the Scarborough First XI he quickly caught the imagination of the local Press, within a few games being tipped for high honours.

In his first full season he came third in the batting averages with 321 runs and an average of 53.5. He had a top score of 81.

Sadly the war interrupted his seemingly automatic selection for Yorkshire and he did not make his debut for the county until 1945.

As match professional for Scarborough his performances became legendary. Spectators paid at the gate to see him bat and when he was out, they left. He won the Yorkshire Council and Yorkshire League batting prizes in 1956 and 1957. Then in 1960 he won the Yorkshire League batting prize again as well as creating a new league record with a score of 180 not out against Hull. This individual record was not beaten until twenty-four years later when another Scarborough batsman, David Byas, scored an amazing 200 not out.

In two hundred innings for the club Ted Lester scored 8,681 runs for an average of just under 55. When he retired from playing the game after the 1961 season he became a highly respected and influential scorer for Yorkshire, a position he still fulfils for home games to this day.

JOHN PADGETT – born 21 November 1861, date of death unknown.
John Padgett was another of those fine cricketers of the 1880s who earned selection for the county. He was a notable right-hand batsman and represented the county six times in all, five times in 1882 and once in 1889, his top score being 22. However, it was said that his fielding let him down and for that reason the county did not persevere with him.

He first played for Scarborough in 1879. The

following season, he played for the Eighteen of Scarborough & District against the Australian Touring XI. His main successes with Scarborough were during the 1880s when the Club could field five or six players who had had county experience.

After the 1889 season, he turned out for Milnrow as a professional and for whom he played for many years.

J.H.(JACK) PEARSON – born 14 May 1915

One of the strange factors of cricket in the 1930s is that Jack Pearson did not play more games for Yorkshire. He seemed to have all the attributes of a county batsman; he had style, technique, an admirable 'eye' and a splendid temperament. Yet he only had three innings for the county, one in each of the years 1934 to 1936. In the second of these, in 1935 against Northamptonshire, he was top scorer in the match, played on a difficult wicket, with 44.

Yorkshire's loss was unquestionably Scarborough's gain. Pearson certainly rivalled Alan Richardson as the club's main attraction throughout the decade and in the matter of averages, his achievements appear to be superior to those of his captain.

Jack Pearson first played for Scarborough as a talented sixteen-year-old in 1931. The following season he scored 285 runs, had a top score of 67 and came third in the club averages. In 1933 he scored 1,001 runs, hit his first centuries for Scarborough and finished top of the averages on 71.5, a remarkable achievement for an eighteen-year-old. As a just reward for his efforts he was awarded the Yorkshire Council Junior and Senior batting awards. The local Press rang with his praise and there were frequent references to his 'flawless' and 'stylish' batsmanship.

From then on he finished either first or second in the club averages. In Alan Richardson's supreme season, 1939, when he smashed several Club and League records, Pearson finished ahead of Richardson with the splendid average of 74.5 to the latter's 71.5. The first four in the averages for that season were Pearson, Richardson, Ted Lester and Vic Wilson. It is unlikely that the Scarborough club has had four more distinguished or exciting batsmen to build an innings.

Of these, Lester rates Pearson as the best.

After the war, Jack Pearson played his League cricket on Teesside but he has always kept in touch with affairs at North Marine Road. He has been a regular attender of the Scarborough players' reunion which is held once a year at the Festival.

J.ALAN RICHARDSON – born 4 August 1908, died 2 April 1985

Alan Richardson was one of the giants of

Alan Richardson, player, captain and president of Scarborough CC and arguably the club's best-ever batsman.

Scarborough cricket. His achievements still stand out to this day as pinnacles of excellence. As a batsman he broke every League and club record imaginable, then as a captain he led the club to unprecedented success. In his day, Scarborough could claim to be the top club in the land.

Alan Richardson started his long association with the club during the time of George Hirst. Indeed it was Hirst who recommended him to Scarborough — as a useful pace bowler! However, it was his batting which caught the eye and in his first season, in 1927, at the age of only eighteen, he finished third in the averages with nearly 350 runs to his credit. There were ten occasions in all when he headed the batting averages, the first one being in 1929 when he scored the club's only century of the season and ended up with an average of 81.6.

Throughout the 1930s he continued to break records seemingly at will. Almost every season he scored over one thousand runs. When he scored 'only' 935 runs in 1938, for an average of 51.94, the local paper complained that he had had a poor season. His top score for Scarborough was 202 in 1932. He won the Yorkshire Council batting prize in 1936, 1937, 1939 and again in 1948. In 1939, he scored 1,359 runs, a club record, for a remarkable average of 71.5.

After the war, he piloted Scarborough to three more Yorkshire Council trophy wins, twice having won it under his leadership before the war. Then in 1957, the club carried off the Yorkshire League title as well, only three years after joining the League.

Alan Richardson retired after the 1958 season, at the age of 50. He kept an active interest in the club he loved and he was elected a vice-president in 1959. In 1980, he became president of Scarborough Cricket Club, a role which he filled with true dignity despite increasing ill-health.

He played a number of games for Yorkshire before and after the war, averaging over 30 runs in twelve innings. In 1947, he played for Yorkshire against the MCC in the Cricket Festival, scoring an impressive 61, his highest score for the county.

Alan Richardson died in 1985, at the age of 76, and he will be remembered by those who knew him as a fine cricketer and a gentleman. His total of 22,000 runs for the club are a record which may never be equalled. In all matches he averaged over 45 runs.

JAMES SHAW – born 12 March 1865, died 22 January 1921

James Shaw was a slow left-arm bowler who joined the Scarborough club in 1894 as a professional. He had a reasonably successful season but he refused the terms he was offered for the following year. During the 1896 and 1897 seasons he played three games for Yorkshire.

Following his departure, Scarborough advertised for a slow left-arm bowler for the 1896 season. Louis Hall, the Yorkshire batsman, recommended a teenager called Wilfred Rhodes. The club, no doubt to its later chagrin, appointed M. Riley and Rhodes went to Galashiels.

GEORGE BAYES – born 27 February 1884, died 6 December 1960

George Bayes was a fast right-arm bowler from Flamborough, who came to Scarborough in the 1910 season and who was an instant success. He took 94 wickets, an achievement which helped him into the county side before the end of the season. In his first Yorkshire Council game for Scarborough, against Pontefract, he took eight wickets. He played in the Festival for Yorkshire at the end of that season, taking two wickets against MCC.

In the five seasons for Scarborough, up to the outbreak of World War One, Bayes took 395 wickets, nearly 80 per season and for most of that time he bore the brunt of the bowling. He returned to Scarborough for just one season, in 1927 when he took 47 wickets.

Bayes was a very popular figure at Scarborough and he played for Yorkshire on eighteen occasions between 1910 and 1921, taking, in all, 48 wickets at an average of 31.95.

JOHN TUNNICLIFFE – born 26 August 1866, died 11 July 1948

John Tunnicliffe is not normally associated with Scarborough Cricket Club but for more than ten years he ran a business in the town. In that time he showed a keen and often shrewd interest in the club. In most seasons he turned out for Scarborough when his Yorkshire commitments permitted.

He regularly attended the annual meeting

John Tunnicliffe, who turned out for Scarborough when his Yorkshire commitments allowed.

of club members and was frequently called upon to speak at banquets by organisers of the Festival.

As a cricketer, 'Long John' Tunnicliffe will best be remembered for his partnerships with Jack Brown of Driffield, in particular their mammoth opening stand of 554 against Derbyshire in 1898, a world record which stood for over thirty years. He scored more than 20,000 runs for Yorkshire and was universally recognised as Lord Hawke's right-hand man. However, in his day, he was equally renowned as a magnificent slip fielder. In the early 1900s he had no equal and he stands alongside the likes of Walter Hammond, Bobby Simpson and Yorkshire's own Phil Sharpe as a snapper-up of unconsidered trifles.

Although his games for Scarborough were few in number, his record was quite impressive, and in 1905 he averaged 222 for the games that he played. His highest score for the club was 160.

CECIL TYSON – born 24 January 1889, died 3 April 1940

Cecil Tyson is probably known best as a fine left-handed batsman who played most of his cricket in the south of the old West Riding. However, he learnt his cricket in and around Scarborough, playing for the town as an amateur and as a professional before World War One.

He was born in Brompton, a village some eight miles west of Scarborough. Brompton is probably best known as the village where the poet Wordsworth was married, but it might well have been known as the place where Cecil Tyson was born, had he not been more interested in financial reward than in fame.

He came to Scarborough to play as a seventeen-year-old in 1906. The following year he played First XI cricket but his early career was marred by illness. However, in 1909 he headed the batting averages with 466 runs and a top score of 79. He also caught the eye as an excellent fielder and a more than useful bowler. As a professional in 1911 he added consistency to his undoubted ability and his fame gradually spread. Sadly the war came along and as it did with so many other blossoming talents, Cecil Tyson's progress was nipped in the bud.

He was not considered for Yorkshire until 1921 when he was thirty-two years of age, but what a sensational debut he made. In his first innings for the county against Hampshire he scored 100 not out, out of his side's total of 220. In the second innings he made 80 not out as his side batted out time for a draw. He played in only two more games — against Lancashire and the Australians — before declaring that

he could earn more as a professional at weekends and down the pit during the week than ever he could playing for Yorkshire. He never played for Yorkshire again.

As a professional at Tong Park and then with Whitwood, he was regarded as the best batsman in the entire county. In 1926, he played two matches for Glamorgan before retiring with a first-class batting average of 45.71.

JOHN S.WARING – born 1 October 1942

In a short career, John Waring took 55 wickets for Yorkshire in 28 matches between 1963 and 1966, at an average of 22.74. These figures included an impressive 7-40 haul in a Roses match.

For some of this time he was living in Scarborough and was able to turn out for the club. His appearances were not as frequent as he would have liked, because there was no keener cricketer to be found anywhere. In three seasons with Scarborough, he took 94 wickets at a miserly cost of 14.3.

In addition to his appearances for Yorkshire, he played in one match for Warwickshire and, later, for Cumberland.

B.B.(BENNY) WILSON – born 11 December 1879, died 14 September 1954

Benjamin Birdsall Wilson was born in Scarborough and joined the Cricket Club as an aspiring bowler in 1897 at the age of seventeen. His progress was slow, although he had a run out in the senior side, also as a bowler, in 1898.

It was his batting which showed most promise and he scored a century for the Second XI in 1900. In 1902, he headed the club's batting averages and had a trial with Yorkshire. His work took him away from the town for a while but on his return he made his name as a reliable, if somewhat dour opening batsman. In 1906 he averaged 44.6 for the club and had a top score of 174 not out. Selection for Yorkshire Second XI was followed by four games with the county First XI at the age of 26.

From then on he was always in the reckoning for a county place, scoring his first century in the 1908 season. In 1909, he scored over 1,000 first-class runs, a feat which he was to achieve on four more occasions. He had his best season with the county in 1914, scoring 1,632 runs at an average of 31.38. These figures gave him third place in the county averages but by then he was in his mid-thirties and when county cricket resumed in 1919, Benny Wilson was released. He played 185 matches for Yorkshire, scoring 8,053 runs at an average of 27.20. After the war he eventually went as coach to Harrow and thence to St Peter's School in York. He never resumed his connections with Scarborough, settling down to spend his later years in Harrogate.

J.V.(VIC) WILSON – born 17 January 1921
One of the significant figures of post-war Yorkshire was Vic Wilson, a farmer from Scampston near Malton. He has the distinction of being the first professional to captain the county this century and the first since Tom Emmett in 1882.

Wilson was a massive left-hand bat who usually batted at number-three and gave the innings considerable solidity. He was a hard-hitting batsman who could drive in front of the wicket with formidable power. He was also a fine fielder close to the wicket, often in the short-leg position, who took many spectacular catches. His fielding ability was such that, when he toured Australia with the MCC in 1954-5, although he did not play in any of the Tests he was called upon to be twelfth man for all five games.

In his 658 innings for the county, he scored 20,539 runs for an average of 31.21 and as captain of Yorkshire from 1960 to 1962, he displayed a firm temperament. This was amply demonstrated on the famous occasion when he sent Fred Trueman home for being late! He led Yorkshire to the Championship in two out of his three years as skipper, in 1960 and 1962.

Vic Wilson learned his early cricket at Scarborough before the war, when he became part of a famous quartet which featured Alan Richardson, Jack Pearson and Ted Lester as well as himself. He came into this very powerful side in 1938 as a promising seventeen-year-old. He immediately attracted the attention of the Press and spectators by his self-confidence and fine striking of the ball. In his two seasons at Scarborough, he finished fourth in the batting averages on both occasions. In 1938, he scored 529 runs in 22 innings for an average of 31.11 and the following season, having scored his first century, he scored 663 runs in 27 innings for an average of 34.9. In the match when he scored his first century he outscored the great Alan Richardson, who was at his peak during his record-breaking season.

During the war, Vic Wilson was lucky enough to be able to continue his cricketing career in the Bradford League.

Scarborough's County Players
The following players also represented the Scarborough club and played at least one game for Yorkshire. Those marked with an asterisk played their cricket for the club before going on to play county cricket.

	Career with Yorkshire
W.J.Threapleton	1881
W.E.Bosomworth*	1872-80
H.L.Walton*	1893
F.J.Whatmough (or Whatmuff)	1878-82
C.H.Wheater*	1880
J.W.Rothery	1903-01
A.D.Towse*	1986
P.N.Anderson*	1988
G.R.Bloom*	1964
J.R.Burnett*	1958-59
J.Lister*	1954
M.Riley	1878-82
E.Peate	1879-87

H.Charlwood and E.Blamires played for Sussex and Surrey respectively as well as playing a number of games for Scarborough. Emmanuel Blamires played for Yorkshire before moving to Surrey.

Memorable Matches

THE North Marine Road ground at Scarborough has witnessed some great occasions and some memorable matches. At any level of the game it is possible to be thrilled and excited about unlikely events unfolding before the eyes and it is from those happenings that memories remain. Being there is the best experience of all, but is also a pleasure to read about such occasions, especially when they cover such a broad spectrum as the matches described in this chapter. For Scarborough Cricket Club has always prided itself on the range of cricket on offer at North Marine Road and in 'Memorable Matches' John Found has chosen as wide a cross-section possible.

1   Yorkshire v Lancashire (1991 County Championship).
2   Scarborough v Moseley (1980 Haig Trophy semi-final).
3   Scarborough v Hull (1984 Yorkshire League).
4   Gentlemen v Players (1885 Festival).
5   T.N.Pearce's XI v Australians (1953 Festival).
6   Hinderwell CP v Bramcote (1987 Primary Schools Under-11's KO).
7   Leveson-Gower's XI v Australians (1934 Festival).
8   Scarborough College v Scarborough HS (1954 Bright Bowl Final Under-19).
9   England v Australia (1951 Women's Test Match).
10   England v West Indies (1976 Prudential one-day international).
11   Yorkshire v Nottinghamshire (1969 Gillette Cup semi-final).
12   XVII of Scarborough & District v Australians (1880 Festival).

Britannic Assurance County Championship
Yorkshire v Lancashire, 1991

ONE need go back no further in time than September 1991 to find one of the most memorable County Championship matches ever to have been played on the North Marine Road ground. That it was played between the arch-rivals Yorkshire and Lancashire, added spice to the proceedings; and that it ended in a win for the home county set the final seal on a truly remarkable match.

Until the fourth and final day, on a pitch deemed by umpires Oslear and Meyer as entirely suitable for a Test Match, the bat had so dominated the ball that the bookmakers were making it odds-on a certain draw. But that was to ignore the glorious uncertainties of the game of cricket.

The Yorkshire captain, Martyn Moxon, declared on the final morning, after becoming the fourth player in the match to score a hundred. He set Lancashire the not-impossible task of scoring 343 to win in a minimum 80 overs. In the process of his innings he had added 145 runs with Phil Robinson for the fourth wicket. Robinson, going on to score 79 not out, took his tally for the game to 268 runs for once out, no mean feat for a player who was by no means an automatic choice for his side.

As the Lancashire openers came to the wicket, the game seemed nicely poised for an interesting finish. The speculation was that if Lancashire lost the initiative in striving for victory, the reliability of the pitch was such that the lower-order batsmen were good enough to hold out for a draw.

How wrong was that speculation! Yorkshire's young pace bowler, Darren Gough, taking advantage of the absence of first-choice openers Sidebottom and Jarvis, tore into the Lancashire batting. In no time at all they had lost seven of their leading batsmen for a paltry 99 runs, with Gough producing his best spell for his side of five wickets for 41 runs in 18 overs. The Red Rose batting was abysmal. It looked like surrender without a struggle. It was — until Philip DeFreitas entered the fray. Never one to submit tamely, he took the battle to the enemy.

Yorkshire, in the form of veteran left-arm spinner, Phil Carrick, decided they would keep Lancashire interested by buying wickets. He was giving the ball plenty of air, hoping, no doubt, that there would be sufficient turn in

YORKSHIRE v LANCASHIRE

Scarborough Cricket Ground, Tues 3rd, Wed 4th, Thur 5th, Fri 6th September 1991

YORKSHIRE	First Innings		Second Innings	
1. M.D.Moxon (Capt)	c Hegg b DeFreitas	4	c Titchard b Watkinson	115
2. A.A.Metcalfe	c Crawley b DeFreitas	2	lbw b DeFreitas	2
3. D.Byas	c Lloyd b Martin	120	c Crawley b Watkinson	21
4. R.J.Blakey (wk)	c Crawley b Watkinson	59	st Hegg b Watkinson	1
5. P.E.Robinson	lbw b Martin	189	not out	79
6. S.A.Kellett.............	c Hegg b Martin	7	c Mendis b Fitton	5
7. P.Carrick..............	not out	36	lbw b Watkinson	3
8. D.Gough	not out	60	not out	5
9. M.Robinson...........				
10. P.J.Hartley............				
11. J.D.Batty				
	Extras	24	Extras	13
	Total (6 wickets dec)	**501**	**Total** (6 wickets dec)	**244**

Fall: 1st inns 1-4, 2-7, 3-18, 4-251, 5-381, 6-426.
2nd inns 1-12, 2-50, 3-79, 4-224, 5-231, 6-237.

Analysis of Bowling	O	M	R	W	O	M	R	W
DeFreitas...................	30.2	5	104	2	6.2	3	7	1
Martin	32	11	71	3	5	1	8	0
Austin	30	6	97	0	6	1	20	0
Watkinson	37	7	117	1	23	1	85	4
Fitton	21.5	3	95	0	29.3	3	113	1

LANCASHIRE	First Innings		Second Innings	
1. G.D.Mendis	c Blakey b M.Robinson	114	lbw b Gough	6
2. N.J.Speak	lbw b Hartley	73	lbw b Gough	11
3. J.Crawley	lbw b Hartley	52	c Gough b Carrick	13
4. G.D.Lloyd	b Gough	51	lbw b Gough	3
5. S.P.Titchard	b Hartley	35	lbw b Carrick	22
6. M.Watkinson (Capt) ...	lbw b Hartley	0	c Blakey b Gough	17
7. P.A.J.DeFreitas	not out	24	c Metcalfe b Carrick	50
8. W.K.Hegg (wk)			c Blakey b Gough	2
9. I.D.Austin	not out	3	not out	101
10. J.D.Fitton ·.............	c Byas b Hartley	33	st Blakey b Batty	34
11. P.J.Martin			c Moxon b Hartley	29
	Extras	18	Extras	6
	Total (7 wickets dec)	**403**	**Total**	**294**

Fall: 1st inns 1-180, 2-211, 3-273, 4-288, 5-356, 6-356, 7-383.
2nd inns 1-18, 2-19, 3-23, 4-48, 5-67, 6-95, 7-99, 8-129, 9-212.

Analysis of Bowling	O	M	R	W	O	M	R	W
Hartley.....................	27	2	100	5	12.5	1	36	1
Gough	17	3	79	1	18	6	41	5
Robinson M	31	3	84	1				
Carrick.....................	32	15	52	0	23	3	184	3
Batty	17.5	2	78	0	7	1	29	1

the aging wicket to induce error. The theory was sound but it contained a fatal flaw. The boundaries at North Marine Road are not sufficiently distant to contain sustained, clean hitting. DeFreitas swung his bat in a full straight arc. Nine times he reached the boundary in an innings of 50, including 28 in one over from Carrick. It was desperate stuff and when he perished with the score on 129-8, the game seemed almost over.

But his innings had been just the stimulus that Lancashire needed to restore lost pride.

Carrick trundled away from the Pavilion End in partnership with the equally gentle Jeremy Batty. The ingredients were there for an explosive afternoon session of unbelievable cricket. The large home crowd's mood turned rapidly from one of anticipation, to amusement and then to near-dismay and total disbelief. Ian Austin, coming in at number-nine, hit the fastest century of the season in a mere 61 balls to turn traditional Roses cricket on its head, smiting 13 fours and six sixes, nearly all of them in the arc between mid-off and mid-on. Not tail-end slogging this, it was sound, controlled hitting.

The ball was there to be hit and hit it was, to the tune of 83 runs in 11 overs, in a stand with Dexter Fitton, who gave excellent support.

As tea approached, Fitton was out stumped and Lancashire still needed 132 to win. Surely this was the end. But no, last man in, Martin, proved every bit as reluctant to surrender his wicket as had Austin, who by now could scent fame if not entirely victory. By the interval the last pair had added a priceless 80 runs. Now victory really was looming on the Lancashire horizon. Whether Carrick and his captain enjoyed their tea we shall perhaps never know. But one thing is certain, Ian Austin would have enjoyed his, for he reached his century just before the players went off.

However, sanity was restored and with the fifth ball after tea, Peter Hartley had Martin caught at slip. So ended a memorable match in which all kinds of records for a Roses match had been broken, including the highest aggregate number of runs. Five splendid centuries had been made and what is particularly pleasing was that the final proceedings were witnessed by over 6,000 people, a remarkable attendance for the fourth day of a County Championship match.

Haig Cup Semi-Final
Scarborough v Moseley, 1980

THE cricket season of 1980 is one that will be remembered and talked about in the town for many years to come. Eleven years on, the supporters of Scarborough still shake their heads in disbelief at the events of 10 August that year. For one player in particular, the Haig knock-out semi-final will be a recurrent nightmare. Indeed, the word 'nightmare' was the word headlined in the local newspaper, to describe the feelings of the home side's opening bowler, Martin Shepherdson.

Omens for reaching Lord's in 1980 seemed good. The Scarborough side was playing well, records had been smashed by the Scarborough opening batsmen at the start of the campaign, a defeat at the hands of Bradford League side Brighouse was overturned because they had fielded an illegal player and above all, the side was brim full of confidence. They were doubly happy to be playing the semi-final match at North Marine Road where they had rarely lost a cup match.

For almost the entire game, Scarborough held the initiative. Batting first they made 198-6 in their allotted 45 overs which, it was felt, was sufficient if not exactly spectacular. The two hundred or so Moseley supporters who had come

by special train from Birmingham were somewhat subdued.

When the scoreboard registered 6-2 wickets only four overs into the Moseley innings, they were utterly silent. There then began a long period of dour attrition. The home bowlers bowled tidily and the fielding was keen. Niggling injuries to two of the bowlers, Nigel West and Brian Close, seemed to give little cause for concern. Only 60 runs were scored off the bat from the first 36 overs, as schoolteacher, Jack Watts and Wright dug in. Their partnership of 97 was at the rate of less than four an over and was to put a considerable burden on the later batsmen.

However, Moseley had a man for just such an occasion in John Taylor, a former Essex Second XI wicketkeeper. In just five balls he totally transformed the Moseley innings to such an extent that their supporters experienced extremes of emotion, from sorrow to ecstasy, in less than five minutes. Taylor swung his bat with such telling effect that he scored 30 runs in those five balls. Shepherdson, the unfortunate bowler whose first six overs were beautifully bowled for just 11 runs and one wicket, suddenly found himself with a final analysis of 8-2-51-1.

The turn-around was so dramatic that even though Taylor was out, the momentum was such that Moseley snatched victory in the dying moments of the match. It was a famous win indeed and the long train ride back to Birmingham was no doubt a very happy one.

Yorkshire League
Scarborough v Hull, 1984

Scarborough matches against Hull have always been keenly fought affairs, relished by players and spectators alike. Ever since the final decades of the last century the contest between the two sides seemed to bring out the best in the players. In 1888, Scarborough's Harry Leadbeater had scored 178 in his side's record total of 613. In 1960, Ted Lester broke the Yorkshire League record when he scored 180 against the Humbersiders.

In the 1920s, thousands flocked to the Anlaby Road ground in Hull when Scarborough included the great George Hirst in its ranks.

By the 1980s rivalry between the sides had lost but little of its keenness for matches and had the added spice of contention for the Yorkshire League title.

In 1984, though, the Hull side had lost some of its potency and when it travelled to Scarborough at the end of that season, all that was left to play for was self-esteem. The result, in fact, was of relatively little importance. Scarborough were to win the title by a record number of points and it is doubtful if the three

SCARBOROUGH v MOSELEY

Scarborough Cricket Ground   Sunday, 10 August 1980

SCARBOROUGH		
1. A.J.Moor	b Turner	30
2. C.Stephenson	c Taylor b Donner	30
3. D.B.Close	st Taylor b Donner	19
4. B.Rennard	b Latham	52
5. P.Hart	c Thompson b Latham	10
6. M.Brown	c Taylor b Thompson	10
7. J.Precious	run out	20
8. D.Byas	run out	3
9. P.Ellis	not out	1
10. M.Shepherdson		
11. N.West		

Extras(B5, LB12, W2, NB2) 21

Total (8 wickets)..........196

Fall: 1-71, 2-77, 3-107, 4-140, 5-163, 6-178, 7-195, 8-196.

Analysis of Bowling	O	M	R	W
Thompson	8	1	21	1
Latham	8	2	17	2
Watts	5	0	19	0
Morgan	8	0	45	0
Turner	8	1	30	1
Donner	8	0	43	2

MOSELEY		
1. R.Milne	Ellis	4
2. M.W.Cheslin	b Shepherdson	2
3. J.Watts	not out	85
4. M.Wright	lbw b Ellis	46
5. M.Heath	b Hart	7
6. J.Taylor	st Brown b West	33
7. P.Morgan	b West	4
8. H.Turner	not out	1
9. A.Donner		
10. A.Thompson		
11. H.Latham		

Extras(B 5, LB 10, NB 1) 16

Total (6 wickets).......198

Fall: 1-4, 2-6, 3-103, 4-137, 5-184, 6-192.

Analysis of Bowling	O	M	R	W
Ellis	8	3	12	2
Shepherdson	8	2	51	1
West	8	1	35	2
Moor	8	1	27	0
Hart	8	0	29	1
Stephenson	2	0	21	0
Close	2	0	7	0

or four hundred spectators who were present on that Saturday afternoon will remember the actual outcome. What they will remember, however, will be the performance of one Scarborough player in particular.

That player was David Byas, then only twenty-one, who was later to make his mark for his county, Yorkshire, gaining his cap some seven years later.

Despite his youthfulness, Byas was acting captain that day in the absence of Tony Moor. He was already earmarked as a county prospect and that season had scored well over one thousand runs for Scarborough. When he opened the innings with veteran Chris Stephenson, who was more than twice his age, he could little have thought that 50 overs later he would be not out, having smashed nearly every Yorkshire League batting record.

The statistics of the innings, fascinating though they are, do not do full justice to an innings of majestic power and savage aggression. Briefly, they are these. His innings of 200 runs was scored off 156 balls and lasted three hours. It contained eight sixes and 21 fours. His first hundred came from 103 balls and the second hundred from only 53!

On reaching 60, he completed 2,000 runs for the season, the only Scarborough player ever to do so. On 146 he beat the existing aggregate record number of runs scored in the Yorkshire League by the great Martin Crowe. A six took him past Ted Lester's record; the same stroke enabled him and his second partner, Tim

Watts, to break the League's second-wicket partnership record. When Watts was out for 85, the pair had put on 244 runs at more than two per minute. This particular record had stood since 1937.

SCARBOROUGH v HULL

Scarborough Cricket Ground
Sunday, 9 September 1984

SCARBOROUGH		
1. C.H.Stephenson	ct & b Brayshaw	41
2. D.Byas	not out	200
3. T.N.Watts	b Cox	85
4. S.J.Dennis	not out	8
5. B.Rennard		
6. R.E.Pockley		
7. P.Woodhead		
8. J.M.Brown		
9. R.V.Southwell		
10. C.C.Clifford		
11. P.Ellis		

Extras (B 3, LB 5, W 1)...9

Total (2 wickets).......343

Fall: 1-80, 2-324.

Analysis of Bowling	O	M	R	W
Garland	7	0	37	0
Flanders	6	0	45	0
Brayshaw	11	0	75	1
Cox	13	1	76	1
McLocklan	4	0	27	0
Ingram	4	0	25	0
Roper	5	0	49	0

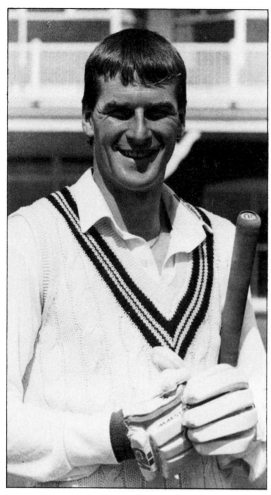

Left: *David Byas, who scored 200 not out for Scarborough v Hull in 1984.* Right: *A young W.G.Grace. 'W.G.' scored 174 for the Gentlemen at Scarborough.*

The Scarborough team total was 343-2: a new League record. It wasn't good enough to secure victory, however! Despite trying eight bowlers, Hull hung on for a draw. Not surprisingly, one of the few players on the Scarborough side who didn't bowl was Byas himself.

Scarborough Festival
The Gentlemen v The Players, 1885

J.M.KILBURN christened 1885 'the year of Grace' and not without reason. The 'Champion' played in all three of the Festival matches that year and those who had made the long journey to Scarborough to see him in action must have thought that it was worth every penny of the fare.

His first match, for the Gentlemen against I Zingari, was unexceptional by his standards. In his one innings he scored 68 out of his side's total of 298. For the MCC against Yorkshire in the final game he scored only four runs (caught Ulyett bowled Emmett). However, for the *cognoscenti* of English cricket in that era, the important match was that between the Gentlemen and the Players.

Both teams were very strong that year with the Players' XI containing five illustrious Yorkshiremen. They were captained by Tom Emmett and they probably fancied their chances of beating their amateur opponents. The Gentlemen, for their part, were captained by Grace himself whose presence alone brought hundreds of extra spectators to the North Marine Road ground.

The weather was fine and warm. Mr Grace won the toss and, as one would expect in a match of this nature, elected to bat. He opened the batting with C.W.Wright but it soon became apparent that the winning of the toss was a doubtful blessing. The newspaper account of the day's play refers to the fact that the wicket played 'somewhat queerly' and that the bowlers' deliveries appeared to 'kick a good deal'. at any rate progress was slow; the bowling was keen and the fielding was greeted with much applause.

Wickets fell at regular intervals, with none of Grace's partners scoring more than 21. Grace himself was dropped before being properly set. The Players' batsmen anticipated, no doubt, that they would be in action before the end of the first day. But it was not to be. A thunder shower held up proceedings in mid afternoon and when play resumed, life in the wicket seemed to be muted.

GENTLEMEN v THE PLAYERS

Scarborough Cricket Ground, Thur 3rd, Fri 4th, Sat 5th September 1885

GENTLEMEN	First Innings	
1. W.G.Grace	c Emmett b Attewell	174
2. C.W.Wright	c Scotton b Barnes	4
3. F.M.Lucas	b Attewell	7
4. Sir T.C.O'Brien	c Hunter b Ulyett	21
5. F.Townsend	b Ulyett	2
6. H.W.Bainbridge	b Attewell	14
7. K.J.Key	lbw b Attewell	4
8. H.V.Page	b Flowers	1
9. A.H.Evans	lbw b Ulyett	14
10. S.Christopherson	not out	9
11. E.W.Bastard	c & b Attewell	7
	Extras (B 5, LB 1)	6
	Total	**263**

THE PLAYERS	First Innings		Second Innings	
1. G.Ulyett	c Christopherson b Grace	14	c Grace b Evans	3
2. L.Hall	c Page b Christopherson	7	not out	30
3. W.Gunn	b Christopherson	6	st Wright b Grace	82
4. W.Barnes	b Christopherson	6	c Garce b Page	3
5. W.Flowers	b Christopherson	10	c & b Christopherson	6
6. W.Scotton	not out	4	b Page	26
7. W.Bates	c Page b Christopherson	0	b Evans	3
8. W.Attewell	c Page b Christopherson	4	b Evans	0
9. T.Emmett	b Christopherson	0	b Evans	0
10. J.Hunter	b Evans	3	c Grace b Evans	0
11. E.Peate	b Evans	0	c Key b Grace	4
	Extras (B 3, LB 2)	5	Extras (B 17, LB 2, W 3)	22
	Total	**59**	**Total**	**179**

Grace resumed where he had left off and went serenely on his way. All wickets were the same to him. Once he had the bit between his teeth, there was no holding him. He scored 50 out of the first 60 runs. When he reached 100 (out of 143) the ground erupted in great cheering. It did not trouble the good doctor that wickets tumbled at the other end. After all, had not the crowd come to see him perform? When stumps were drawn at the end of the day's play, Grace's contribution was 163 out of the team's score of 234-8.

On the second day the wicket seemed to have eased and an even larger crowd blocked the entrance to the ground before play commenced. Grace was soon out, for 174 and the Gentlemen's innings folded for 263. But the Players were never in the picture and were skittled out for 59. They did slightly better in their second innings but they were still defeated by an innings and 25 runs.

Grace's contribution on an uncertain wicket cannot be over-emphasised. He thoroughly demoralised his opponents, standing out as a man amongst mere boys. In the entire match only one other player scored more than 30 runs. Little wonder, then, that the local paper proudly announced that 'Dr.W.G.Grace will play with MCC on Monday'!

Scarborough Festival
T.N.Pearce's XI v The Australians, ꜱber September 1953

Many people will remember the year 1953, Coronation Year, as being a very significant and exciting one. Nowhere was that significance more apparent than in the world of English cricket. It marked the occasion when the England side, after many years in the doldrums, restored itself to where it felt it rightfully belonged: on top of the cricketing world. The Ashes had been challenged for and had been deservedly won, following one of the most enthralling Test series ever.

It was also a highly significant year for Scarborough Cricket Club. The local teams had had a particularly successful season, with both First and Second XI winning their respective League competitions. Club secretary, Alfie Rutherford was prompted to call the 1953 First XI one of the best ever to represent the town.

Interest in that year's Festival, then, was at an all-time high. And what a Festival it turned out to be; again one of the best ever. In his 'Centenary Festival Brochure', published in 1986, John Herbert selected the 1953 Scarborough Cricket Festival as being the one he would most like to have seen.

T.N.PEARCE'S XI v THE AUSTRALIANS

Scarborough Cricket Ground, Wed 9th, Thur 10th, Fri 11th September 1953

T.N.PEARCE'S XI	First Innings		Second Innings	
1. L.Hutton	c Langley b Hill	49	st Langley b Hassett	102
2. R.T.Simpson	c Craig b Johnston	86	c Graig b Johnston	12
3. W.J.Edrich	b Johnston	5	c Langley b Davidson	33
4. P.B.H.May	lbw b Hill	29	c Hassett b Hill	43
5. T.W.Graveney	run out	24	c Hassett b Hill	66
6. N.W.D.Yardley (Capt)	b Hill	6	c Benaud b Davidson	19
7. T.E.Bailey	lbw b Benaud	35	not out	24
8. T.G.Evans (wk)	c Hassett b Hill	10	st Langley b Hill	1
9. J.H.Wardle	not out	17	st Langley b Davidson	10
10. A.V.Bedser	c Craig b Benaud	40		
11. R.Tattersall	lbw b Benaud	4		
	Extras (B 13, LB 2)	15	Extras (B 4, LB 2)	6
	Total	**320**	**Total (8 wickets dec)**	**316**

Fall: 1st inns 1-71, 2-145, 3-182, 4-188, 5-206, 6-219, 7-243, 8-290, 9-307.
2nd inns 1-24, 2-167, 3-213, 4-258, 5-262, 6-292, 7-293.

Analysis of Bowling	O	M	R	W	O	M	R	W
Johnston	26	4	93	2	14	1	71	1
Davidson	11	3	27	0	22.3	5	72	3
Benaud	17.2	1	98	3	8	0	41	0
Hill	24	6	65	4	15	2	94	3
Hassett	3	0	17	0	5	0	18	1
Morris	1	0	5	0				
Hole					2	0	14	0

THE AUSTRALIANS	First Innings		Second Innings	
1. A.L.Hassett (Capt)	c Yardley b Bailey	74	c Evans b Bedser	25
2. A.R.Morris	b Tattersall	20	b Tattersall	70
3. G.B.Hole	run out	52	c & b Bedser	26
4. R.N.Harvey	b Tattersall	41	lbw b Wardle	3
5. I.Craig	lbw b Wardle	9	c Tattersall b Bedser	2
6. J. de Courcy	lbw b Tattersall	0	b Wardle	8
7. R.Benaud	c & b Bedser	29	c May b Bedser	135
8. A.K.Davidson	c Wardle b Bedser	39	not out	27
9. C.J.Hill	c Edrich b Bedser	18	not out	9
10. G.R.Langley (wk)	b Bedser	25	c Wardle b Bedser	9
11. W.A.Johnston	not out	0		
	Extras (B 9, LB 1)	10	Extras (B 4, LB 6, NB 1)	11
	Total	**317**	**Total (8 wickets)**	**325**

Fall: 1st inns 1-36, 2-69, 3-117, 4-123, 5-190, 6-190, 7-274, 8-276, 9-317.
2nd inns 1-163, 2-209, 3-218, 4-237, 5-246, 6-278, 7-287, 8-309.

Analysis of Bowling	O	M	R	W	O	M	R	W
Bedser	22.5	6	66	4	26.5	3	86	5
Tattersall	24	4	70	3	13	1	98	1
Wardle	22	3	97	1	23	2	107	2
Bailey	15	2	74	1	7	1	23	0

In truth, it was a most marvellous occasion, fully worthy of the spirit of that memorable year. All three Festival matches were played before record crowds, with secretary Rutherford having to exhort spectators, via the public-address system, to move up and make more room for more on the Popular Bank. In those three matches nearly four thousand runs were scored, as well as ten individual centuries, one of them a double century by, appropriately enough, Len Hutton. As an added bonus, all nine days were blessed by fine, often sunny weather.

The climax of the 1953 Festival was the traditional one between the tourists and a side representing the cream of English cricket selected by T.N.Pearce. The strength of both sides was such that the match merited the title of a 'Sixth Test'. Only the home skipper, Norman Yardley, had not played in the 1953

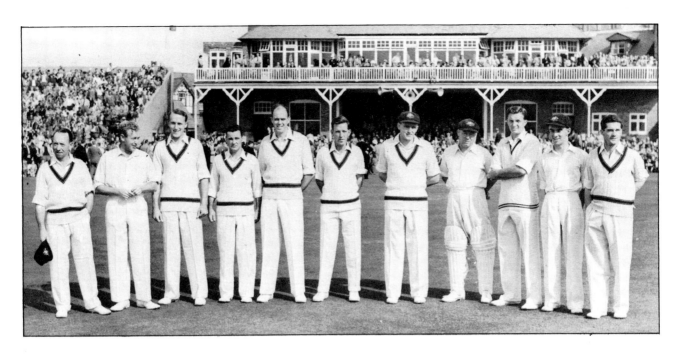

The Australians at Scarborough in 1953. Left to right: A.L.Hassett (captain), A.R.Morris, G.B.Hole, J.de Courcey, W.A.Johnston, C.J.Hill, A.K.Davidson, G.R.Langley, R.Benaud, I.Craig, R.N.Harvey. This was Hassett's last appearance in England, in a match in which Benaud hit 135 including eleven 6's.

Test series. How the crowds flocked to this game. At 8.30am on the morning of the first day, queues of people stretched down North Marine Road as far as the eye could see. The groundsman, Jack Meads, was compelled to mark a new boundary line in order to accommodate hundreds of spectators on the grass. Observers estimated that there were almost 20,000 spectators present.

Yardley won the toss and Hutton and Simpson gave the innings just the right start with a cultured opening stand of 74, before Hutton shocked his fans by getting out one short of his half-century. Simpson scored a splendid 86 and most of the batsmen chipped in with useful if not spectacular scores. Number-ten, Alec Bedser, ensured a score in excess of 300 by scoring a valuable 40.

Skipper Lindsay Hasett, in his farewell match, top-scored as the Australian innings stuttered falteringly to within three runs of the home side's total. Honours even! Pearce's XI's second innings contained what all the vast crowd wished to see, a Hutton century, before the master finally surrendered his wicket in true Festival spirit, to Hassett. The innings was given added momentum by the two rising stars, Peter May and Tom Graveney. Yardley a peerless Festival captain was able to declare, leaving the Australians around three and a half hours to score 320 to win the match.

There was to be no suggestion of playing for a draw. Hassett entrusted the number-one spot this time to the young Richie Benaud, making his first visit to Scarborough. How well he responded to the challenge. It was a situation tailor-made to his cavalier instincts. In 90 minutes he and his partner, Arthur Morris, had taken the score to 163 before the latter was out. It was the Australians' best opening partnership of the summer.

This achievement was particularly memorable because it was not in the nature of the opening bowlers, Alec Bedser and Trevor Bailey, to give runs away. Bedser, in fact, was given his head by Yardley and he responded splendidly, bowling 27 overs for 86 runs and five wickets, and on a pitch that was a batsman's paradise.

There was no containing Benaud though. By the time he was out for 135, the visitors were well on their way to a famous victory. He hit eleven massive sixes, a record for the ground and for his last 35 runs he required only seven balls, five sixes, one four and a mishit single. Four of the sixes were from the first four balls of a Roy Tattersall over.

When Benaud was out, wickets tumbled and although runs kept coming, both sides had their sites set on a victory. Finally, the last over of the day arrived with the Australians needing five runs to win, but, with only two wickets to fall, it was anybody's game. Then, when the scores were level, Hill pulled Bedser for six to produce an unforgettable ending to a memorable match.

Esso Primary Schools Cup
Hinderwell CP School v Bramcote School, May 1987

ONE match more than any other stands out in the mind of the author to illustrate the glorious uncertainties of cricket. It was not a match played by county teams, nor even club sides; it was a game played by schoolboys — and primary schoolboys at that. It should also serve as a warning to those who wish to write-off the chances of one team against another,

HINDERWELL CP SCHOOL v BRAMCOTE SCHOOL
Scarborough Cricket Ground   Monday, 18 May 1987

BRAMCOTE		HINDERWELL	
1. Graham ..... c Smith b Blades 3		1. R.Hartley....... c Matthews b Wilson 4	
2. Matthews .... b Dockerty 15		2. I.Comins ...... b Johnson...............20	
3. Lazenby ..... c Blake b Dockerty 14		3. D.Blake......... lbw b Buchanan..........1	
4. Whitaker .... c Shepherdson b Dockerty 9		4. I.Clarke......... b Buchanan 4	
5. Kitching..... not out 7		5. S.Blades .... c Howard-Vyse b Johnson 0	
6. Howard-Vyse c & b Dockerty............0		6. P.Dockerty ..... not out 22	
7. Johnson ..... not out 2		7. P.Parker .... b Johnson 0	
8. Wilson		8. A.Smith .... not out 1	
9. Buchanan ...		9. Shepherdson ...	
10.		10. Blake	
11.		11.	
Extras (B 1, W 5) 6		Extras (LB 1, W 3, NB 1) 3	
Total (5 wickets) 56		Total (6 wickets) 57	

Fall: 1-7, 2-26, 3-34, 4-51, 5-51.   Fall: 1-27, 2-28, 3-32, 4-32, 5-43, 6-43.

Analysis of Bowling	O	M	R	W	Analysis of Bowling	O	M	R	W
Blades	4	0	9	1	Buchanan	4.4	2	12	2
Smith...............	4	0	11	0	Wilson	4	1	18	1
Clarke	5	1	11	0	Lazenby	4	0	14	0
Comins.............	1	0	5	0	Johnson	3	0	11	3
Dockerty............	5	1	13	4	Whitaker	1	0	1	0
Sellers	1	0	6	0					

no matter how one-sidedly the cards appear to be stacked.

The match in question was in the first round of the Esso Primary Schools competition at North Marine Road in 1987. Bramcote, a preparatory school, were the holders of the trophy, as indeed they had been for most of the seasons in which they had entered the competition.

The presence of the two Scarborough prep schools had always rankled with one or two of the local state school heads, for it must be said that circumstances and facilities for playing the game of cricket were very much in favour of the private schools. For some of the county primary schools the Esso competition provided the only opportunity that some of the boys ever had at primary school, of playing organized cricket. Indeed, for some of the lads, it was the first time they had ever touched a hard cricket ball.

Be that as it may, the first round pitched the might of Bramcote School against a school drawing from one of the poorest areas of Scarborough, Hinderwell County Primary School. The holders were playing against a school side which rarely progressed beyond the first round. The contrast between the two sides was remarkable, the immaculate uniform gear of the Bramcote Boys as opposed to the rather motley outfits of the local lads.

Bramcote batted first and the Hinderwell boys took the field, looking anxiously to their captain to see where they should field. The two Bramcote openers, Graham and Matthews, came to the middle and the match began. An early wicket was looked upon as a slightly bizarre aberration when Graham was caught off Bales for three. For ten overs or so out of the 20 allotted to each side, Bramcote made unworried if unspectacular progress. Hinderwell chased and fielded well and with the advent of Dockerty to bowl, wickets started to tumble and the scoring rate slowed down almost to a halt. Eventually time ran out with the Bramcote total showing 56-5 wickets, Dockerty 4 for 13.

If the low Bramcote total was a surprise, the nature of the Hinderwell reply was an eye-opener. Runs started to flow, 11 off the second over would you believe? The fielding of the private schoolboys, usually a feature of their cricket, became ragged and catches were dropped. The opening pair put on 27 with Comins hitting four fours in his 20 runs.

When a few wickets tumbled and it looked as if Bramcote might indeed pull off a win, in came bowling hero, Dockerty who swung his bat to great effect, scoring 22 not out as his side passed the opposition's total for the loss of six wickets with plenty of overs to spare, much to the delight of the parents and teachers from Hinderwell who were there to lend vocal support to their boys. It was certainly one of the greatest days in the career of Don Booth, the Hinderwell boys' games teacher.

Scarborough Festival
H.D.G.Leveson-Gower' XI v Australians, September 1934
THE traditional match in which the touring team played an England XI assembled by

Mr H.D.G.LEVESON-GOWER'S XI v THE AUSTRALIANS

Scarborough Cricket Ground, September 1934

THE AUSTRALIANS   First Innings
1. W.H.Ponsford .... c & b Nichols 92
2. W.A.Brown .... b Farnes 3
3. D.G.Bradman .... st Duckworth b Verity.......132
4. S.J.McCabe .... c Duckworth b Farnes........124
5. W.M.Woodfull........ lbw b Verity 9
6. L.S.Darling .... b Bowes......................19
7. A.G.Chipperfield ..... b Farnes 53
8. W.A.Oldfield.......... c Duckworth b Nichols.......18
9. H.I.Ebeling .... c Nichols b Farnes............16
10. W.J.O'Relly........... c Duckworth b Farnes 9
11. L.O'B.Fleetwood-Smith not out........................1
     Extras (B 2, LB 9, W 1, NB 1)   13

     Total 489

Analysis of Bowling	O	M	R	W
Farnes	31.3	4	132	5
Bowes	23	2	111	1
Nichols	28	5	126	2
Townsend	3	0	23	0
Verity	21	3	84	2

H.D.G.LEVESON-GOWER'S XI   First Innings   Second Innings
1. Mr R.E.S.Wyatt .... b Ebelling 7   b McCabe.......................3
2. H.Sutcliffe .... run out 7   b Fleetwood-Smith 36
3. M.Leyland .... c & b Ebelling 27   run out 48
4. E.Hendren .... b Fleetwood-Smith 0   b O'Reilly 48
5. Mr J.H.Human .... c Darling b Fleetwood-Smith 31   c Brown b Fleetwood-Smith 9
6. M.S.Nichols........... lbw b O'Reilly.................75   c Ebeling b Fleetwood-Smith 17
7. L.F.Townsend .... lbw b O'Reilly.................37   not out 30
8. H.Verity............... c Ebelling b Fleetwood-Smith 3   st Oldfield b Fleetwood-Smith 0
9. G.Duckworth .... not out 22   c Ponsford b Fleetwood-Smith 1
10. Mr K.Farnes........... b O'Reilly 0   b Fleetwood-Smith 0
11. W.E.Bowes .... b Fleetwood-Smith 2   b O'Reilly 20
     Extras (B 3, LB 9) 12   Extras (LB 6) 6

     Total 223   **Total** 218

Analysis of Bowling	O	M	R	W	O	M	R	W
Ebelling	22	5	54	2	11	2	35	0
McCabe	3	1	5	0	5	2	15	1
Fleetwood-Smith	32.5	8	111	4	31	5	90	6
O'Reilly	16	5	35	3	25.5	5	72	2
Chipperfield	2	0	6	0				

H.D.G.Leveson-Gower, was always the highlight of the annual Cricket Festival. To the Australians it was regarded as being almost a Sixth Test. This was particularly so in 1934, when thousands of Yorkshiremen and women flocked to the ground in September that year to see if the England side could erase some of the humiliation inflicted upon them in the Leeds Test Match.

In that match a certain Donald Bradman had put all the home bowlers to the sword when he had scored 300 runs in a day and when Test cricket had seemed totally one-sided.

The Australian side included ten players who had figured in Test Matches, Grimmett standing down, while the England side contained seven Test players as well as Townsend who had been twelfth man. The additional players were J.H.Human, George Duckworth and the young Essex pace bowler, Stan Nichols.

The match was made memorable by the batting of Bradman, in an innings which is still talked about today. In 90 minutes before lunch on the first day, coming in when the Australians had reached 14-1 in 20 minutes, he scored 132 amazing runs.

Bradman, who was missed at slip early on, played an unforgettable and uncontainable innings. He completed 50 out of 65 runs in 40 minutes and 100 out of 145 in 80 minutes. He completely overshadowed Ponsford, his partner, even though the latter was in impressive form. At this point, he added 31 runs in two overs, taking 19 of them off one over by Verity. It was breath-taking stuff, with no hint of slogging. His ability to pierce the field at will and to farm the bowling over after over was almost supernatural.

In three innings in Yorkshire that season, he had scored 576 runs — 140 versus Yorkshire at Sheffield, 304 in the Leeds Test and now 132. This innings he regarded as being probably his best ever in England and it was played before a packed house of over 14,000 people. Never was an innings greeted with such approbation as that one of Bradman's. In it batsmanship reached new heights of technical achievement. Just for the record, the Australians won the match by an innings and 48 runs. The experienced Englishmen were outclassed, outplayed and in the end overrawed by one of the most exciting sides ever to play in the Scarborough Cricket Festival.

Bright Bowl Final
Scarborough College v The Boys' High School, July 1954

OVER the years, Scarborough Cricket Club has sponsored many competitions for local clubs. None have been more keenly or fiercely contested than the Bright Bowl competition for boys of secondary school age, the age limit varying over the seasons.

Recently, the competition has been contested almost exclusively by school teams but this was not always the case and it was certainly not the intention of the early organisers of the competition that it should be so. In the 1950s a number of the larger villages were able to field a junior side. Be that as it may, the outstanding side of the early years of that decade was drawn from the local independent school, Scarborough College.

Their cricket coach in those days was none other than the redoubtable Percy Holmes, the former great Yorkshire opening. The successes of the College side won somewhat grudging admiration from the local Boys' High School side, who had had to play second fiddle to their independent neighbours.

So it was with some delight that the state school side savoured the prospect of settling a few old scores when success in the 1954 competition saw them drawn to play the College in the Final. However, the portents were not particularly favourable. The College had a decidedly strong side, there was no question about that; they were the current holders of the Bright Bowl, having won it for the two previous seasons. Had Ladbrokes had a marquee on the ground in those days they would undoubtedly have made the College XI odds on favourites!

The night of the Final was a dull one with intermittent drizzle making conditions for cricket difficult in the extreme. As it was an

Scarborough College win the 1953 Bright Bowl by beating Scarborough Juniors.

evening start well on into the month of July, whoever was able to bat first would have much the better light. As is so often the case, fortune favoured the favourites and the College were pleased to take first strike. The opening batsmen, Clowes and Richardson, went straight out for runs and put on 50 in the first ten overs. The pair put on 59 for the wicket before Richardson was bowled by High School skipper, Norman Overfield.

Thereafter, the College innings faltered and aided by some suicidal running by some of the College batsmen, the High School team clawed their way back into the match. After their allotted twenty-five overs, the College innings closed on 120-7, with Overfield having taken 5 for 60.

In reply, the High School's innings started falteringly and it had only reached 37 after ten overs. The 50 came up after 13 overs, less than four an over when five an over were required for victory. Batting at number-four, the High School captain tried to speed things up but wickets fell with some regularity and with only seven overs remaining, the score stood on 69-4, 52 runs still required.

Worse still, the light had deteriorated further as rain started to fall. But High School had a 'secret weapon' in opening bowler, Howard Reynolds. Promoted to number-six, he batted in the only way he knew, with extreme violence, hitting two rapid fours and a six and scoring 19 priceless runs in a matter of a couple of overs.

Runs were now scampered off almost every ball but with three overs to go, 15 were still needed. Man of the match, Overfield, was then out for 27 and it was left to two fifteen-year-olds, Found and Beanland, to score the winning runs, amidst scenes of great jubilation from the considerable High School support.

It had been a splendid game of cricket played in a fine spirit between two evenly-matched sides. It reflected great credit on the youngsters of both of the schools involved.

Women's Test Match
England v Australia, June 1951

AFTER the privations of World War Two, people in this country wanted life to return to normal as soon as possible. One of the institutions which benefited most from this understandable attitude was the world of cricket. As a result, the Scarborough Cricket Festival went from strength to strength as record crowds flocked into the ground, producing record receipts at the turnstiles.

True to its proud traditions, the club committee ploughed much of the profits back into improving the facilities on the ground. The proud boast at the time was that the North Marine Road ground was to become the 'Lord's of the North'. It was hoped that Scarborough would be recognized not only as the spiritual home of festival cricket but also as a venue for cricket at the highest level. Certainly, there were suggestions from time to time that Scarborough might be an appropriate arena on which to play Test matches.

So it was with great satisfaction that Scarborough greeted the news that in June 1951 a Test Match would be played on the ground, and a Test between England and Australia at that. The fact that this was 'only' to be a Women's Test Match did not matter one little bit, for it was an acknowledgement from the cricketing authorities that Scarborough was in their mind.

When Mollie Dive, the Australian captain, brought her girls to Scarborough in June of that year, she was quick to appreciate the facilities that the club had to offer. Indeed, back in those austere post-war days, North Marine Road offered them for only the second time on the tour, a chance to have showers after the game.

The Australians were at full strength for the match but the England side were without their captain, the incomparable Molly Hide, who was nursing a twisted ankle. In her absence, the team was captained by opening bat, Myrtle MacLagan. When the England opening pair, MacLagan and Celia Robinson, opened the innings on the Saturday morning, 6,000 people were present, some doubtless sceptical about the ability of women to play the game of cricket. If there were sceptics in the crowd matters were soon set to rights by the performance of both sides. Spectators were particularly appreciative of the skills and athleticism of the Australian fielders who strove hard to contain the experienced England openers.

The two openers were in tip-top form and 95 runs were realised for the first wicket before Myrtle MacLagan was out caught for 56. By mid-afternoon, a big score looked assured as the England score had reached 130-1. Celia Robinson, in particular, was batting well and was well on her way to a century. The advent of the slower bowlers wrought a change in the innings, however, and wickets fell at regular intervals, so that by the end of the first day's play, England's score was 260-8, seven wickets having fallen to just double the score.

Next morning, the home side added another 23 runs before being all out for 283, five of the touring team's bowlers having taken at least one wicket. It had been a good performance by both sides and the second day's crowd, which almost equalled that of the first day, were in no doubt as to the ability of both sets of contestants.

ENGLAND v AUSTRALIA

Scarborough Cricket Ground, Sat 16th, Mon 18th, Tues 19th June 1951

ENGLAND	First Innings		Second Innings	
1. M.Maclagan	c Schmidt b Hudson	56	b Craddock	35
2. C.Robinson	c Paisley b Hudson	105	c Larter b Hudson	36
3. W.Leech	lbw b Craddock	15	c & b Craddock	2
4. M.Duggan	c Jones b Paisley	4	not out	21
5. J.Wilkinson	lbw b Paisley		c Schmidt b Whiteman	20
6. H.Sanders	run out	53	run out	14
7. M.Spry	not out	21	c Jones b Wilson	7
8. W.M.Johnson	st Larter b Wilson	2	c Larter b Wilson	9
9. B.Murrey	lbw b Wilson	2	run out	33
10. A.Geeves	b Whiteman	5		
11. M.Lockwood	lbw b Craddock	0		
	Extras (B 7, LB 4, NB 1)	12	Extras (B 1)	1
	Total	**283**	**Total** (8 wickets dec)	**178**

Analysis of Bowling	O	M	R	W	O	M	R	W
Jones	29	11	37	0	5	0	15	0
Whiteman	39	16	64	1	14.3	4	35	1
Wilson	34	10	59	2	23	2	55	2
Craddock	28	8	56	2	22	7	39	2
Hudson	10	2	21	2	4	0	19	1
Paisley	14	1	34	2	7	1	14	0

AUSTRALIA	First Innings		Second Innings	
1. J.Schmidt	c Lockwood b Duggan	4	run out	31
2. M.Allitt	b Duggan	30	c Geeves b Leech	8
3. A.Hudson	c Lockwood b Maclagan	70	not out	48
4. U.Paisley	c Maclagan b Leech	2		
5. V.Batty	c Murrey b Maclagan	31	not out	22
6. B.Wilson	c Geeves b Johnson	81		
7. M.Dive	c sub b Maclagan	0		
8. L.Larter	b Maclagan	5		
9. N.Whiteman	lbw b Maclagan	10		
10. M.Craddock	run out	0		
11. M.Jones	not out	2		
	Extras (B 10, LB 1, NB 2)	13	Extras (LB 1, W 1)	2
	Total	**248**	**Total** (2 wickets)	**111**

Analysis of Bowling	O	M	R	W	O	M	R	W
Duggan	16	4	28	2				
Johnson	22	7	65	1	13	4	17	0
Geeves	7	2	21	0	5	1	20	0
Leech	20	6	54	1	11	3	23	1
Maclagan	28	13	43	5	8	2	12	0
Wilkinson	5	0	24	0	7	2	24	0
Sanders					2	0	13	0

When Australia batted, the left-handed Mary Duggan soon accounted for opener, Joan Schmidt, and they were 4 for 1. Most of the visiting girls were out just when it appeared they were set for a reasonable score. Wickets fell regularly and the score reached 176-7 before Betty Wilson (81) and Amy Hudson (70) gave the Australian score a semblance of respectability. They were all out at the end of the second day for 248. In mitigation of the visiting side, it must be said that the conditions were far different from what they were used to, the weather being unseasonably cold and damp.

On the third day, the English girls tried to push the score along in order to leave themselves with enough time to bowl out their opponents. However, they came unstuck against the Aussie spinners and, after a bright start, they slumped to 115-6 until the injured Duggan helped Murrey put on 41 for the eighth wicket. This was enough to make the game safe for the England side but there was not sufficient time left to set Australia a reasonable target.

The tourists needed 214 to win in only 135 minutes, a target they made no effort to chase and the game ended quietly with Australia being little troubled as they proceeded to 111-2.

*The Australian Ladies'
team, led by Mollie
Dive, take the field at
Scarborough in 1951.*

By common consent it had been a splendid match, enjoyed by both teams and by the large crowds of spectators who had turned out in indifferent weather to watch. The game had been a very considerable coup for the Scarborough Committee and it was hoped that this was the precursor of similar games to come.

Prudential Trophy
England v West Indies, August 1976

CONSIDERABLE interest was shown in the town when it was announced that North Marine Road was to be the venue for the first match in the Prudential Trophy series of one-day internationals between England and the West Indies. This was the first occasion in which the ground had been chosen for a full international match.

The ground had hosted Women's Test matches and Under-19 internationals, but never before had two official Test teams contested a match of this status at North Marine Road. Rumours were that the game would be a 'sell-out' and this proved to be the case. Half an hour before the scheduled start the gates were closed with a crowd of over 13,000 eager to see the two teams. 'Wisden' was moved to remark that the interest shown in the match at North Marine Road should advance 'the claims of Scarborough for further representative cricket in the future'.

The weather, in this loveliest of hot summers, was dry but there was a suggestion of sea fret in the air when the two captains, Alan Knott of England and Clive Lloyd for the West Indies, came out to toss up. Lloyd called correctly and he had no hesitation in inviting the home side to bat first. If there was

to be any movement of the ball it was bound to be in the opening overs.

His judgment proved correct for no sooner were the spectators settled for the start of play than England were a wicket down. Barry Wood, the opening batsman, missed Andy Roberts' opening ball, a medium-paced sighter, and was bowled for nought. England 0-1. It was soon 18-2 and then 23-3 as the full might of the tourists' opening attack in the persons of Roberts and Michael Holding, gave the visitors a stranglehold on the match which they were never to relinquish.

Some resistance was offered by Graham Gooch and the young Middlesex left-hander, Graham Barlow, playing in his first international match. They advanced the score to 136 before the fifth wicket fell but then it was a regular procession and slow going until the 55 overs ran out with the England score a disappointing 202-8.

It was disappointing because the boundaries at Scarborough, by Test Match standards, are relatively short and the outfield was like lightning. The innings was interesting, historically, for it provided Ian Botham with the opportunity of playing in his first international match. He was yet to have to prove himself, however, for he was disappointingly caught off Holding for a single. Graham Barlow was not out at the end, scoring a hard-hit 80.

A total of 202 was never going to be a total to test the might of the West Indian batting line-up with Richards and Lloyd in imperious form. So it proved. There was an early success for England when Roy Fredericks was clean bowled by Mike Hendrick for 1 when the total

ENGLAND v WEST INDIES

Scarborough Cricket Ground		**Thursday, 26 August 1976**

ENGLAND			WEST INDIES		
1. D.L.Amiss	b Julien	34	1. R.C.Fredericks	b Hendrick	1
2. B.Wood	b Roberts	0	2. C.G.Greenidge	b Wood	27
3. D.S.Steele	c King b Roberts	8	3. I.V.A.Richards	not out	119
4. R.A.Woolmer	c Murray b Holding	3	4. C.H.Lloyd(Cpt)	b Underwood	20
5. G.D.Barlow	not out	80	5. L.G.Rowe	c Hendrick b Botham	10
6. G.A.Gooch	c Holder b Roberts	32	6. C.L.King	not out	14
7. I.T.Botham	c Fredericks b Holding	1	7. D.L.Murray(wk)		
8. A.P.E.Knott(Cpt,wk)	run out	16	8. B.D.Julien		
9. D.L.Underwood	c Julien b Roberts	14	9. V.A.Holder		
10. J.K.Lever			10. M.A.Holding		
11. M.Hendrick			11. A.M.E.Roberts		
	Extras(LB 11, W 1, NB 2)	14		Extras(B 8, LB 8)	16
	Total (8 wickets)	**202**		**Total** (3 wickets)	**207**

Fall: 1-0, 2-18, 3-23, 4-72, 5-136, 6-145, 7-181, 8-202.

Fall: 1-3, 2-77, 3-116, 4-176.

Analysis of Bowling	O	M	R	W	Analysis of Bowling	O	M	R	W
Roberts	11	0	32	4	Lever	9	1	38	0
Holding	11	1	38	2	Hendrick	9	3	38	1
Holder	11	3	30	0	Wood	8	2	29	1
Julien	11	2	37	1	Underwood	9	1	34	1
King	6	0	25	0	Botham	3	0	26	1
Lloyd	5	1	26	0	Woolmer	2	0	16	1
					Steele	1	0	9	0

was 3 but this served merely to bring in Viv Richards, already the most exciting batsman in the world, and he treated the England bowlers as if this was just a practice session.

Knott tried seven bowlers but they all came alike to Richards as he played shots all around the wicket. The result was a formality long before the end and when Collis King hit a six into the Trafalgar Square enclosure to win the match, there were still 14 overs to go. The West Indies won by six wickets, sending them off to Lord's for the second game of the series in a very happy frame of mind.

For the Scarborough club, the game had been a huge success. Favourable comments were received regarding the arrangements and the facilities. The weather had been dry and sunny, albeit rather chilly, and a capacity crowd had more than amply justified the choice of the ground for international cricket. The club was rewarded two years later when it staged a similar international when the New Zealanders were the visitors.

Gillette Cup Semi-Final
Yorkshire v Nottinghamshire, July 1969

THE Gillette Cup semi-final between Yorkshire and neighbours, Nottinghamshire, was played at North Marine Road on 30 July 1969 before a packed house. The occasion, the size of the crowd and the very tangible atmosphere made this a very special cricket match indeed.

Yorkshire had only once previously won the Gillette Cup and here was an opportunity to

bury for good, the notion that the county was not interested in one-day cricket. For their opponents, led by the incomparable Garfield Sobers, it was a chance to restore lost pride and put themselves back in the forefront of major cricket, where they at least felt that they belonged.

The day dawned fair and turned out to be a scorcher. When officials turned up at the ground, they were greeted by the beginnings of what would eventually be a vast throng of expectant spectators. The first enthusiasts, correctly anticipating a packed house, turned up to queue at 6am, although the gates were not to open for some three hours or so. By the time the gates were opened the great queue stretched back through the streets surrounding the ground for approximately a mile. People joining the queue found that they had to go into Dean Road.

Matters were even worse on the roads into Scarborough. AA reports suggested that one thousand cars an hour were queuing for some three miles on roads into the town. All the car parks were packed and every roadside space was filled for a radius of about a mile from the cricket ground.

It became obvious to late-comers that they would not get in to see the game. Nevertheless there was little trouble, only a little pushing as the crowd divided up to reach the various turnstiles. By the time the game began at 11am, some 12,000 people were inside but there were still thousands outside. Many missed the

YORKSHIRE v NOTTINGHAMSHIRE

Scarborough Cricket Ground Wednesday, 30 July 1969

YORKSHIRE		
1. G.Boycott	c Murray b Stead	0
2. B.Leadbeater	c Murray b Stead	1
3. P.J.Sharpe	c Murray b Forbes	67
4. D.E.V.Padgett	c Murray b Halfyard	46
5. J.H.Hampshire	lbw b Forbes	15
6. R.A.Hutton	b Taylor	3
7. J.G.Binks(Cpt,wk)	c Murray b Sobers	22
8. D.Wilson	b Taylor	16
9. C.M.Old	b Stead	4
10. P.Stringer	not out	5
11. A.G.Nicholson	run out	2
	Extras (LB 8, NB 2)	10
	Total	**191**

Fall: 1-2, 2-3, 3-104, 4-132, 5-134, 6-142, 7-165, 8-179, 9-183.

NOTTINGHAMSHIRE		
1. J.B.Bolus	b Hutton	15
2. M.Harris	b Old	31
3. R.A.White	b Wilson	8
4. M.J.Smedley	c Binks b Hutton	2
5. D.L.Murray(wk)	b Old	1
6. G.S.Sobers (Cpt)	c Binks b Old	20
7. S.B.Hassan	c Binks b Stringer	18
8. M.Tayor	lbw b Nicholson	0
9. C.Forbes	b Stringer	9
10. D.J.Halfyard	c Old b Stringer	1
11. B.Stead	not out	4
	Extras (B 9, LB 5)	14
	Total	**123**

Fall: 1-40, 2-49, 3-52, 4-89, 5-90, 6-95, 7-106, 8-110, 9-117.

Analysis of Bowling	O	M	R	W
Sobers	12	8	12	1
Stead	11.4	1	46	3
Taylor	12	0	51	2
Halfyard	12	1	41	1
Forbes	12	2	31	2

Analysis of Bowling	O	M	R	W
Nicholson	12	3	28	1
Hutton	12	2	23	2
Wilson	12	5	22	1
Old	10	0	32	3
Stringer	4.5	1	4	3

dramatic opening overs but people in the packed boarding houses surrounding the ground gave a running commentary on the game to those waiting in the queue.

Even representatives of the Gillette Company which was sponsoring the occasion found it difficult to park and then get into the ground.

The gates were closed at around 12.30pm with a large number of people still outside, many having made the long journey from Nottinghamshire. The hope was expressed that they might be opened later when the crowd was fully settled but this must have been a forlorn hope because the spectators were packed solid with many having to sit uncomfortably on the grass. The official attendance was 15,242 making receipts of £5,230 but it was reported by many that some gained admittance by climbing over the perimeter wall. It would seem that in reality some 16,000 or 17,000 actually watched the game.

The game itself was by no means a classic but the vibrant atmosphere made it seem so at the time. The atmosphere was reminiscent of a Wembley Cup Final and indeed the roar that went up when Sobers was out could hardly have been bettered by a winning goal.

Yorkshire took first strike and their start could not have been more disastrous; both openers were out to Barry Stead before the folk in the crowd were properly settled. The scoreboard read 3-2 wickets. Man-of-the-match, Phil Sharpe restored some Yorkshire pride with a combative innings of real class and with his partner Doug Padgett in tenacious mood the

pair put on a further 101 runs. Sharpe was out immediately before the luncheon adjournment but the Yorkshire supporters ate their sandwiches in a reasonably contented frame of mind. Indigestion may have set immediately afterwards because some 45 minutes later the score was 142-6 with only the bowlers to come in. Despite some brave resistance from Binks, captaining Yorkshire that day, and Don Wilson, the innings folded in the 60th over for 191.

The wicket though playing slowly, was a good one and the sceptics in the crowd thought that the home total was insufficient. Their doubts seemed justified when Nottinghamshire openers, Bolus and Harris, put on an unflurried 40 runs for the first wicket at more than three runs an over, entirely within the required striking rate. However, Yorkshire bowlers, Wilson and the young Chris Old, playing in his first full season, thought otherwise and, suddenly, wickets started to tumble. White went for 8, Smedley for 2 and wicketkeeper Murray for 1.

Enter 'King' Sobers. The Yorkshire supporters held their breath, the Notts supporters crossed their fingers. Sobers, batting at number-six was renowned for pulling lost games out of the fire. He batted with caution but no real discomfort until Old found one to clip the edge of the bat and Binks took a comfortable catch. The ground erupted, the crowd rose to their feet as one man. The cheer, I dare say, could be heard in Filey and the match was as good as over. The wicket of

Sobers, out for 20, knocked the resistance out of Yorkshire's opponents and they were all out for 123, still 69 runs short of victory.

It had been a famous win on a day that is still talked about to this day in the bars and clubrooms of Scarborough. The local club had experienced nothing like it, not even in the very great days of the Cricket Festival. Yorkshire went on to beat Derbyshire in a somewhat undistinguished Gillette Final at Lord's. The real Cup Final had been fought at North Marine Road.

Challenge Match
XVIII of Scarborough & District v Australians, August 1880
SINCE the early years of its existence no game can have attracted greater interest than the visit to the Scarborough club of the 1880 Australians. They came to play against eighteen men of Scarborough and District and all that summer they had remained invincible.

The Scarborough side, it must be said, was a strong one and contained a number of players who had achieved or were to attain county

SCARBOROUGH & DISTRICT v THE AUSTRALIANS

Scarborough Cricket Ground, Thur 19th, Fri 20th, Sat 21st August 1880

SCARBOROUGH	First Innings	Second Innings
1. Swithenbank	c Murdoch b Palmer 23	c Bonner b Spofforth 1
2. H.Taylor	b Spofforth 7	b Boyle 7
3. M.Myers	c Palmer b Spofforth 4	c Palmer b Spofforth 18
4. J.R.Buchannan	c McDonnell b Palmer 26	b Spofforth 6
5. J.Hunter	lbw b Palmer 0	lbw b Boyle 1
6. G.Watson	c Palmer b Spofforth 16	c McDonnell b Spofforth 0
7. H.Charlwood	c Jarvis b Spofforth 2	b Spofforth 0
8. D.Eastwood	b Boyle 4	not out 17
9. M.Riley	b Palmer........................19	b Boyle 0
10. C.H.Wheater	run out 33	b Boyle 0
11. D.Bookless	st Blackham b Palmer 0	b Palmer.......................19
12. T.Harrison	c Jarvis b Spofforth............3	run out 1
13. S.F.Yeoman	c Murdoch b Spofforth 0	c Blackham b Boyle.............2
14. J.Frank	b Spofforth 7	run out 4
15. H.J.Dewhurst	b Spofforth 7	st Blackham b Boyle 4
16. H.O.Wellburn	not out..........................8	
17. J.Padgett	thrown out Blackham 4	b Palmer.......................5
18. H.Mossley	b Spofforth 0	st Blackham b Boyle 0
	Extras 9	Extras 0
	Total (sic) **170**	**Total** (sic) **96**

Analysis of Bowling	O	M	R	W	O	M	R	W
Spofforth	50.2	20	72	9	26	15	26	3
Palmer	32	9	44	4	11	4	17	2
Boyle	29	14	45	2	30	9	43	7

AUSTRALIANS	First Innings	Second Innings
1. A.C.Bannerman	c Watson b Mossley.............0	c Taylor b Frank................9
2. W.L.Murdoch	c Mossley b Buchannan 1	b Mossley 6
3. T.U.Groube	run out 0	b Frank 1
4. P.S.McDonnell	c Yeoman b Mossley...........20	not out 26
5. F.R.Spofforth	b Mossley 1	b Frank 22
6. J.M.Blackham	run out 6	c Wheater b Mossley 1
7. G.J.Bonner	c Yeoman b Bookless 35	c Swithenbank b Mossley.......9
8. H.F.Boyle	b Buchannan 4	b Frank 0
9. G.E.Palmer	not out 17	b Frank 4
10. A.H.Jarvis	b Frank 0	run out 1
11. W.H.Moule	b Frank 1	c sub b Buchannan 11
	Extras 11	Extras 10
	Total **96**	**Total** **80**

Analysis of Bowling	O	M	R	W	O	M	R	W
Mossley	19	7	25	3	27	14	41	3
Buchannan	21	6	41	2	1.2	0	2	1
Frank	8	5	3	2	28	12	27	5
Bookless	5	3	16	1				

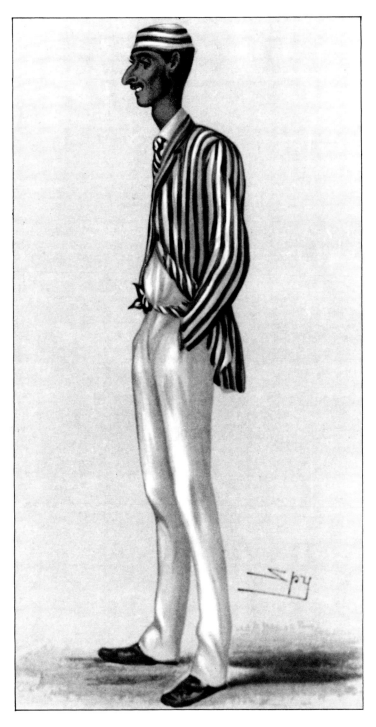

A cartoon of 'The Demon', F.R.Spofforth, who suffered a serious injury whilst playing at Scarborough.

was well supported and some of the players were highly regarded throughout the county.

For their part the Australians were a force to be reckoned with and they contained some very fine players, such as Bannerman, Murdock, Bonner and above all the 'Demon' Spofforth, the greatest fast bowler of his time.

The facts of the match are these: Scarborough XVIII 170 all out and 96, Australians 96 and 80, Scarborough winning by 90 runs and in so doing they inflicted the first defeat of the tour on the visitors.

The match caused a sensation at the time, not so much because of the Australians' defeat but because of the bowling of the Helmsley cricketer, Joseph Frank. Frank was highly rated as one of the best bowlers in the county but, partly no doubt due to the controversy surrounding his bowling in this match, he rarely secured a place in first-class matches.

During the Australians' second innings, the opener, Bannerman, drew back and refused to play Frank's bowling, on the grounds that he threw. The umpire declared his action to be legal and ordered the batsman to continue, whereupon Frank had him caught by Henry Taylor. Soon afterwards Spofforth came in to bat and a ball from Frank struck him on the hand shattering some of the small bones there. Spofforth was to play no more cricket that season.

The attitude of the Australians and in particular their captain, Murdock, prompted calls from the spectators for the local side to leave the field. There were subsequent catcalls to the visitors to 'play the game', the taunts going on for some time. However, the game proceeded and the home bowlers, Frank in particular, did a superb job and the Australians were bowled out in their second innings for 80. The home players were cheered to the echo when they finally left the field.

There was an inquest after the match was over but it was rightly pointed out that the tourists had earlier played against Joseph Frank in a game at Malton without ever questioning his action. Indeed, Bonner, one of the tourists, had commented that Frank was the best bowler they had come against in Yorkshire. Joseph Frank's figures for the match were 2 for 3 and 5 for 27 (in 28 overs).

status. In the thirty or so years since it was founded the local team had gone from strength to strength and in the 1880s it was to achieve some of its greatest feats. Cricket in the town

Scarborough Cricket Club Recollections

THE views and opinions expressed in this chapter are those of a few of the people who, over the years, have been at the sharp end of keeping Scarborough Cricket Club in the mainstream of English cricket. Oral history has had a chequered existence, but with modern communications technology, recordings of the spoken word will undoubtedly be of greater significance in the future. The motivation for this chapter is the great American oral historian from Chicago, Studs Terkel, whose conversations with people from all walks of life and on-the-spot interviews around the world are classics of the tape-recording genre. The first four interviews were obtained in August 1985, the rest in 1991.

The extracts themselves concentrate on different aspects of the club's activities. The first one is concerned primarily with ground development over the years as an element of club policy. The second reflects on the standing of Scarborough Cricket Club in local cricket circles, as well as looking at the importance of visitors to Scarborough as a source of finance to the club. The third interview casts light on how the close relationship of the club with the Borough Council was formed and also examines the general financial policy of the club since World War Two. The fourth interview is primarily about the playing side of the club in the successful years of the 1970s. The fifth features the chairman of the club in the years when the structure of cricket at first-class level was beginning to change to bring problems for the Festival, whilst the sixth interview concerning current ideas, policies and problems, is with the present chairman of the club. Finally are some of the recollections of Scarborough Cricket Club's oldest member, whose continuing enthusiasm for the game of cricket is an inspiration.

Frank Winn

Frank Winn joined the club in 1918. He was playing member and captain of the 'A' team

Frank Winn, player, committee member and chairman of Scarborough CC. He served the club from 1918 to 1987.

for many years and became a member of the committee in 1933. In 1948 he became chairman and honorary treasurer of Scarborough Cricket Club. He retired in 1957, but continued to attend committee meetings as a vice-president of the club until his death in 1987. Frank Winn's service to Scarborough Cricket Club totalled more than fifty years.

His first match for the club was against an Army team from Catterick, whose colonel bowled underarm, although this was the only time Frank experienced such a form of bowling. His early memories of the club are significant in that they are about the ground, which he considered to be a central policy area of the club in his time. He talks about the club after the World War One.

The field had not properly recovered; it was occupied by the Army people during the war. When we played on it, well, Alf Fatterini was groundsman in those days and had got the pitch ready, but that was about all you could say. The outfield was really dreadful.

Frank was a batsman and bowled only occasionally. The best batsman, as he recalled, was a man called Esherleigh, the agent for Lord Derwent.

He was a very good bat. He used to worry us as he always used to turn up, what I really call full togs, everything, blazer and all the lot. Of course Robin — W.S.Robinson who was chairman of the committee — was also skipper of the first team and he was a useful all-rounder. We had a pretty good side.

Yes, I played with George (Hirst) quite a while. First time I ever played with George was at Sheffield and you know what Sheffield crowds are like. "Did George 'Irst teach thee to catch like that?" — if we dropped one. Sheffield used to get terrific crowds; the stand was always full and a lot of people in the pavilion. They had some good players and were usually near the top of the Yorkshire Council.

Frank went on to say that in his opinion there were far too many teams in the Yorkshire Council and he welcomed the formation of the Yorkshire League in 1951, which had fewer teams of better quality. He then talked about practising and the nets.

We were lucky with coaching at Scarborough. First we had David Hunter, the old Yorkshire wicketkeeper, and he used to be down (to nets) every night. He used a bat like a feather. He used to stand in the net, behind the wicket and wave his bat as if it was a piece of straw. Then, of course, we had George (Hirst). He was a great coach was George. We had five nets going all evening. We never had enough.

I asked him about the quality of match wickets.

Wickets were very good. We were lucky to get Alf Fattorini, who came to us from Headingley. A good groundsman was Alf.

Frank had views on the secretaries he knew.

Leadbeater was a marvellous secretary. The way he got about was marvellous. He was a cripple, you know. He had a three-wheel bicycle and used to come down on that. Everyone knew him in the cricket world. He was a first-class organiser. He was a sort of stockbroker with an office in Westborough, but

he spent nearly all his time at the cricket ground. He used to get on the pavilion balcony. "Good shot, good shot, very good shot, do it again".

J.H.Goodall followed William Leadbeater as secretary in 1930.

Jimmy Goodall had done the assistant secretary's job before. He was, of course, involved in his estate agency business. (Goodall eventually became the largest property owner in Scarborough). He carried on for quite a while, not, we thought, as successfully as he might have done, because he wasn't able to put the time in that Leadbeater had for a start. In fact, that started the real trouble. Later on we had the real clear out. That would be 1947. The committee was completely divided by that time. It was absolutely chaos. In the end, there was about five younger chaps on the committee, a thing they'd never had before and it came to the boil. One evening we had a meeting at Jimmy Goodall's. It finished at half past one in the morning, this meeting. We had such a row. A lot of things were brought up. It was announced in the Press that night that Goodall and Hoyle, who was chairman, had resigned. We were on our own then and from there was the real start. The ground was bad and the first thing to do was to get the ground in decent shape and get some buildings on it.

I asked Frank Winn whether, or not, things had been done in the 1930s to take advantage of the situation built up by Leadbeater.

No, no I wouldn't and that really started the trouble. We felt that not enough was being done on the ground. We still had the old cowsheds. We still had the urinals out of the way behind the Pavilion. Every Festival we had an awful job. I have seen people being lifted over the heads of folks so that they could get out of the urinals on to the ground again. It was absolutely chaos. Of course, we recognised something had to be done to the ground pretty quickly as well, to get it into shape. We spent an awful lot of money in those nine years I was chairman. It wouldn't sound a lot nowadays, but we spent about sixty thousand quid, just on the ground itself. That would be a lot of money nowadays.'

The views of Frank Winn confirm the consistent central theme of club policy regarding investment in the ground. He then spoke about Alfred Rutherford.

I remember Alf coming, he was very raw in those days. He came on recommendation. Jack Knowles and Alan Richardson knew him. He worked night and day for the club, night and day. We had 1,900 members. When Alf cleared off we had 4,250. We recognised we needed the members' subscriptions for a nucleus to start the season off with. I don't think any special effort was made to entice members, but it was what we were giving them from a cricket angle which seemed to bring them in. One Australian year we had about six hundred new members in that year.'

I asked Frank about general maintenance, especially about repairs to the stands, which were to cause financial headaches in later years.

I think quite honestly, that was the committee's fault. There were too many delays. You know how things are. Whenever steel reinforcement goes it goes very rapidly. It is very difficult, very difficult and, of course, the inclination is to delay and it is really the worse thing you can do. I remember when the stand first started going (North Stand). Not the big job, the one before. It cost six thousand pounds. We got the shock of our lives. We had no idea. We didn't realise anything was wrong.

I can still see the meeting. 'Robin' was chairman. He announced that we had just got a letter from Scarborough Corporation and they were prepared to offer us all the land behind the new stand for five hundred. "We can't afford it gentlemen," he said. It was turned down. Just imagine. We could have had all the land to Woodall Avenue for five hundred pounds. Think what we could have done with that!'

Len Halstead

Len Halstead's earliest connection with the club was as an office boy 'cum runaround' for William Leadbeater. One of his duties was to keep the president informed of what had happened in the day's play, on days when the president was not able to attend. Len used to cycle from Leadbeater's office in Westborough to Holbeck Hill, where the president lived and give him the news.

Len first appeared for the 'Possibles' (fourth team) in 1930 and later became a regular and successful member of the 'A' team. He joined the committee in 1949 and became honorary treasurer in 1977. Len Halstead's affiliation to Scarborough Cricket Club is that of a lifetime; his official playing and committee service spans more than sixty years.

First, I asked Len Halstead about players and, in particular, Alan Richardson.

Yes he had twenty odd years as a skipper. He was a great person to be with. He was a wonderful story-teller. He could tell tales and even up to his death he could tell of his experiences. He was a great cricketer, batsman particularly. He beat all records at Scarborough.

We then talked about the Yorkshire Council and I asked him about travelling at that time.

We used to hire a coach that was tacked on to the rear of the train and when we got to

York we would be pushed into a siding until a Doncaster train came from Newcastle and we were then tacked on to the back of that and dropped off at Doncaster. A coach would be waiting to take us to a restaurant for lunch and then the coach would take us to all the places where we played. Then the reverse journey back. It was all laid on, not a penny to pay. It is only recently that the players have had anything to pay. We have had to cut that down. Now they have to pay for their own lunch, unless it is a special occasion; and fifty pence match fee to cover teas.

The next topic of conversation concerned the capacity of the North Marine Road ground, especially with reference to photographs of spectators sitting on the grass inside the normal boundary. I put it to Len that some official attendance figures would have been quite revealing.

I contend that we must have had the best part of twenty thousand in those days. Until Yorkshire played Nottinghamshire in the Gillette semi-final in 1969 we never knew how many we could get into this ground. Everybody had to pay for that match, committee, everyone had to pay. So that was the first time we ever found out. The figure was £15,250.

The discussion turned towards the importance of membership as a source of income to the club and the suggestion in Minute Books of earlier periods, of a certain amount of apathy of Scarborians towards the club.

I still think it applies. Of our membership

Len Halstead at work in the Committee Room at North Marine Road.

now only approximately one-third are local people.

I asked Len why that should be.

I think there is more cricket played now in and around Scarborough than there ever was and they won't become members of this club as well as their own small club, whereas at one time we were the big club in the town. Well we still are, but they hadn't alternatives then and so they became our members.

But the boarding house people, I can quote you a while ago how we tried to get a boost to the membership. We got the chairman of the Hoteliers' Association to contact all the boarding houses and hotels in Scarborough to see if he would do it. He was on a percentage basis and he went round and he got quite a lot of them to become members, pressurised them I think, because the following year ninety per cent of them dropped off and now we're trying to get them back again.

There followed a discussion about the relationship between the club and the town. Len made the point that, because of the motor-car, more people were coming to Scarborough for much shorter periods of time. In that respect it seems ironic that the factor which contributed to Scarborough's development as a tourist resort in the nineteenth century — increased transport and communications — is now working against the town and the cricket club. Road has largely replaced rail and people often delay their journey to Scarborough, in order to find out weather prospects and do not commit themselves so early to visit the town and the cricket club.

Len had forthright views about visitors, the ground and finance.

I contend that we don't use this ground enough during the season. Apart from the matches played on this ground and one Donkey Derby there is no use made of this ground at all and I contend that especially in July when the Scots visitors are here — and they are the people that come and stay the week — if we could only utilise this ground and put on entertainment for them, because it proves when we had the Donkey Derby after the thunderstorm and there was no sign that they had ever run on the course, so that it isn't as though the field is going to be damaged in any way. There are certain people, when we first put this proposition of the Donkey Derby, they thought, oh crickey, no it will spoil the surface, and all that sort of stuff. There has been talk of having a dog track around here. Some people would like to have a running track after they had seen what Foster has done at Gateshead, but you would encroach too much on the ground itself for that.

We talked about fund raising in general.

I have always been hoping that we could have something to raise funds, not necessarily on this ground, but even at the Open-air Theatre, or somewhere. There is the outside possibility that the council would let us have say, the Spa, or the Floral Hall and put on a big concert, same as James Last. When they came, they sold out before the concert started and had a £60,000 gate. I won't say they made such a lot of profit as the overheads must have been tremendous, but even so you're going to make some money. It is a headache at the moment, financially because we are running with this big overdraft and it seems whatever we do we just cannot reduce the figure because of the interest charges.

I pointed out that the club had occasionally had a big overdraft before.

Yes, but they cleared it very quickly. They had a big overdraft for that particular time in 1956. It was considered to be a big overdraft to build the West Stand, but within five years or so, five Festivals, it was wiped out. I think we are coming to a time where we shall have to have an appeal, with the one hundredth Festival coming up.

Len Halstead's words proved prophetic. There was a Centenary Festival Appeal in 1986, which raised £28,873. Furthermore, in March 1986, the club was bequeathed a sum of £100,000 in the will of Jack Knowles, a farmer and former First XI player of many years' standing, although the terms of the will did not allow for the immediate benefits of that bequest to be realised. Nevertheless, the immediate financial problems were alleviated.

Harry Wilson

Harry Wilson was Scarborough Borough Council treasurer until 1964. He preceeded Len Halstead as honorary treasurer of Scarborough Cricket Club in the years of 1958 to 1977 and was thus in a position to influence the two bodies which proved to be useful in bringing a closer relationship between the club and the Corporation. Harry Wilson, a kindly man, keen golfer and a regular supporter from the Trafalgar Square enclosure rather than the committee balcony, died in 1991. Here, in 1986, he describes the treasurer's position, when he took office in 1958.

In the past the treasurer to the club was the Midland Bank manager in Scarborough. Then there was a change in bank manager as far as I can recall and it happened that at that time Francis Whittaker, who was patron of the club, he had been president on at least two occasions, he said that he thought there ought to be a closer relationship with Corporation. He was my chairman of the finance committee at the Town Hall as well.

He suggested to the committee that instead of letting this nominal managership be with the bank, it should pass to the treasurer of the club. The only reason the bank was manager was that the money was paid in, but the secretary at the time did all the work. He did the treasurer's work and also the secretary's job. There was first of all Alf Rutherford and then, following him, we had John Midgely. When Francis Whitaker made his proposal for me to do it I said that it wasn't a question for me. I should like to take it on, but before I do that I wanted to ask the finance committee if they would agree to me doing this extra job.

I was full-time Borough Treasurer, you see, and that was my job. Anyway I went to the finance committee and they were quite happy. They thought it was a very good idea and it would bring a closer relationship. So I took it on in 1958.

Harry Wilson then went on to describe how he understood the situation to have been before.

This is purely heresay, but I understand that there was a former chairman of the cricket club committee, he was the chairman before Frank Winn, a chap called W.S.Robinson. Well, W.S.Robinson was very, very anti-Corporation and he was always afraid that if ever they had any contacts with the Corporation at all, officially, it would be the beginning of the end so far as the cricket was concerned. He thought the Corporation would come in and take over, which was quite ridiculous, because they just couldn't have done. Robinson thought that once the Corporation got in they would want to rule the club. I think that was really at the back of his mind.

I asked whether Robinson might have been concerned about the Corporation taking over the ground for building purposes as the land would be of prime value.

Oh no, no, no. He was thinking that once the Corporation got a foot under the table, as you might say, the Corporation would want to take the club over and run it, which, of course, just wouldn't have happened. The club had no stronger supporter than Francis Whittaker. He'd been a member of the club since he was a small boy and the Whittaker family had supported the club, but that is how I came to be the first treasurer, the first one who actually was a member of the committee.

On Francis Whittaker's death in 1962, no one specially assumed his role in relation to the club and the Corporation. We then discussed finance.

When I took over in the 1957-8 period there was a £17,000 debt outstanding and John Harrison, who was the local manager of the Midland Bank at that time, he was worried about this, so Francis Whittaker and I went

Harry Wilson (left) with Brian Sellers, president of Scarborough CC in 1965 and a great supporter of the Festival.

to London to the Head Office and I said to them you needn't bother about this. I'll guarantee we'll repay the lot within five years, because at that time we were having really good Festivals. Well, in fact, I think we had it paid off in three years, or thereabouts. It was no problem.

Harry was concerned about the current overdraft of the club, due to the investment in the sponsor's room in the pavilion. I suggested that the club had always been prepared to invest in ground facilities and investment always carried a degree of risk.

This is very true, but I think you have got to remember this, that at the time the investments were being carried out — I'm not talking about this development in the Pavilion — when we were developing the ground in the past, we had an adequate income to do this from the Festival. Now one of the things which, in my opinion, did a tremendous lot of damage to the Scarborough Cricket Festival, was the end of the Gentlemen v Players era. I think that did us a tremendous amount of damage; it was a popular event. Of course it's gone now and our Festival income has almost disappeared.

Harry's point is that a competitive match like the Gentlemen v Players, or North v South match, was replaced by, what would he would call, 'exhibition' matches and so interest declined, especially among cricket enthusiasts who were the backbone of the Festival. The one-day fixtures have attracted good crowds, but a different sort of following which did not have the deep-rooted commitment to the Festival.

In other words you can't rely on the activities of the cricket club to provide the finance that is needed to keep the ground. Now the income you need to maintain the ground can no longer be found from cricketing activities. It must have sponsorship to enable any profit at all to be made out of the Festival.

In 1905, John Tunnicliffe, a famous Yorkshire player of the time, gave a speech at a dinner in Scarborough, in which he strongly advised the club to try to be self-sufficient, regardless of the Festival. Harry Wilson had qualified sympathy with that viewpoint.

Well, they could only have done that at the time by increased subscriptions and by carrying out all sorts of other activities to raise money. And they did have patrons like Londesborough.

I asked Harry whether, in his opinion, membership subscriptions had been rather low in the past.

I think probably immediately after the war, the fees were too low. If I remember rightly the ordinary member's ticket was thirty shillings and the enclosure member's ticket was fifty shillings, or something like that. Well, it was quite ridiculous when you consider you could go every Saturday afternoon and many Wednesday afternoons and you could see a good local cricket match. Then you got the Festival for nothing. Oh yes, the Yorkshire matches as well. Considering that, I think the charges for subscriptions were too low. Now, I wouldn't say they were too high either. They are much higher than they used to be but even so, I still think they are reasonable.

Annual subscriptions in 1986 were:
Ordinary: £21.50 per annum (£39.50 in 1992)
Enclosure: £24 per annum (£43 in 1992)
There were a number of other categories of membership including
Life Membership: £240 (£360 in 1992)
Note that in 1978, Life membership was £50.

Tony Moor
Tony Moor was captain of the First XI in 1973-9 and 1983-4. He joined the committee in 1973 as captain of the club, I asked him

how he first became associated with the club.

First of all I lived in North Marine Road, just behind the Pavilion and, so I mean, I was in the ground every spare minute of the day, as it were and so got into it in that way. In those days Alfie Rutherford was secretary and there were probably eight or nine nets going then and it was paced with kids and the change nowadays is quite amazing. I got into what was called 'The Possibles', I think. There was the First XI the 'A' team, the Reserves and the Possibles and I think I was in that side when I left school at fifteen. I very quickly got into the 'A' Team and then I got into the first team.

I always remember the first game, it was at Headingley. I got picked one Bank Holiday Tuesday, when a lot could not get off work. Alan Richardson was captain and we were put into bat. I was down to bat at six or seven and we were quickly 15-4 or 5 and I was in before I could really think about it and I batted right through and got 40 some not out, very slowly probably, but I was very proud of myself and I played then for two or three years and got dropped once, for one game only. I then got back in the first team and played for twenty-odd years.

The club employed professionals at the time and Tony remembered professionals like Reg Holton, Peter Rochford and, in particular, Hughie Croskill, who was particularly good with young players.

Tony was also a professional footballer and for ten years his cricket activities were curtailed. There can be few cricketers in Yorkshire better qualified to pass opinion about the relative merits of League cricket in the county, particularly the long running dispute over which is the stronger League in Yorkshire, the Yorkshire League, or the Bradford League.

I think probably now the Bradford League is a stronger League than the Yorkshire League, although there are two points of view on it, I think the Yorkshire League is probably a better League for cricket, simply because the wickets are better and they have more balanced sides in the Yorkshire League, whereas the Bradford League sides have three or four professionals who are doing all the batting and the bowling and they are made up with six or seven not-so-good players. Grounds are smaller and don't encourage slow bowlers.

We discussed the national club trophy teams.

1972 was the first time we won, that was the D.H.Robins Cricket Club Trophy. We entered, I think, the year before that and we lost in the first round on a toss up, which I understand was made by telephone and Geoff (Geoff Dennis, the captain) let the chap at the other end toss and we lost! That was against Pocklington Pixies and they went on to the

Tony Moor receives the Haig Trophy at Lord's after the victory over Reading in 1979.

Final which they lost. The first time we really played anything like in the competition, we played at Lord's and won it. I think the highlight of the match was Colin Oxtoby's wicketkeeping. Looking back that was a tremendous side we had at that particular time.

Geoffrey retired at the end of that season and I took over as captain. We've had five wins at Lords and for me the best of the lot was 1976. We also won the Yorkshire League and the National Six-a-Side knock-out, but in that year in 1976, we had six players who were playing their first year in Yorkshire League cricket, which was quite amazing. We lost one game all season, which believe it or not was at Halifax, who were bottom of the League, but that's cricket isn't it?

I asked Tony what, in his opinion, were the outstanding qualities needed to win the national trophy.

I think in probably four out of five Finals we have looked like getting beaten, and I just think that we have really stuck at it; really kept going and fielded like demons.

Was Scarborough's experience of playing on big grounds like Scarborough and Headingley an advantage in such circumstances.

I think it's a help there, certainly, I think also that after the first visit we, have always had three or four who have played previously, which gives you that experience of playing there and I think that is a great advantage over sides that haven't played there before, because

I think sides are overawed really before they start. If we won the toss we put the other side in because we thought it was worth one wicket, if not two wickets early on, through players being so tied up with the emotions of the day as it were.

We discussed who were the outstanding players Tony had played with during his career at Scarborough, starting with the best bowler.

No question really, Bill Foord. He used to make the ball talk at times. I just wish that I had played a few more years with him whilst he was still a good bowler. I never saw him bowl badly.

There was more difficulty with the batsmen.

I think it would have to be Harry Halliday. If I was picking for someone who was very sound and you could rely on nine out of ten to get runs. If you wanted an entertainer you couldn't beat Ken Stockwell in his heyday. He used to flash a few over the slips, but when he started hitting a few cover drives you wouldn't see better anywhere. For sheer guts and determination you wouldn't find better than Chris Stephenson who is playing now. He's got a tremendous record.

Bill Foord played fifty-one matches for Yorkshire; Halliday 182 matches. I asked Tony's opinion about the ability of the current Scarborough captain, David Byas, who the previous year, 1984, had broken the Yorkshire League runs record aggregate.

Again he is a tremendous entertainer. As a

Waid Wood, chairman of Scarborough Cricket Club, shows HRH the Duchess of Kent around the North Marine Road ground on the occasion of her visit to the 1976 Festival when she was its president.

club cricketer I would say there won't be many better in the country. His only fault is that he hits too many in the air, if he wants to play county cricket. When you think that last season his last two knocks were 177 not out and 200 not out. To get 200 not out in a 50-overs-a-side game is quite something. He's got a tremendous eye.

After early struggles, Byas went on to play for Yorkshire and, in 1991, established himself in the county game, making over 1,500 runs at an average of 44.48, including five centuries. He learned to hit less deliveries in the air!

The conversation turned to changes in local cricket.

There's not the loyalty today that there was. In 1976 I could always get them down for extra fielding and things, but not today. I can remember in my early days when Ted Lester, who would be in the top six players, was scoring loads of runs. I remember going to Sheffield twice, Halifax and Rotherham and not even putting my pads on. If that happened nowadays these youngsters would be up to see the captain to say they wouldn't play in this team. They'd want to go, but for me, playing with a lot ex-county players, I was just pleased

to be in the side. I was honoured to be there and you waited your chance and when you did get in you thought that you were bloody well going to take it now.

Tony felt that, apart from fielding, the standard of cricket was not as high as when he first started, especially in bowling. He thought that batting was easier, due to wickets being covered. Evidence to support his feeling that standards overall were not as high, was perhaps tied up with his initial remark about net practice. We agreed that reductions in practice automatically reduces basic skill levels. First-class cricketers, by the nature of their job, have greater opportunity and incentive to practice and so any reduction in standards is rather less apparent than at local level. Perhaps the gap between local level and the first-class game is wider than ever before.

Waid Wood

Waid Wood became a committee member of Scarborough Cricket Club in 1948, having been a playing member since 1930. He succeeded Frank Winn as chairman of the club in 1958 before resigning in 1980, thus joining the select group of persons completing fifty years of service to the club. A solicitor by profession, Waid Wood was not always the most popular of chairmen, as his forthright manner, desire to get things done and inability to suffer fools gladly, led to clashes with people less decisive than himself.

Yet his chairmanship of twenty-one years was in a period when cricket was undergoing many changes and without imaginative and clear-sighted leadership, it is unlikely that Scarborough Cricket Club could have continued to keep pace with events. In the event many of the initiatives taken by the club in the 1960s and 1970s — the introduction of sponsorship, single-wicket contests, one-day cricket, the Fenner Trophy — bore the stamp of a Waid Wood idea, I asked Waid what were the immediate problems when he took over the chairmanship in 1958.

Financial. He (Frank Winn) gave up the chair because he said medically he was off-colour etc. and I was put in the chair and I sat down at the first meeting and when it came to any other business I said "Yes, I want a sub-committee appointed to go into the whole financial affairs of this club."

And it was appointed, three of us, and the first lot of accounts coming out, showed curtailment of expenditure under every heading in the club and I started from that base onwards on the financial position . . .And I said at that meeting, I said, this is just like a farming enterprise, its finances are dependent on the weather. That was the immediate concern, getting all the financial side on a satisfactory basis.

I asked Waid whether he was looking at the financial side in terms of reducing costs, or increasing income.

Both, really, but the latter was very difficult to deal with and became immediately more difficult, because immediately, the Festival was interfered with for the first time. Within about two years of my chairmanship, the county championship was extended into September and that meant that every player in England was no longer available as he had been and, consequently, it bore on the fact of what you could do. But at that time, the whole of cricket was of a standard format, except Gillette came in, that was the first thing. And when Gillette appeared (1963), not long after that, I realised that by such-and-such a date nearly all the teams were out and were not otherwise engaged in those days. I wanted Midgley, the secretary, to look into the whole business of having a mini-Festival at the date of the semi-finals of the Gillette. And he was a chap, he was perfect at maintaining what was there, but he didn't want to be bothered with development.

That was the tragedy of it and the oppor-tunity was lost, I think. I always had it in the back of my mind that, if things got desperate with the extension of cricket into September, we could switch back to the mini-Festival and blow it up in July, or whenever it was.

Waid went on to talk about how expenditure was not really great at that time and finances were steady, with inflation yet to become a serious factor. Before he became chairman, he had already been rebuffed with one idea whilst a member of the ground committee.

I proposed we raise £50,000 by a form of loans, say three per cent, because at that time, Dalton (the Chancellor of the Exchequer) *had put two-and-a-half per cent stock on the market for the Labour Government and I said, get so many, we could repay them out by drawing for lots each year, gradually. And I said, with £50,000, let us put this ground in order from top to bottom, including getting rid of the gas light burners in the dressing-room, I remember that, remember that. But it was too much, too much for 'em. Oh, I regret that.*

A favourite saying of Waid Wood during his chairmanship was "Look after the grass," meaning not just the playing surface, but the whole of the ground and he paid tribute to those who had contributed to the quality of the North Marine Road ground.

The place has always been kept very, very well. Very, very well. Its been a pleasure to be in the ground.

We discussed playing conditions.

That grass, principally the wicket, has priority. I saw first-team cricket every Saturday for thirty years. You sit there and you're satisfied with Scarborough, the way they are playing and so you think of other things. I noticed how, from the top of the pavilion, there were areas appearing of coarse grass, circles of it all over and all the other was, sort of, miserable, poor grass. So I said, it would be Midgeley. Get Bingley over. I explained it to the chap, I don't know the first thing about grass.

And he took out a sort of hunting knife and took a piece out and he said, "Look, Mr Wood," he said, "you can put all the manure you like on this," he said, "this coarse grass is really in a hollow, that poorer grass is higher up. It all washes into the hollow and you get coarse grass because there is too much artificial manure for it and the other is starved anyway."

That winter, I don't know how many lorry loads of grass was raked off. It was enormous. When I saw that ground, it looked like a field that had been ploughed. I was scared stiff, oh yes. Oh, it worked, Bingley were right. I would always have liked to have seen it levelled you know. It would have made it look bigger.

The next topic of conversation was the

Carling single-wicket tournament in the 1960s.

Of course, I brought back single-wicket. Aye, I was reading a book about this blessed single-wicket and I rang up Pearce and I said, "What the hell is it?" He said, "I don't know a lot, Waid, but I'll find out all what used to take place. I'll have a word with them at Lord's". We spent hours picking the people in the first contest. We wanted all-rounders, an average of so much and so many wickets etc., and they failed us miserably! They couldn't get any runs and we didn't know how to keep it going when we produced it. Yes, I brought that back.

The single-wicket experiment led to the tournament being transferred to Lord's for several years, with reasonable success.

Waid's next venture involved an England XI versus The Rest of the World XI (presented by Rothmans of Pall Mall). It is interesting that sponsorship was not a word generally used at the time, although a heading thanking sponsors was introduced into the Annual Report in 1964.

The match itself came about in the following manner.

The West Indians were touring (1963) and there had been a piece in the 'Daily Mail' which said that on the official schedule they weren't due to come again for an awful long period, because previously they had had no standing. But that tour party was fantastically successful. At the Grand Hotel that night, I said to Trevor Bailey, talking about that article, I said, "Where are they all next year?" and he said a lot of them were pro'ing up and down the country. I got Pearce on the Saturday morning and if we could get them up together, I said, if we could get the biggest part of the present XI we couldn't go wrong and that's how it started.

It was taken up and I cannot remember what happened . . .Charlie (Griffiths) was supposed to be chucking it, 'cause the verandah top was covered in Press men. We had to give them tables in the open air and pray it didn't rain. We'd never seen so many Press men in our lives.

The Rest of the World XI matches lasted for four Festivals and the success of one-day cricket had wetted the appetites at Scarborough. The John Player Sunday League, too, began in 1969 and, if the Festival was not to fall behind the times, something needed to be done. The result was the Fenner Trophy competiton in 1971, but the background to it was somewhat accidental.

I used to read all papers to see what was interesting about cricket and I noticed that a fellow called Hainsworth, who was then on the Yorkshire committee, had given the gates at the entrance (to Headingley) called the Sutcliffe Gates, because he was such an admirer of Herbert. And I thought well, if this chap, we'd better get him over to the Festival, see. This was before we had got any sponsorship at all.

Well, we got chatting and the outcome was, I suggested to him that he would like to, in the name of Fenner, entertain so many guests per day and give an honorarium of so much. Within a couple of years, I'd got rid of the cost of all the Festival tent, which was full of non-members and cost us so much per day, that is what I had in mind . . .Well I became such close friends with him that what with this business about Gillette going on and what not, I said I think we ought to do something and he backed the first Fenner.

The Fenner Trophy competition boosted the Festival receipts and continued for ten years. Waid had views on why, eventually, the Fenner Trophy tournament declined.

What happened was, the cricket, in my humble opinion, the cricketers gradually, bit by bit, let us down on what they produced. In fact that's an interesting business about cricketers letting us down. I subsequently said that when you were here and the New Zealanders appeared you got 'em to play.

That was my humble opinion and I said also about that match, Meredith Whittaker of the local newspaper, wanted to make a payment of about £2,000 to benefit the players and I said, until I know their best team is coming and secondly that they're going to play, we don't want your money. They played a marvellous match, if I remember rightly. Sidney Hainsworth loved cricket and I think he would be the first to say that they (Fenners) really gave it up because the cricket went down.

Waid hastened to add that in recent years the sides had played very good cricket and the club were to be congratulated on the quality of sides fielded in the recent Festivals.

On the local scene, Waid was of the opinion that the club prospered at the time Harry Halliday was club coach and was in favour of the club having a professional to act as coach for the benefit of all clubs in the area. He could not account for the fact that, despite running several sides, only very few came through the lower teams into the first team and many of the first-team players came from away from Scarborough. He thought the jump from local cricket to Yorkshire League level was often underestimated.

During the late 1970s, Waid attempted to develop the cricket ground at Oriel Crescent on South Cliff, in order to relieve pressure of matches on North Marine Road. For a while the Reserve team played on the ground, quite successfully, but the arrangement with the Oriel Cricket Club eventually ceased.

Finally, Waid looked back at the years of the Festival.

You see, you ask me about the cricket in the Festival? Once I became chairman I didn't see a fat lot of it! My concern was always with the cricketers, build up the goodwill. Members, do the same; and with the festival people who kept appearing. I used to welcome all these people to the Festival. I saw very little cricket. But I was always concerned about the wicket.

Since Waid retired as chairman, the financial arrangements between Scarborough Cricket Club and Yorkshire have changed. Scarborough club members have always been admitted to Yorkshire matches at North Marine Road without charge, but whereas in previous times, the county club paid a fee to play at Scarborough, now the situation is that the Scarborough club pay a levy to Yorkshire to play at North Marine Road, based on the total number of full and business members of the Scarborough Club. In 1991 the levy totalled £6,808 plus VAT. As ever, Waid Wood was forthright in his comments.

I don't know that I would have put up with that. There is a big asset there (the ground), which should have a big fat rent on it!

Fred Robson

The current chairman of Scarborough Cricket Club is Fred Robson. A retired headmaster, he came to Scarborough from his native Durham in 1963 and was a useful club cricketer. His proudest boast is that he played league cricket in six decades, having played for Durham City at the end of the 1930s and playing one match for Scarborough 'A' team in the 1980s. He is hopeful, but doubtful, about being called on in the 1990s! He joined the committee in 1968, became vice-chairman in 1980, before succeeding Geoffrey Smith as chairman in 1987.

I put it to Fred Robson that by the mid-1980s the Festival was beginning to look threadbare. Moreover, the club was becoming financially insecure, because of a substantial overdraft and that it was really the fortunate windfall of the Jack Knowles Deceased Trust legacy, followed by the contribution made by Don Robinson, which put things on an even keel once more. Fred Robson agreed that the assessment was fair overall, but needed a little qualification.

I wouldn't think that the Jack Knowles legacy had a direct influence on the improvement we have seen since those mid-1980s. I would put much greater stress on Don Robinson's involvement. Previous to that, in the last year of the Asda sponsorship, (Sir Noel Stockdale, chairman of Asda-MFI was president of Scarborough Cricket Club in 1987) they had already signified their intention to pull out. Scarborough Building Society had also done that and around 1984 and 1985 time we had a bank overdraft of about £33,000.

Now, from the election of Don Robinson as president, he seemed to instill into the Festival. Certainly that's where it emanated from. A vigour from a president which I don't think, certainly in my experience, we'd ever seen before; an active involvement.

Previous to that, through a long line of very distinguished presidents, basically they had been figureheads, who had appeared at the Festival and played a very worthwhile role and function at the Festival. But throughout the year they were not involved. Now Don Robinson, when he was asked to be president, he indicated that he didn't want to be just a figurehead. He wanted to take an active part, which he certainly did!

The election of Robinson as president was a bold and somewhat surprising move. Robinson had been on the Scarborough scene for many years and his success in business ventures in the entertainment industry and at Scarborough and Hull City football clubs, meant he had a high profile in the area. He was well known as a person who 'got things done' and for Scarborough Cricket Club to approach him to become president after such a long period of time, was an indication of a change of attitude within the committee, brought about by a recognition that the club was beginning to slide into a serious situation. Sponsorship was a crucial element.

The whole basis for successful Festivals these days, not as it was perhaps a number of years ago, is successful sponsorship. And with the pulling out of Asda, it was obvious that we were going to have difficulty unless we could find successful sponsors. Now I knew the reputation of Don Robinson. I didn't know him personally, although I'd met him once, but I had a feeling, because of his previous record of success in anything he undertook, and I had the same impression from people who know him better than I do, that he would not countenance failure.

And so I approached him. I went to see him at the outdoor pool, swimming pool, one Saturday afternoon. Put the case to him. Would he be interested in having his name put forward, nominated, as president? We discussed it fairly briefly and he agreed to do it.

Immediately, when he saw what was required, that Asda and The Scarborough Building Society were pulling out, he set about looking for alternatives. And one of the first things he was able to do again because of his

Personalities at the 1989 Festival. From left to right: Fred Robson (chairman), Michael Parkinson, Don Robinson (president), Bill Mustoe (vice-chairman). They are pictured during the match between Michael Parkinson's XI and MCC.

previous contacts with Yorkshire Television, he persuaded them to get involved. That was the catalyst, as it were, for commercial firms to be interested too, the thought that there might be more television exposure.

From then on, again as vice-chairman of Kunick plc, a leisure group, he happened to have on his board, I think at the time the chairman of Kunick, who was a member of MCC. And I think it was through me telling Don that the chairman of Tesco was on the MCC . . .that was the intro to Tesco.

Wheels within wheels. Back in the 1870s, Lord Londesborough and C.I.Thornton had established the important link between Scarborough Cricket Club and MCC in a formal way. Here in the 1980s, the MCC connection was still important, albeit in a more informal manner.

Several other sponsorships accrued. Joshua Tetley, McCains, Plaxtons, Wards, Northern Electric, became involved in the ensuing Festivals, as well as several smaller companies. Confidence was restored in the Festival and to the club. Fred Robson explains.

Now Don, in addition to getting sponsorship which is absolutely essential, he had a lot of experience with the media. In addition he had what one might call a bit of showbiz, razzmatazz, attached to it, which didn't necessarily go down with everybody, but it generated a new sort of interest in the Festival. Something. Some spark, seemed to take off and people were talking about it, largely because of his efforts. A great publicist.

Don also is a local lad with tremendous loyalty to Scarborough, a devotion to it. Not just the cricket club, or soccer club, but to the town. He has remained here . . .just in this morning's paper, there's a release that he's gone into Bulgaria, built a casino, operating a casino there. Yet here he is, still in Scarborough.

And, because of the amount of sponsorship which he attracted, we were able to make essential improvements to keep the ground in the twentieth century with twenty-first century facilities.

We paid him a tremendous honour, it was a two-way thing, of course, because he was helping us as well, of inviting him to be president for a second year, which was a fairly rare occasion in the history of the club. It was two-edged certainly, but it was a great honour, I think to Don, to be invited a second time. It also ensured a continuity of the sort of approach he'd begun.

Don Robinson's second term of office continued to benefit the club financially, as profits reflected the increasing interest taken in the Festival by sponsors and public alike. And the pattern was continued in 1991 and 1992 with the election as president of Charles (Mac) McCarthy, deputy chairman of McCain Foods (GB) Ltd. His regular attendance at committee meetings reaffirmed the new style of presidential involvement. The decision to broaden the brief required of the president is currently paying dividends, although Fred Robson was anxious to dispel any notion that the change of emphasis was irreversible and, at some earlier stages of the club's development, even desirable.

Certainly during my time as chairman, the presidents, apart from Michael Parkinson, *have been connected with business. Now whether there is any significance in this as a sign of the times, or whether it is something to do with me, the way I look at it, who knows. What we have attempted to do is to try and keep the presidency in a varied form.*

Not only business, but sporting connections, probably the world of television and so forth, big names, that way, but I would hate to think that we should lose the connection with the, for want of a better word, aristocracy, where we've had some very powerful, important people as our president, albeit they probably took no significant part in the running of the club. I would hate to think we were moving away from that and concentrating entirely on the business world.

The general problems of running a unique Festival in the modern world was the next topic of conversation.

I have been aware, whilst I have been chairman, and I am sure Geoffrey Smith was equally aware of it, that the days have gone when you could ensure a successful Festival by gates and membership.

I suggested that the ability to adapt to the times was one of the key factors in the longevity of the club.

It's been one of the strengths I think, of the committee of the club that at all times, certainly while I've been on the committee, they have been aware of this and without it the Festival would fold. Its the life-blood of it really. Nowadays, so long as you have got successful companies backing you, there is no reason why the Festival shouldn't continue for another hundred years. No, the big problem that the committee is faced with over the Festival now, at this instant, because we have got the sponsors, who will disappear and we will be looking for new ones, obviously, they don't stay there for ever, the big problem is getting the fixtures right. There is more and more congestion of fixtures and this is where I come back to TCCB. When we had MCC playing we could ask the MCC to supply us with a team, suggest players, whatever.

At the end of the day, it was the clubs that would release them. If the TCCB are wanting the players, the counties themselves, we would be ending up with an MCC side which, at the last minute, would include two or three Lord's groundstaff and they were just not strong enough, in a cricketing sense, to compete with a World XI, or attract people to come and watch. So we had to do something to redress that and, sadly in many ways, the MCC has been dropped as a team.

We should always like the tourists to come and I am heartened by the fact that South Africa are back in the fold. Also, why I wouldn't be

able to identify a reason for it, part of it is probably financial, but the number of international players who, having played there (North Marine Road) want to come again. They've enunciated this to us that they want to come back, which they didn't before. Some of that, as I say, may be financial. Some of it is the class of cricket that they're playing.

And I think also they may be surprised when they come to Scarborough for the first time and see such a glorious wicket, particularly to bat on. And they get this crowd atmosphere, which even touring teams don't always get at county grounds and they have, if not a full stadium to perform in, at least a very well attended one, much better than most of the county matches and better than some days of Test matches . . .I have a suspicion that some counties, who have not been invited to the four counties knock-out, may wonder how they get in on it.

Eventually, the conversation turned back to the central issue of how the club had survived for so long. After recognising the loyalty and long service of many members over the years and emphasising the importance of good leadership throughout the history of the club, Fred Robson's thoughts turned, inevitably, to the ground.

I think visitors coming for the first time are absolutely astounded when they enter that ground and look at it. And if you go now, here we are in the middle of January, it looks a picture. You go in there to this green area, with beautiful facilities, which many many, many county grounds, I suspect, would be proud of . . .Without that ground, or one of a poorer standard, you wouldn't attract the players. At least we've got that as a starting point.

Fred Robson's welcoming of South Africa back into the world of cricket gave Scarborough Cricket Club another opportunity to demonstrate its ability to keep up with the times. A Press release early in February 1992, announced that the first team of South African cricketers to play in England since reconciliation took place would take part in the 1992 Festival. Eastern Province, captained by Kepler Wessels, who led South Africa in the 1992 World Cup, would play two one-day matches against a World XI.

Tom Walker

The last word in this section of Scarborough Cricket Club recollections goes appropriately enough to the oldest living club member. Tom Walker was born in 1901 and his father played for Scarborough Cricket Club in the more important matches which took place in the

Castle Yard, before the club began to develop the ground at North Marine Road.

The family were tenants of The White Horse pub at Seamer, now The Copper Horse, which was on Lord Londesborough's estate, where cricket was the main topic of conversation in the bar. On the paddock at the rear of the pub a man called Brucknell used to coach Tom and his brothers, but because Brucknell batted left-handed and bowled right-handed, he taught all the boys to play in the same way. That is until Tom's father discovered what was happening and sent Brucknell packing. Brucknell's teaching must have been effective as Tom continued to bat and bowl in the way he had been taught.

Tom Walker was eight years old when he attended his first Festival. The only thing he can remember of that occasion was of Ran-

Tom Walker, the oldest living member of Scarborough CC. He remembers Ranjitsinhji playing in the Festival before World War One.

jitsinhji taking a catch in the slips and pretending that the ball had gone past him. Tom also remembers that his father had many friends.

George Hirst, Schofield Haigh and of course, don't forget the local man, David Hunter, they were all friends of me Dad's, David Hunter was wicketkeeper. He was a very nice fella; he lived down Columbus Ravine and kept canaries. Very nice was David, fatherly.

Tom talked about playing cricket in the playground at Scarborough High School, where the girls had a very good team, although Tom bowled a little too fast for a girl called Peggy Ibbotson and after hitting her twice on the hip he was taken off. When he was seventeen he went in the Army to serve in World War One and whilst stationed near Cologne he bowled in the nets to some of the officers who were about to play a match against I Zingari. After the war he joined Scarborough Cricket Club and went down to the nets. I asked Tom about the secretary at the time

Mr Leadbeater? 'W.W.'? Formidable. He was a hard man, he was, honestly, his whole attitude. He ran the club and I never, ever saw him smile. He was lame in one leg . . .he used to have a stick . . .he never clipped me, I should have clipped him back. No, he never clipped me.

Tom played a few matches for the First XI, but thought the team was 'very clannish', although he remembered travelling to the West Riding in style in the special coach reserved for the Scarborough team and attached to the train at York. Mainly he played for the 'A' team, whose matches with Pickering were always competitive affairs.

Our battles were really with Pickering, always with Pickering. By gum. What did they call 'em, the Franks? By gum, four of 'em. And it always seemed like when we played them, they always had somebody who wasn't connected with Pickering at all!

I asked Tom about net practice and the numbers invovled.

You had a few overs, that's all, just a few, then you had to field out. I remember splitting my hand. There was a huge roller and everyone rolled the wicket.

John Tunnicliffe lived in Scarborough, Long John. There was a lot of good cricketers in the county (village) teams. There was a lad called Tom Abraham, I believe he came from Snainton, a big strong lad, a fast bowler and John Tunnicliffe got him accepted by Glamorgan. The story goes that he didn't play much cricket he married the secretary's daughter and packed up . . .ha, ha, ha!

Talking of secretaries

Jimmy Goodall was a sort of relative of mine

. . .dear old Jim. Frank Winn once told me, he was doing the books or something, and he said, "Jim where's the . . .there must be some money somehwere?"

"Oh, no" he (Goodall) said, "I pay every-thing cash."

"Have you any receipts?"

"No, I haven't any receipts, I just pay as it goes on, like that."

It all seemed to be alright, but Frank couldn't make head nor tale of it. And, yes, he was an accountant!

Tom was a dental surgeon and worked in Hull and when he came back to Scarborough he felt things were not the same. The faces had changed and so he went to play for Scalby. He talked of Eric Bowker, a well-known Scarborough player.

The best leg-break bowler who never played for Yorkshire. I was once fielding close in to him and you've heard of the saying, 'he made the ball fizz?' Now this actually did. I heard this thing fizz . . .phhuutt, like that. Now, only twice have I heard that. Cyril Slightall was a good off-break bowler and we played against a team, Dr Sokill was the captain, he was batting and Cyril bowled him with an off-break which . . .phuut, it seemed to go like that.

I asked Tom if there were more spin bowlers then than there are now, but he was unsure whether that was the case.

John, the farmer. Damn, I've forgotten his name. He was a spin bowler. I don't remember much about them really. They got hammered, I know that! Especially if they went in the country.

Perhaps even in Tom Walker's long lifetime, not a lot has really changed in local cricket, at least for spin bowlers!

The Big Hits — From Scarborough to Trafalgar Square

SCARBOROUGH was originally a fishing port, although today the industry has declined considerably from that in previous times. Fishing still takes place, however, and tourists can satisfy their curiosity about the size of fish by taking a stroll on the harbour to see the fishermen at work with their razor-sharp knives, gutting and preparing the catch for the fish market.

The size of fish is a crucial element in many a fisherman's tale. Likewise is the enormity of the hit when people start to talk about the big hitters in the history of the game of cricket. Albert Trott, Arthur Wellard, Gilbert Jessop, Jim Stewart, Ian Botham — all names which spring immediately to mind in such a context. But the notion that someone has hit a cricket ball from Scarborough into Trafalgar Square beats most of the fishermen's tales on record. Especially when told to someone who has little knowledge of cricket.

Of course, cricket followers believe it. Or do they? For even accepting that the Trafalgar Square referred to is not in London, but borders the south side of the North Marine Road cricket ground at Scarborough, the idea that someone should hit a ball straight over the roofs of the multi-storey lodging houses and small hotels that stand between the ground and Trafalgar Square itself, takes some believing.

Like a fisherman's tale, the story improves with the telling and claims have been made on behalf of many mighty hitters that they have actually succeeded depositing a ball from the pitch at North Marine Road into Trafalgar Square itself. Sadly, many of the claims are invalid. Either the ball went through the single gap between the houses; or it hit the roof and trickled over; or accredited witnesses have not verified the happening. It appears that throughout the 150-year history of Scarborough Cricket Club, only three batsmen have performed the feat — C.I. Thornton, G.F. Wells-Cole and C.G. Pepper.

The first of the big hits took place in 1886. Appropriately, the person involved was C.I. 'Buns' Thornton, the doyen of the Scarborough Cricket Festival. By common consent, Thornton was the biggest hitter of his day. He hit a ball over the Pavilion at Lord's during his undergraduate days at Cambridge and had several hits measured at over 160 yards in practice. One hit of over 150 yards was recorded in a match at Canterbury when he was playing for Kent.

The relevant match at Scarborough was between the Gentlemen of England and I Zingari. The unfortunate bowler was A.G. Steele, who had already been savaged by Thornton's hitting and eventually conceded eight sixes to the great man, as Thornton made 107 in only 29 strokes. One of the eight sixes carried the ball over the houses into Trafalgar Square.

That the ball cleared the houses is supported by a report of the game appearing in the local newspaper on the occasion of Thornton being presented with the Freedom of the Borough of Scarborough in 1921. The report recalls how the ball went 'over the third chimney pot from the space between the houses'. In his reminiscences in 1922, S.F. Yeoman also describes seeing the ball going 'clean over the houses'.

Following the death of C.I. Thornton in 1929, George Hirst paid a tribute:

Of his wonderful feats I have heard much, particularly of the great hit at Scarborough which carried the ball over a four-storey house into Trafalgar Square. I had great hopes of equalling this particular feat, and I once

Left: C.I.Thornton, the first of the big hitters, who cleared the houses in Trafalgar Square in 1886. Right: Cec Pepper, who also achieved that feat when playing for the Australian Services against Leveson-Gower's XI in 1945.

succeeded in hitting the chimney of the house over which Mr Thornton drove the ball. If the chimney had not been there I might have equalled that hit. I should very much have liked to have done so.

Yet there are conflicting accounts of the passage of the ball for Thornton's hit. In his biography 'Recollections & Reminiscences' (1924) Lord Hawke states:

At Scarborough I was in the field to the biggest hit I ever saw C.I.Thornton make — or that he ever did make as a matter of fact . . .'Buns' helped himself to 107 in just over an hour. His mightiest slog was just from the Pavilion End, when he drove a ball straight over the screen, so high that it hit a chimney on the roof of one of the houses outside the ground. In golfing parlance, it was the 'longest carry' I have ever known. He hit another full-pitch through the window of an adjoining house, only just missing the hands of a lady who was knitting. A third he hit through the gap between the houses, and the ball went into Trafalgar Square.

Fredrick Andrews, who became a distinguished headmaster of the Quaker School at Ackworth, wrote a letter to the 'Scarborough Mercury' published in August 1921.

Sir — The near approach of the Cricket Festival, coinciding as it does with the honour which the Corporation is proposing to confer upon Mr C.I.Thornton, recalls a personal incident of more than forty years ago, which may be of interest to your readers. From 1872-76 I was a member of the Scarborough cricket

eleven. On the eve of the Yorkshire and Middlesex match in 1875, if I remember right, the Scarborough club played a team of visitors, seven of whom were members of the Middlesex eleven. The two first batsmen for the visitors were C.I.Thornton and I.D.Walker. The latter rested on his oars until the hurricane at the other end had run its course. When the first wicket fell the score stood at 53, of which C.I.Thornton claimed 51.

I happened to be in the outfield with my back against the fence at the Trafalgar Square end. At that time there were neither stands nor seats in that part of the ground. Suddenly Thornton ran some yards down the pitch, caught the ball in the middle of his bat, and away it sped well out of reach, perhaps to my inward satisfaction. I still see in memory that ball, as it flew so high in the air that its flight was only arrested when it came into contact with a chimney stack of one of the houses in Trafalgar Square. Tradition says that this was not the biggest hit Mr Thornton made in Scarborough; the palm is given to a drive on the old cricket ground on the Castle Hill. This, however, I did not see . . .

This would seem to be an entirely different match to the one in 1886. What is certain is that C.I.Thornton hit sufficient balls in the direction of Trafalgar Square in the matches he played at Scarborough, that some confusion is likely to exist. Suffice to say, he was indeed one of the really big hitters.

G.F.Wells-Cole is the least known of the celebrity hitters, although at the turn of the century his reputation was widespread in and around Lincolnshire where he was a gentleman farmer and successful breeder of Lincolnshire longwood sheep. He attended Winchester College before going on to Jesus College, Cambridge, where despite much success for the college team — once scoring three successive centuries in consecutive days — he did not obtain a Blue. On leaving university, he played regularly for the Lincoln Lindum XI and Lincolnshire and was much in demand to play for MCC and I Zingari, making 535 runs in a single week during an MCC tour of Sussex. His highest innings for Lincolnshire was 220 not out against Durham, but his best individual performance was a really staggering affair which took place in August 1901.

Playing as a guest for Scarborough against the Gentlemen of Yorkshire, he made 387 in four and a half hours. Included in that mammoth score was a six into Trafalgar Square. Harry Leadbeater, one of Scarborough's best-ever left-handed batsmen, was featured in a local newspaper article on 1 July 1905, which stated:

Mr Leadbeater holds that Mr G.F Wells-Cole has made the biggest hit over the houses into Trafalgar Square. An on-drive which rose six or seven feet above the house tops, with a clear drop into the square. Mr Thornton has also lifted at least one over the house-tops, but, in Mr Leadbeater's opinion, the biggest hit ever made into Trafalgar Square was the one he mentions by Mr Wells-Cole, as it was higher up the Square, and also higher in the air, than the one by Mr Thornton.

On 2 August 1922, an article by S.F.Yeoman appeared in the Scarborough newspaper:

Speaking of 'tall' scores and big drives, the best drive I ever witnessed on the cricket ground was one by Wells-Cole, which went clean over the chimney pots of the houses in Trafalgar Square. I also witnessed C.I.Thornton in 1896 when he made no fewer than eight drives out of the ground, most off A.G.Steel. One of them soared clean over the Trafalgar Square houses.

The third of the big hitters is Cec Pepper, the formidable Australian all-rounder, who later became a first-class umpire in this country (1964-79). He claims that far from three people having hit a ball into Trafalgar Square, in fact, he is the only person to have genuinely done so. The claim is made on the basis that one of the gatemen, who was on duty when he made his hit, also witnessed the hit that C.I.Thornton made some sixty years before. The gateman assured Cec that Thornton's hit went through the gap between the houses, which provides the entrance to the Trafalgar Square enclosure section of the ground and Cec is adamant that Keith Miller and Lindsay Hassett witnessed the gateman's comments.

The match itself took place in 1945 and was between H.G.D.Leveson-Gower's XI and the touring Australian Services XI. Cec Pepper made 168 and took 6-121 in the match, as the Australians won by an innings and 108 runs. Cec still describes the event with great gusto.

Ask Miller where it went. He was the other batsman and still tells people about it, I actually hit one square off R.W.V.Robins which probably went further, but its always more spectacular when it goes straight. And of course, it went so high.

Eric Hollies was the bowler and he was shell-shocked. He told Bob Wyatt he couldn't believe what had happened and wouldn't bowl at me again.

No, it wasn't pre-determined in the sense that I decided on that particular delivery, but I had certainly got my eyes on the target, because a few overs before, Arthur Wood, who

Two views of the Trafalgar Square Enclosure. The houses overlook the square. In the history of the club only three people have hit a ball over them. The bottom picture shows the view towards Trafalgar Square when batting at the Pavilion End. A few balls have been hit through the gap.

Mr H.D.G.LEVESON-GOWER'S XI v AUSTRALIAN SERVICES
Scarborough Cricket Ground, Wed 5th, Thur 6th, Fri 7th September 1945

AUSTRALIAN SERVICES   First Innings

1. R.W.Whitington	st Wood b Robins	79
2. C.F.Price	lbw Matthews	5
3. J Pettiford	c Edrich b Hollies	38
4. K.R.Miller	c Coxon b Robins	71
5. C.G.Pepper	st Wood b Hutton	168
6. A.L.Hassett	c and b Robins	19
7. R M Stanford	b Matthews	19
8. S G Sismey	b Matthews	78
9. R.G.Williams	st Wood b Hutton	8
10. A W Roper	c Robins b Matthews	10
11. R S Ellis	not out	0

Extras (B 6, LB 5) 11

Total 506

LEVESON-GOWER'S XI   First Innings   Second Innings

	First Innings		Second Innings	
1. L.Hutton	lbw b Pettiford	42	c Roper b Williams	0
2. L.B.Fishlock	c Sismey b Williams	95	lbw b Ellis	37
3. W.J.Edrich	b Ellis	22	c Whitington b Ellis	18
4. R.E.S.Wyatt	c Miller b Ellis	3	c Roper b Pepper	8
5. G.Cox	b Ellis	3	c Pepper b Ellis	0
6. R.W.V.Robins	st Sismey b Ellis	3	b Pepper	12
7. A.Coxon	b Pepper	1	c & b Pepper	8
8. A.Wood	b Ellis	2	c Pepper b Ellis	16
9. A.B.Sellers	c Whitington b Pettiford	27	not out	3
10. A.D.Matthews	c Pettiford b Pepper	0	c Hassett b Pepper	25
11. E.Hollies	not out	1	b Ellis	3

Extras (B 22, LB 6, NB 1) 29   Extras (B 8, LB 2) 10

Total 258   **Total 140**

Trafalgar Square pictured c.1886 around the time that C.I.Thornton smote a cricket ball out of the North Marine Ground and into the Square.

was keeping wicket said, "I bet you can't hit one over the houses." As you know, I'm not likely to refuse a bet, especially as Woody said he would bet me a bottle of whisky and for a Yorkshireman to do that was really something. He paid up though.

I suppose I wasn't surprised it went over, as I knew I had caught it right, but then again,

Trafalgar Square as it is today, still recognisable from the time of Thornton's feat over 100 years ago. The only changes appear to be in the vehicular traffic and the rooftop extensions to the houses.

it was a surprise to see it rise and rise — will it, won't it — and then go over the top! There was a terrific crowd in and they gave me a standing ovation. Handshakes all round. A few beers afterwards, I can tell you.

The match is recorded in 'Wisden':

This innings by Pepper stood out as the feature of the match and of the revived Festival, for it included six sixes and eighteen fours. One of the sixes off Hollies cleared the roofs of the houses in Trafalgar Square, so repeating the effort by C.I.Thornton in 1886 off A.G.Steel, when batting for Gentlemen of England against I Zingari. Pepper's lofty drive probably did not carry as far as a hit that went into an empty house at the wet end of the Square.

I asked Cec about the weight of the bat he used and whether the hit at Scarborough was the biggest he had achieved.

About 2lb 3/4 oz I think. Not like the mallets they use now. Its not the weight that matters.

Biggest hit I made was at Sydney Cricket Ground. To the left of where the teams come out. It went out of the ground and must have bounced on the road, because they fished it out of the lake a couple of hundred yards further on. Kippax Lake its called, after Alan Kippax. They reckoned it bounced, but no one can be sure! That was the biggest.

I also hit one off Gupte at the Brabourn Stadium in Bombay into the Consul's residence. Worrell was at the other end. I also hit one against the clock at Lord's.

The one at Scarborough gave me a lot of satisfaction though. Third chimney to the left of the gap, that's where it went. Ask Miller. They still talk about it; all over the world.

All over the world. Like fishermen's tales, the big hits in cricket are discussed and analysed. And wherever and whenever such a discussion takes place, it is quite likely that someone will say, perhaps mischievously, "Yes, that may very well be so, but is it really true that a ball was hit from Scarborough to Trafalgar Square?"

Conclusions

SCARBOROUGH Cricket Club was established for two main purposes. First, to provide opportunities for local people to participate at cricket, which was becoming a more organised leisure activity in Victorian England. Second, to make provision for cricket matches between locals and visitors.

The first objective has remained unaltered. The second became modified as a result of the challenge match in 1871 between Lord Londesborough's XI and C.I. Thornton's XI. This match, usually regarded as the forerunner of the Scarborough Cricket Festival, altered one of the original purposes of the club by substituting a second visitors' team in place of the local team. Ostensibly, this was to raise the standard of play, but it seemed more specifically designed to satisfy Lord Londesborough's aim of being involved in an

acceptable leisure pursuit which had acceptable social advantages. The desire of the aristocracy for class exclusivity may well have been another factor in the formation of the two visiting teams.

As financial considerations became important with the need to improve the ground for a better class of cricket, income to the club became a central issue. Despite aristocratic patronage, greater funds were required and the necessity for attracting spectators became a prime objective. At this point the aims of the club and the interests of the town coincided, as both needed to attract visitors to carry on their business successfully.

The town has succeeded in carrying on its business to the extent of remaining one of the premier seaside resorts in the country. It has done so by adapting to changing leisure

Hedley Verity, who had just heard that he had been included in the MCC touring party for Australia, taking time off from the 1932 Scarborough Festival to oversee an impromptu game on the beach. Mrs Verity is batting whilst young Wilfred Hedley Verity studies the game at close quarters.

patterns and providing attractions beyond the natural benefits of coast and countryside. The Borough Council has played an increasing role in advertising the resort and developing its facilities, but in an age of increasing leisure and rising living standards the character of holiday making has changed. The stylish carriages of the seventeenth and eighteenth centuries, which brought the gentry to Scarborough for 'the season', have given way to the more functional motor car, which now transports all social classes to Scarborough often just for the day. Between such two extremes the town experienced the railway age of the ninteenth and early twentieth centuries, when excursion trains symbolised the coming of the annual weekly holiday into the British way of life and eager holidaymakers flooded into the town, Scarborough responded in two ways.

First, there was a rapid population increase from 13,000 in 1851 to 38,000 in 1901. Second, many of the new inhabitants were commercially minded. The result was that hotels were built and shops, cafes and businesses increased. Scarborough's tourist trade became established.

Two important geographical factors have had considerable effect on that tourist industry.

Scarborough is situated on the north-east coast of England. The climatic effect is that the tourist season is a relatively short one of about thirteen weeks. Scarborough is also forty miles from a major population centre and, until the improvement in the road systems in the early Eighties, particularly the Tadcaster and Malton by-passes, visitors tended to stay weekly, fortnightly, or even longer. Reflecting the era of train travel and those weekly and fortnightly holidays, Saturday is still referred to locally as 'change-over day'.

The two geographical influences have historically conditioned the outlook of people who make their living out of the tourist trade. Profits have to be made quickly; leisure facilities have to be extensive. In this equation, cricket has played an important part in the commercial development of the town and the business community is well aware of the benefits of staging the Festival and first-class cricket at North Marine Road. The relationship was highlighted by the Mayor of Scarborough, Councillor David C. Jeffels, on the eve of the 97th Cricket Festival in 1983:

The value of the Festival to Scarborough's economy is substantial and is greatly appreciated by the shops and other businesses as a major contribution to their holiday business.

The Victorian costumes may be a reminder but this picture shows a scene a long time away from the Queen Hotel and Castle Hill. The players are pictured before a match at North Marine Road in 1980.

The statement reflects the mutual self-interest, which has existed between the Scarborough Cricket Club and the town almost from the club's formation.

It is impossible to quantify the number of people attracted to Scarborough simply to watch cricket. It is usually the case that people visit Scarborough for a combination of reasons, depending on their interests. Nevertheless, it is certain that a substantial number of Yorkshire members travel to Scarborough for the sole purpose of watching their team play at North Marine Road. There are no more partisan supporters of cricket than Yorkshire members and attendances recorded at Scarborough bear testimony to that claim. Whenever Yorkshire play at North Marine Road, telephone enquiries regarding prospects of play flood in to the club's offices from 7am onwards and continue until early afternoon. The majority of these enquiries are from members living in the West Riding, now only a couple of hours drive away.

For Yorkshire and Scarborough Cricket Club members, the entrance gates open half an hour earlier than for the general public and queues begin to form two or three hours before the start of play. Supporters who have attended for many years, seek to reserve their favourite spots on a ground which holds fond memories often from childhood. Having reserved a seat by means of a coat, a blanket, or even a Yorkshire speciality, the hired cushion, a steady stroll along North Bay to taste the salt is usually called for. After that the serious business of the day can be attended to. Woe betide anyone if the coats have been disturbed!

As far as the Festival is concerned, advance bookings invariably include a number of followers who automatically book for the following year's Festival whilst attending the current one. This trend is less prevalent now than in the years when the traditional Festival following was very strong. Photographs which show spectators sitting on the grass within the normal boundary at several post-war Festivals, indicate the popularity that Festival cricket has enjoyed at various times.

At local level, Scarborough Cricket Club continues to fulfil its purpose of providing cricket playing opportunities for as many people as possible. The premier status of the club and the superb ground at North Marine Road is an incentive for all young aspiring cricketers in the area and a vigorous policy of encouragement of young talent has long been pursued. In the past, attendance at practice and high quality coaching have always been a priority and, since 1920, three, often four and sometimes five teams have represented the club at different levels.

As the desire to practise has waned in the face of other attractions, the club is acutely aware that a greater struggle is in prospect to regain the outstanding playing record of the past, as reflected in Yorkshire Council, Yorkshire League and national competitions.

Another geographical factor is important. Away matches for the First XI in the Yorkshire Council and Yorkshire League, involve long journeys and considerable expense. Quite clearly a club that could arrange for a special coach to be attached to the Edinburgh-London train and indulge in pre-match meals at high-class hotels, was engaged on serious business. Team spirit and collective will developed on those trips and Scarborough players appreciated the speciality of the situation and of the club. The Yorkshire League title is now overdue at North Marine Road and the club cannot afford to let its playing standards slip in Yorkshire and national club cricket circles.

All organisations require clear aims and objectives. Scarborough Cricket Club has succeeded throughout its history in fulfilling its twin purposes in respect of local and first-class cricket. This has been achieved by providing members and spectators with a sufficiently attractive product to enable the club to finance its activities. Key elements include the historical and cultural aspects of cricket, which seem to be embedded deeply in the psyche of cricketers and cricket followers in Yorkshire. Cricket is not quite a religion in Yorkshire, it just seems like it at times. Cricket at Scarborough mirrors that intensity of outlook.

The important links with MCC and the support of the Yorkshire County Cricket Club have been vital. Also, the club has been exceedingly well served at crucial points in time, by three outstanding secretaries in Robert Baker, William Leadbeater and Alfred Rutherford. They, along with a sizeable number of shrewd and knowledgeable committee members, were not slow to take advantage of the entrepreneural possiblities offered by a national pastime like cricket in a seaside resort like Scarborough. The ability of the management of Scarborough Cricket Club to judge and, when necessary, anticipate the changes which have taken place in the social and economic sphere and link them with advantage to the cricket world, has enabled the club to operate successfully for more than 140 years.

Two points deserve further emphasis. First, leisure has always been treated as a business in the history of Scarborough Cricket Club. Today, commerical considerations are as important for the club's survival as they ever have been and the competition is greater. In sport the role of sponsorship is worthy of close

examination, particularly when placed alongside other commercial interests needing to promote goods and services and surrounding themselves with plausible images of sport. How far, for example, has sport benefited from sponsorship, other than in narrow financial terms? Does sport benefit from an association with a product to the same extent that the product benefits from its association with sport? This aspect of the growth of advertising and sponsorship and the place of the leisure sector in the economy deserves more detailed study, so that the achievements of Scarborough Cricket Club can be weighed in relation to the rest of cricket and to sport in general.

Second, Scarborough Cricket Club can justify claim to be a unique club. The uniqueness does not lie simply in its longevity. It does not lie in its capacity as an organisation to continue to satisfy the demand for cricket by the inhabitants of Yorkshire and wider afield. It does not lie in the special connection with national cricket which undoubtedly gives the club status. The uniqueness really lies in the absolute necessity for the town to attract visitors, which, when joined with the self-interest of the local cricket club, as projected through the Festival, has interwoven a cultural pattern into the social fabric of Scarborough life itself. The people of Scarborough value their club and the club values its people. That is why it has sustained its vigour and vitality. An organisation is only the people in it and Scarborough Cricket Club, from the time of Robert Baker onwards, has succeeded in capturing the loyalty of members, spectators and players alike for cricket at Scarborough.

Officials of Scarborough Cricket Club

Presidents

Sir Harcourt Johnson Bart (Lord Derwent) 1863-1866
Mr John Haig, JP 1866-1874
Mr E.H.Hebden, JP 1874-1877
Mr W.E.Woodall 1877-1881
Mr C.W.Woodall, JP 1881-1897
Mr Henry Darley, JP 1898, 1903
Mr Gilbert Wilkinson 1899-1900
Sir G.Everard Cayley, Bart. 1901-1902
The Rt Hon The Earl of Londesborough 1904-05, 1912
Mr G.Alderson-Smith, JP, DL 1906
Mr J.W.Drew, MA 1907-1908
Mr B.B.Popplewell 1909-1911, 1914
Mr T.H.Good 1913
Lt Col T.G.Hawdon, JP, DL 1915-1919, 1922
Mr T.L.Taylor 1920-1921, 1923, 1935, 1957
Mr C.C.Graham, OBE, JP 1924-1925
Col The Rt Hon Viscount Downe, CMG, DSO 1926
Alderman George Whitfield, JP 1927
Sir W.G.Middlebrook, JP 1928
The Rt Hon Lord Hawke 1929-1930
Mr Claud S.Norton 1931-1932
Sir Paul Latham, Bart. 1933
Dr G.W.Thompson 1934
Dr J.H.Thornley, MC 1936
Alderman F.C.Whittaker, JP 1937, 1946, 1951, 1963
The Rt Hon Viscount Downe, OBE, JP 1938, 1955
Mr M.E.Hodgson, OBE 1939-1944
Mr H.Huggan 1945
Sir Kenelm Cayley, Bart. 1947-1948
Sir Wm.A.Worsley, Bart. 1949, 1953
Mr H.D.G.Leveson-Gower 1950
The Rt Hon Lord Derwent 1952
Alderman J.W.Hardcastle, CBE 1954
The Rt Hon Lord Grimthorpe 1956
Mr W.E.Harbord 1958
Lt Col Sir J.Dunnington-Jefferson, Bart., DSO 1959
Lt Col R.T.Strannyforth, CVO, MC 1960
H.R.H.The Duke of Edinburgh, KG, KT 1961
His Grace The Duke of Norfolk, KG, PC, GCVO 1962
The Rt Hon The Earl of Halifax, DL 1964
Mr A.B.Sellers, MBE 1965
The Most Hon The Marquis of Normanby, MBE, HML 1966
The Rt Hon The Earl of Harewood, LLD 1967
Mr H.Sutcliffe 1968
The Rt Hon The Viscount Downe 1969
Mr A.B.Sharman 1970
Mr T.N.Pearce 1971
Mr S.B.Hainsworth, CBE 1972-1973
The Rt Hon Lord Netherthorpe 1974
Sir Leonard Hutton 1975, 1986
HRH The Duchess of Kent 1976
Sir Kenneth Parkinson 1977
Sir Meredith Whittaker 1978
Mr J.Palmer 1979

Mr J.A.Richardson 1980
Mr N.W.D.Yardley 1981
Mr M.B.Henderson 1982
Mr B.A.Johnston, OBE, MC 1983
Sir Marcus Worsley, BT, JP, DL 1984
Sir Michael N.Shaw JP, DL, MP 1985
Sir A.Noel Stockdale, LLD 1987
Mr D.Robinson 1988-1989
Mr M.Parkinson 1990
Mr C.M.A.McCarthy 1991-1992

Chairmen

1902-1908 Herbert Walton
1908-1945 William S.Robinson
1946-1948 J.Hoyle
1949-1957 Frank Winn
1958-1979 Waid A.Wood
1980-1986 Geoffrey H.Smith
1987-date Fred Robson

Secretaries

1869-1896 Robert Baker
1896-1897 Richard Bent
1897-1930 William Leadbeater
1930-1949 J.Lucas Goodall
1949-1961 Alfred Rutherford
1961-1975 John Midgley
1975-1978 Donald Briggs
1978-1979 Ian W.Hall
1979-1985 Lt Commander Harry Wood
1985-date Colin Adamson

General Manager

1989 John Maw

Chief Executives

1990-1991 Roland Davies
1991-date Cecil Snell

Commercial Manager

1981 John Bridgeman
1982 Philip Hart

Captains

1907-1921 W.S.Robinson
1922-1934 A.H.Fawcett
1935-1958 J.A.Richardson
1959-1960 D.M.Douglas
1961-1972 G.H.Dennis
1973-1979 A.J.Moor
1980-1982 B.Rennard
1983-1984 A.J.Moor
1985-1988 D.Byas
1989-1990 P.R.Hart
1991-date P.R.Hart & S.C.E.Hardy

Scarborough CC Playing Records Since World War Two

The following records refer to most of the leading figures of Scarborough's first team who have represented the club since Second World War. It must be emphasised that the club's records are incomplete and it has not been possible to include all the details that we would have liked. Where a player also played before the war, all his matches have been included. Wartime matches have been included where a player also played before the war. These players are indicated with an asterisk.

Batting

Name	Extent of career	Innings	Not/Out	Total	Highest Score	Average
E.S.Alcock*	1934-51	137	40	2,616	102*	26.97
G.R.Bloom	1959-76	294	33	7,342	123*	28.13
P.Bowes	1987	41	5	609	42	16.90
W.K.Bradshaw	1947-58	88	10	1,319	105	16.91
J.M.Brown	1978-84	111	37	1,281	44	17.30
J.R.Burnett	1954	13	2	146	51*	13.30
D.Byas	1980-	200	35	6,742	200*	40.86
K.A.Calvert	1962-69	136	17	2,254	87*	18.94
J.A.Claughton	1954-58	98	18	2,492	106*	31.15
C.C.Clifford	1963	297	133	2,786	86	16.99
D.B.Close	1979-80	33	4	715	72	24.65
M.W.D.Cowell	1987	46	5	1,246	123*	30.39
H.O.Crosskill	1950-52	64	8	1,467	90	26.20
A.Dalby	1981-82	60	8	2,123	127	40.80
M.Davison	1973-89	109	14	1,720	109*	18.10
G.H.Dennis	1948-72	279	65	2,839	61*	13.27
D.M.Douglas	1957-60	57	12	1,563	126*	34.70
G.Downes	1963-66	31	8	252	30	10.96
A.J.Grayson	1985	71	13	1,442	98	24.86
S.Gormley	1987	24	-	522	80	21.75
D.Greenlay	1990	42	6	752	71*	20.89
H.Halliday	1960-63	46	15	1,402	114*	45.22
L.Halstead*	1936-48	55	6	685	49	13.98
R.L.Halton	1953-55	73	23	2,457	97	49.14
P.R.Hart	1970	271	71	3,616	77*	18.08
K.Hudson	1952-58	23	6	347	45	20.41
C.T.Hugill	1986	129	20	3,195	113*	29.30
C.A.Hurd	1969-75	53	11	551	38	13.10
J.A.Hutton	1955-77	272	50	5,192	108	23.39
M.Kirkland	1965-72	76	20	1,250	78	22.32
J.R.Knowles*	1936-48	165	37	3,273	110*	25.57
E.I.Lester*	1938-61	200	42	8,681	180*	54.94
J.Lister	1953-54	30	3	950	103	35.19
A.J.Moor	1958-84	447	88	13,086	127*	36.45
B.C.Moor	1952-643	149	29	3,754	135	31.28
J.W.T.Mustoe	1972-90	26	3	521	100*	22.65
M.Naylor	1956-59	39	8	721	59	23.26
W.Pincher	1970-83	126	27	2,315	113*	23.38
J.Precious	1978-82	48	15	678	47	20.55
R.E.Pockley	1983-84	41	11	670	64*	22.33
B.Rennard	1968-85	445	77	10,480	100*	28.48
J.A.Richardson*	1927-58	573	113	22,244	202	48.36
F.Robson	1963	8	1	90	30	12.86
G.M.Shepherdson	1952-54	54	11	1,136	84	26.40
M.Shepherdson	1975-80	48	20	279	31	9.96
R.Sherwood	1975-82	130	31	2,070	69*	20.90
G.H.Smith*	1938-52	177	26	3,370	87*	22.30
C.H.Stephenson	1978-85	221	33	7,494	138*	39.86
K.C.Stockwell	1949-79	525	71	13,195	139*	29.06
F.Temple*	1929-47	281	47	5,747	112	24.56
C.D.Watson	1990	41	4	1,093	92*	29.54
T.N.Watts	1983	210	34	5,443	124*	30.92
A.P.Wood	1989	50	15	724	55	20.69
G.B.Wood	1958-62	46	15	454	42	14.65
D.A.Woodhead	1984-89	84	18	1,193	61	18.08
P.Woodhead	1984-87	50	6	935	76*	21.25
P.Woodliffe	1976-79	89	18	2,014	99	28.37
B.A.Young	1984-85	43	7	1,264	100	35.10

Bowling

Name	Extent of career	Runs	Wickets	Average
P.N.Anderson	1986-87	1,008	52	19.38
E.Bowker*	1934-35	3,033	251	12.08
D.Byas	1980	2,190	93	23.55
J.W.Cammish	1948-533	2,033	158	12.87
C.C.Clifford	1963	18,195	1,080	16.85
D.B.Close	1979-80	806	51	15.80
R.Coward	1956-66	2,425	131	18.50
N.Cowton	1990	1,635	43	38.02
H.O.Crosskill	1950-52	2,052	131	15.66
A.Dalby	1981-82	680	30	22.67
G.H.Dennis	1961-72	10,696	668	16.01
S.J.Dennis	1978-84	1,960	110	17.82
R.A.Diggle	1951-56	3,130	178	17.58
P.Ellis	1980	5,213	258	20.20
C.W.Foord	1941-71	16,149	1071	16.01
P.S.Glaves	1974-79	4,482	219	20.47
P.R.Hart	1970	9,406	531	17.71
R.L.Halton	1953-55	2,025	142	14.26
M.Heath	1966-76	3,150	175	18.00
P.F.Judge	1948-49	820	49	16.73
C.W.Kirby	1972-74	323	27	11.96
J.R.Knowles*	1936-48	446	29	15.37
E.I.Lester	1938-61	506	45	11.24
A.J.Moor	1958-84	5,914	445	13.29
J.W.T.Mustoe	1972-90	532	27	19.70
M.Naylor	1956-59	1,204	100	12.04
W.Pincher	1970-83	4,800	295	16.27
J.Rigby	1947-49	632	33	19.15
M.Shepherdson	1975-80	2,344	115	20.38
R.Sherwood	1975-82	619	38	16.29
J.D.Snowball	1940-51	3,057	225	13.59
K.C.Stockwell	1949-79	3,520	233	15.11
A.D.Towse	1986	909	47	19.34
R.Tye	1973-74	784	56	14.00
J.S.Waring	1965-68	1,344	94	14.30
C.D.Watson	1990	622	26	23.92
N.J.West	1980-82	680	35	19.43
A.P.Wood	1989	2,282	62	36.81
G.B.Wood	1958-62	2,158	134	16.10
D.A.Woodhead	1984-89	460	24	19.17
P.Woodhead	1984-87	417	10	41.70
P.H.Woodliffe	1976-79	1,353	81	16.70

Twenty-two of the Best

One of the happiest ways of whiling away the time when cricket has been rained off is to indulge in that line of fantasising so beloved of cricket writers: the all-time great eleven. Here one can run one's eye down the old bowling and batting averages and select eleven players to take on the rest of the world.

If one can enlist the expertise of former great cricketers, then one has a chance of being only marginally awry; and if these same experts have over one hundred years of first-hand experience between them, then one should be just about spot-on with one's selections.

Accordingly, we asked two of Scarborough's most notable former players to play our game for us. Len Halstead's connections with the club go back to 1924. He was asked to pick a side from players who appeared for Scarborough regularly in the years between the two world wars. Bill Foord, who first played for the club in the early 1940s and represented one or other of its sides for over forty years, has selected an eleven of post-war cricketers.

Despite their endeavours, some of their selections will be open to discussion. So much the better. It would not be cricket if we were all in complete agreement! They both agreed, however, that where they were in two minds about a selection, each time they opted for the player who was the better fielder.

So here they are then, Len Halstead's XI (1919-1939) versus Bill Foord's XI (1945-1991).

Bill Foord's XI	Len Halstead's XI
E.I.Lester	J.A.Richardson
K.C.Stockwell	J.H.Pearson
D.Byas	G.H.Hirst
A.J.Moor	J.V.Wilson
H.Halliday	E.P.King
J.W.T.Mustoe	J.R.Knowles
G.H.Dennis	Joe Johnson
C.C.Clifford	J.F.Temple
C.Oxtoby (wkt)	E.R.Bowker
C.W.Foord	A.H.Fawcett (wkt)
J.Cammish	J.Meads

Scarborough CC Professional Players

1867 First recorded professional, John King of Snainton
1868 Probably no professional
1869   ”
1870   ”
1871 P.Woodruff
1872 John Reed Joy
1873 J.King (30s per week plus benefit)
1874 J.King
1875 J.King
1876 J.King
1877 J.King
    H.Reynolds of Notts
1878 Alf Willey of Kent
    W.Clarke, Notts.
1879 John Waterfall of Alfreton
    John King
1880 David Bookless
    John King
1881 H.H.Webster of Birmingham
    J.King
1882 R.McLeod of Kelso
1883
1884 Jack Marshall of Guisley
1885 J.H.Duckworth of Bolton
1886 J.H.Duckworth
1887 D.Bookless (part-time)
    E.Peake

1888
1889 J.H.Duckworth
    G.P.Harrison
    D.Bookless
1890 J.H.Duckworth
    D.Bookless
    G.P.Harrison & others
1891 J.H.Duckworth
    Henwood & others
1892 H.Butler
    H.Eastwood
1893 H.Butler
    probably Shaw
1894 F.Watmough
    Shaw
1895 F.Watmough
    F.Borton
1896 F.Watmough (sacked)
    J.Riley
1897 J.Riley
1898 J.Riley
1899 J.Riley
1900 R.Blades & W.Oakley
1901 R.Blades & W.Oakley
1902 R.Blades & W.Oakley
1903 R.Blades & W.Oakley
1904 R.Blades & W.Oakley
1905 W.Oakley
1906 W.Oakley
1907 F.Barker
1908 F.Barker
1909 A.E.Johns
1910 A.L.Richardson (from County) & G.Bayes
1911 C.Tyson & G.Bayes & J.Rothery
1912 C.Tyson & G.Bayes
1913 G.Bayes & F.Bale
1914 G.Bayes & F.Bale
1920 J.T.Green
1921 J.T.Green
1922 J.T.Green & G.H.Hirst
1923 J.T.Green & G.H.Hirst
1924 J.T.Green & G.H.Hirst
1925 J.T.Green & G.H.Hirst
1926 J.T.Green & G.H.Hirst
1927 E.Hutchinson & G.H.Hirst & G.Bayes
1928 W.H.Barber & G.H.Hirst
1929 W.H.Barber & G.H.Hirst
1930 E.P.King
1931 E.P.King
1932 E.P.King
1933 J.Meads
1934 J.Meads
1935 J.Meads
1936 J.Meads
1937 J.Meads & J.Johnson
1938 J.Meads & J.Johnson
1939 J.Meads & J.Johnson
1950 H.Crosskill
1951 H.Crosskill
1952 H.Crosskill
1953 R.Halton
1954 R.Halton
1955 R.Halton
1956 E.I.Lester
1957 E.I.Lester
1958 E.I.Lester
1959 E.I.Lester
1960 E.I.Lester
1961 E.I.Lester

Scarborough CC East Yorkshire Cup XI Captains since World War Two

1946-49 F.Winn
1950-55 L.Halstead
1956-64 C.R.Atkinson
1965-70 F.Robson
1971-75 G.Downes
1976-80 C.A.Hurd
1981-82 M.Davison
1983-88 G.Downes
1989 R.V.Southwell
1990 N.C.Stephenson
1991 A.J. Grayson

Ridings XI Captains

1981-85 J.A.Hutton
1986-87 J.T.Riley
1988-90 J.W.T.Mustoe
1991 J.T.Riley

Scarborough CC Wicketkeepers since World War Two

1946-47 R.Candler
1948-49 F.H.Stephenson
1950-51 P.Rochford
1952 F.H.Stephenson
1953-65 A.Marston
1966 G.R.Bloom/J.B.Mitchell
1967 J.B.Mitchell
1968-75 C.Oxtoby
1976-77 D.Kneeshaw
1978-84 J.M.Brown
1985 B.Young/C.Burdass
1986 C.Burdass/S.C.E.Hardy
1987-91 S.C.E.Hardy

Scarborough CC Groundsmen

c.1882-1912 John King (to age 78)
1912-1943 Albert Fattorini
1944-1945 L.Dyson (temporary)
1946-1959 Jack Meads
1960-1980 Bernard Pearson
1981-1983 Bill Pincher
1984-date Mike Corley

Individual Awards

Brian Johnston Trophy (Players' Player of the Year)
1983 D.Byas
1984 D.Byas
1985 C.C.Clifford
1986 C.C.Clifford
1987 J.T.Riley
1988 P.W.Bowes
1989 J.W.T.Mustoe & A.P.Wood
1990 M.W.D.Cowell
1991 C.D.Watson

Castle Colour Services Trophy (Club Player of the Year)

1984 D.Byas
1985 No Award
1986 C.T.Hugill
1987 C.C.Clifford
1988 C.T.Hugill
1989 A.P.Wood
1990 J.W.T.Mutoe
1991 C.D.Watson

J.W.Hardcastle Trophy (Young Player of the Season)

1989 G.Pickup
1990 C.D.Watson
1991 G.Pickup

Edgar Slack Trophy (Season's Best Bowling)

1988 C.C.Clifford
1989 P.R.Hart
1990 P.W.Bowes
1991 A.S.Parvin

Trophies won by Reserve and Junior XIs

Scarborough & District League   1946
Scarborough & District Hospital Cup   1950
Scarborough & District Beckett League   1960 (Div 'B')
Scarborough & District Beckett League   1973 (Div 'C'), 1979
Cayley Cup   1972 (Div 'B'), 1973 (Div 'C')
Bright Bowl   1962, 1964, 1967, 1969, 1976, 1977, 1978, 1987
Derwent Valley Junior League   1985, 1986, 1987, 1988, 1990
League Cup   1985, 1986, 1990

Primary Schools KO Competition

Winners 1981-1991
1981 Bramcote
1982 Seamer & Irton
1983 Bramcote
1984 Bramcote
1985 Bramcote
1986 Bramcote
1987 Brompton & Sawdon
1988 Bramcote
1989 Bramcote
1990 Seamer & Irton
1991 Bramcote

Scarborough Cricket Festival
One-day Trophy Winners (50 overs-a-side)

Fenner Trophy
1971 Kent beat Lancashire by 66 runs
1972 Yorkshire beat Lancashire by 60 runs
1973 Kent beat Yorkshire by 28 runs
1974 Yorkshire beat Warwickshire by 7 wickets
1975 Hampshire beat Yorkshire by 7 wickets
1976 Hampshire beat Yorkshire by 32 runs
1977 Hampshire beat Essex by 44 runs
1978 Northants beat Yorkshire by 8 wickets
1979 Leicestershire beat Yorkshire by 9 runs
1980 Leicestershire/Hampshire rain — Trophy shared
1981 Yorkshire beat Essex by 2 runs

Asda Trophy
1982 Derbyshire beat Lancashire by 9 wickets
1983 Lancashire beat Hampshire by less wickets lost in tie
1984 Hampshire beat Yorkshire by 7 wickets
1985 Derbyshire beat Lancashire by 8 wickets
1986 Hampshire beat Essex by 87 runs
1987 Yorkshire beat Lancashire by 4 wickets

Ward Four-Counties Knock-out Cup
1988 Essex beat Yorkshire by 94 runs
1989 Yorkshire beat Essex by 1 run

Scarborough Cricket Festival Trophy
1990 Hampshire beat Essex by 5 wickets

Joshua Tetley Festival Trophy
1991 Yorkshire beat Essex by 5 wickets

The White Horse Yorkshire Ashes: Yorkshire v The Yorkshiremen (55 overs-a-side)
1988 The Yorkshiremen beat Yorkshire by 8 wickets
1989 Yorkshire beat The Yorkshiremen by 3 runs
1990 Yorkshire beat The Yorkshiremen by 8 wickets

Northern Electric 'Super' Bowl
1991 The Yorkshiremen beat Yorkshire by 3 wickets

Index

SUBSCRIBERS

Presentation Copy
1 Scarborough CC

2 Ian W Hall
3 John Found
4 MCC Library
5 John Grainger
6 Anton Rippon
7 Ron K Frost
8 J A Harris
9 J C Parkinson
10 Ernest Elliott
11 Andrew Stevens
12 J G McKinney, MBE
13 Mac Fattorini
14 Angus J McCarthy
15 Andrew C McCarthy
16 Charles M A
   McCarthy
17 Martin John Wall
18 John Wall
19 L Halstead
20 Mike Webdale
21 Edward G Lancaster
22 Waid A Wood
23 K D Procter
24 Ken C Stockwell
25 Alfred G Hey
26 Roy Young
27 G W S Cawthorn
28 J M Sellers

29 Richard L Grunwell
30 Dominic L Grunwell
31 James H Grunwell
32 Eric Wright
33 Jack Grafton
34 T B Speak
35 W G E Lewis
36 Joseph Henry Ball
37 Richard Hodgson
38 Donald Briggs
39 Roland S Davis
40 Professor Derek
   Colville
41 Eric Stitt Alcock
42 Derek William
   Ferdinand
43 B Howes
44 Mr N D Hopkin
45 Mrs H Hopkin
46 T J Fletcher
47 Bob Harrison
48 Joseph Hunter
49 Andrew Rowe
50 Mr A Bates
51 Sports Marketing
52 Anthony Jones
53 Another Brunts OB
54 Denis Stagg

55 Andrew D Marr
56 Ernie Thompson
57 Gordon Hunter
58 Fred Robson
59 Anthony Woodhouse
60 John Featherstone
61 Dr J R B Turner
62 Robert A Hilliam
63 Paul Bannister
64 G W Pearson
65 Colin T Adamson
66 J Moss
67 Stephen Boville
68 Ian Petrie
69 W Kneale
70 Mr B A Young
71 Clive Ronald
   Marrison
72 J Gardiner
73 Mr J S Burrell
74 David Gregg
75 Mel Brown
76 Norman White
77 Nicholas H D Brown
78 John Pickering
79 Steve Davies
80 Malcolm Ferguson
81 Paul Atkin